ALDOUS HUXLEY

A COLLECTION OF CRITICAL ESSAYS

Edited by
Robert E. Kuehn

Prentice-Hall, Inc. *Englewood Cliffs, N.J.*
A SPECTRUM BOOK

Library of Congress Cataloging in Publication Data

KUEHN, ROBERT E   comp.
   Aldous Huxley: a collection of critical essays.

   (A Spectrum Book)
   Bibliography: p.
   1. Huxley, Aldous Leonard, 1894–1963—Criticism and
interpretation.
PR6015.U9Z745   823'.9'12   74–11444
ISBN 0–13–448514–9
ISBN 0–13–448506–8 (pbk.)

10 9 8 7 6 5 4 3 2 1

PRENTICE-HALL INTERNATIONAL, INC. (*London*)
PRENTICE-HALL OF AUSTRALIA PTY. LTD. (*Sydney*)
PRENTICE-HALL OF CANADA LTD. (*Toronto*)
PRENTICE-HALL OF INDIA PRIVATE LIMITED (*New Delhi*)
PRENTICE-HALL OF JAPAN, INC. (*Tokyo*)

Contents

Huxley as Biographer: *Grey Eminence*
and *The Devils of Loudun*

Introduction

by Robert E. Kuehn

Aldous Huxley's career resembles that of several other eminent twentieth-century writers: he began as an *enfant terrible* and ended as a sage. The descendant of two immensely distinguished Victorian families—the Huxleys and Arnolds—he was nevertheless a distinctly twentieth-century man. In the rich cultural overlap of the two centuries (one thinks of James and Proust, of Mahler and Strauss, of Yeats) Huxley had no part. Each of his novels, from *Crome Yellow* through *Island,* is indisputably modern, even though the later books differ so radically from the earlier ones. Huxley seems to have been born mistrustful of received attitudes and disdainful of those creeds that provided his forebears with a sense of order, continuity, and spiritual composure. His intellectual temperament, if one may call it that, was skeptical, restless, experimental. In his youth he was a debunker of moribund truths; in middle age he became an ardent seeker of new truths or of fresh combinations of old truths. His zestful assault on the old order of things in *Crome Yellow, Antic Hay, Those Barren Leaves,* and pre-eminently in *Point Counter Point* gave way in time to a strenuous and eclectic attempt to find a new order, to fashion a "perennial philosophy" from disparate fragments of the human past. The transition was not quite as abrupt as it is sometimes made to seem: the road to mysticism is as clearly implied in *Those Barren Leaves* as is the road to orthodoxy in *The Waste Land.*

Huxley has always been a hero to the young, for his interests have consistently matched those of the generation just coming forward. Men fifteen years younger than Huxley have testified to the "liberating" effect of his early stories and novels; he was one of the first to understand, appreciate, and promote the work of D. H. Lawrence; he was an advocate of pacifism long before pacifism became an unarguable mark of sanity; his loathing of technology when it is allowed to develop without ethical imperatives and his fear of the terrible consequences of over-population and the despoliation of

1

nature were subjects of his fiction and essays years before they became subjects for the popular press; the preoccupations of his final
books—mysticism, parapsychology, "psychedelic" drugs—offended or
embarrassed the set-in-their-ways (probably some of those very men
who had been liberated by *Antic Hay*) but not so the generation
under thirty, to whom these subjects are important and respectable.
And yet Huxley never courted the good will of the young or of any
other group. His mind was free and adventurous, and his books were
unfailingly of their time and place.

Huxley's novels are original in the sense that no one else could
have written them: each is stamped with Huxley's peculiar mode of
invention and with that witty inflexion that is his alone. We find in
the novels an odd array of characteristics that constitute the Huxley
vision and the Huxley style: an impressive and sometimes showy
awareness of culture in all its multiplicity; enviable clarity of argument and facility of expression; the ironist's relentless tendency to
demonstrate the differences between appearance and reality in
things great and small; a love of unlikely, learned, and sometimes
gruesome comparisons; and that "foible" that Peter Quennell describes as "his love of following up an irrelevant train of ideas, regardless of literary consequences." The novels are the very antithesis of the revered Jamesian model. They are quirky, full of ideas
and lively debate, richly reflective. Better novelists have not succeeded in describing the age—roughly 1920 through 1960—with
anything like the massive and significant detail that we find in
Huxley's fiction. Faulkner, for example, is a better novelist, but who
would read Faulkner for a picture of twentieth-century life? Faulkner's universe is closed, neither conceived in time as ordinary mortals perceive it nor really related to history. The highest forms of
fictive art may indeed be timeless in just this sense, but some other
forms of fiction are not; they are lashed to the decade or even the
very year that generated them. *Point Counter Point* is 1928 London,
and part of its value for us lies in its brilliant, dense, and authentic
evocation of life at just *that* moment in English civilization.

I would suggest that the proper way of viewing Huxley is as a
moraliste, a writer who has more in common with Montaigne and
Pascal than with, say, Hardy or Conrad. Huxley's well-developed
interests in philosophy, biology, sociology, economics, religion, an-
thropology often intrude upon the design of his novels because these
interests were, for him, more important than design. Huxley is a
cerebral rather than a poetic novelist. He is a satirist and a prosely-

tizer of humane values who used the novel form because he found it sufficiently congenial to his purposes. He was a writer more passionately interested in truth as fact than in truth as myth, a writer who had the courage always to do as he pleased and who consequently displeased many, especially those whose definition of the novel was more rigid than his own.

A history of this critical displeasure may be summarized in a few paragraphs, since the complaints against Huxley were few and have been repeated many times.

Huxley came to prominence very early in his career. He had the best possible credentials for success—a famous name, an Oxford education, a wide circle of acquaintances in literary London—plus a youthful talent of the first order. Contemporary reviewers of his early novels were charmed by their freshness, their sprightly erudition and casual impieties. But the praise faded as Huxley, the "amused Pyrrhonic aesthete" of those early years, became increasingly obsessed with the problems of modern life. His somewhat presumptuous attempt to dramatize these problems in his fiction met with disapproval, and the disapproval persisted. His colleagues in the arts—Eliot, Maugham, Virginia Woolf, to name only three—found his books unsatisfactory, and many subsequent critics have concurred: David Daiches, Arnold Kettle, D. S. Savage, Sean O'Faolain, William York Tindall. The case against Huxley was put succinctly by Daiches in his first version (1939) of *The Novel and the Modern World*:

> The fact is that Huxley is no novelist; he has never mastered—is not really interested in—even the elements of form and structure in fiction. We may note how frequently he makes his heroes write long diaries or autobiographical documents or makes them utter long philosophical monologues. His novels are either a series of character sketches or simple fables or tracts. The suggestion of mature technique in *Point Counter Point* and *Eyeless in Gaza* is quite misleading. It is as though Huxley deems it necessary to keep up with contemporary innovators in the technique of fiction by doing some jumping about in time and space, splitting up the action and taking it out of its chronological order, all of which devices are wholly unnecessary, having no functional purpose in building up the story at all. The musical analogy in *Point Counter Point* is quite false and the tampering with chronology there quite purposeless. As for the technique of *Eyeless in Gaza*, it would be comic if it were not so irritating. The novel would have been much more effective as straight autobiography or as the straightforward history of the development

of his hero. Other innovators in technique have had some compelling reason, in terms of plot and structure, for the innovations they introduced, but Huxley seems to be doing it only because he feels that it is expected of him. His real genius is as an essayist. He has a gift for brilliant discussion, for sketching an atmosphere or a character, for making a point. His essays are always quite brilliant affairs technically. He is not really aware of the problems that face the writer of fiction of his day, but he does know how to handle—in isolation— exposition, argument, and description.

Professor Daiches' indictment is clear, penetrating, authoritative, and answerable. Huxley himself acknowledged that he lacked the "congenital" novelist's interest in character and plot. In a famous passage in *Point Counter Point,* Philip Quarles, a novelist very like Huxley himself, makes this revealing entry in his diary:

> Novel of ideas. The character of each personage must be implied, as far as possible, in the ideas of which he is the mouthpiece. In so far as theories are rationalizations of sentiments, instincts, dispositions of soul, this is feasible. The chief defect of the novel of ideas is that you must write about people who have ideas to express—which excludes all but about .01 per cent. of the human race. Hence the real, congenital novelists don't write such books. But then, I never pretended to be a congenital novelist.

Huxley's modest defense of his aims is taken up again in an essay called "Tragedy and the Whole Truth" (1931), in Anthony Beavis's journal in *Eyeless in Gaza* (1936), and eloquently in a letter of 1945 addressed to Jean E. Hare (*Letters,* p. 538):

> [The structure of *Point Counter Point* represents an experiment] . . . in the technique of narrative and of the exploration of the mind carried on by one who is not congenitally a novelist and therefore is compelled to resort to devices which the born novelist would never think of using—being perfectly capable of covering the necessary ground without departing from straightforward techniques.
>
> The conclusion of *Point Counter Point* is the concerned expression of that kind of aesthetic mysticism which runs through the book and which is the analogue on another plane (perhaps even, to some extent, it is the homologue) of the ultimate, spiritual mysticism. Anyhow, it was through the aesthetic that I came to the spiritual—having begun by rejecting the spiritual in favour of the aesthetic and by identifying it with the aesthetic, making the part include the whole. The sense that even the highest art was not good enough, that if

this was all it was a pretty poor thing to be man's final end—this was, at bottom, the impelling motive.

Daiches's charges of ineptitude of technique in *Point Counter Point* and *Eyeless in Gaza* are fully answered in the essays by Peter Firchow and Peter Bowering that are reprinted in this book. His more general complaint against the discursive element in Huxley's fiction is probably a just complaint; but for Huxley, as he makes clear in the letter quoted above, mere art was never enough, and hence his novels are maddeningly encyclopedic. Few writers have imposed upon fiction quite the weight of exposition which Huxley would have it bear, and perhaps only Tolstoy, in *War and Peace,* has done this successfully. Huxley's contrivances—his "long diaries or autobiographical documents"—may bore or disappoint the reader whose expectations have been shaped by long and exclusive familiarity with the novel of sensibility. But Huxley's novels are a deliberate departure from this tradition and we are misguided in blaming him for failure to conform to the canons of that tradition.

The English novel from its inception has had two great models: Fielding and Richardson. *Tom Jones* and *Clarissa* are both superb works of art, and yet their differences in authorial posture and tact, in narrative method, in atmosphere, tone, and range could not be more pronounced. In the twentieth century, the tradition of Richardson—a "congenital" novelist if ever there was one—has prevailed, and writers who have veered from it have been undervalued. Huxley is no Fielding—he was never quite able to combine the instincts of the novelist with the habits of the essayist in the happy fashion of Fielding in *Tom Jones.* But Huxley's unsentimental view of man, his moral passion, his dependence upon humoural characters to convey his meaning are comparable to Fielding's; and like Fielding, he made his novels the carriers of diverse accumulations of experience and learning. *Tom Jones* is a great encyclopedia of eighteenth-century life, an aesthetic whole with layers of incidental reflections on fashion, social class, law, morals, education, sexual mores—an immensely rich sociology as well as a lasting fable of good and evil. Few British novels of the twentieth century, aside from *Point Counter Point,* are comparable to *Tom Jones* in their intellectual energy, diversity, and thoroughness.

On this vexed question of "congenital" versus "noncongenital" novelists, Peter Firchow, in his sound and illuminating study of Huxley, makes a point worth repeating. Comparing Huxley to Lawrence, he comments:

In the useful terminology employed by Erich Auerbach in *Mimesis,*
Huxley is a hypertactic writer, Lawrence is a paratactic one; Huxley
is the Hellene who must see and elaborate all the connections which
go to make up an experience, Lawrence the Hebrew who intimates
and suggests rather than states; Huxley is the Platonic rationalist
who finally prefers history to fiction, Lawrence the Aristotelian who
knows that art can be truer than life. (*Aldous Huxley: Satirist and
Novelist,* p. 8.)

Huxley's reputation is of course problematical. Most readers prefer the early, Peacockian satires; others—Christopher Isherwood, for
example—prefer the wisdom and gravity of the later works. But
even the most hostile of Huxley's critics would probably admit that
our literature would be greatly diminished without him. The man
we meet in the books is arresting, for we see Huxley struggling
heroically with those very problems that have made our century so
turbulent and imploring us again and again to reason patiently, to
view life clearly, and to be better. His moral seriousness and intellectual honesty are awesome. Isaiah Berlin, in an essay that he wrote
for a Huxley memorial volume, isolated the main theme of Huxley's
mature books and pointed out his enduring claim on our attention:

. . . he always returned to the single theme that dominated his later
years: the condition of men in the twentieth century. Over and over
again he contrasted on the one hand their powers to create works
of unheard of power and beauty and live wonderful lives—a future
far wider and more brilliant than had ever stretched before mankind
—with, on the other hand, the prospect of mutual destruction and
total annihilation, due to ignorance and consequent enslavement to
irrational idols and destructive passions—forces that some individuals had, and all men in principle could, control and direct. Perhaps
no one since Spinoza has believed so passionately or coherently or
fully in the principle that knowledge alone liberates, not merely
knowledge of physics or history or physiology, or psychology, but an
altogether wider panorama of possible knowledge which embraced
forces, open and occult, which this infinitely retentive and omnivo-
rous reader was constantly discovering with alternate horrors and
hope. (*Aldous Huxley 1894–1963,* p. 148.)

In editing this collection, I have tried to select a dozen essays (if
the short "Symposium" pieces may be counted as two) that comment
on various aspects of Huxley's art (not only the fiction, since Huxley
never saw himself as only a novelist) and that open up some of the
crucial questions about the merits and defects of his writings. The

collection is not meant to provide an historical summary of critical views of the past forty or fifty years; in fact, all but the essay by Frederick J. Hoffman and *The London Magazine* pieces have been published since Huxley's death ten years ago. All the articles except Professor Hoffman's are reprinted here for the first time. A quiet but steady and sympathetic reappraisal of Huxley is underway by academic critics in America and England, aided by such recent volumes as Grover Smith's edition of the *Letters* (1969), Donald Watt's *Collected Poetry of Aldous Huxley* (1971) and Sybille Bedford's *Aldous Huxley: A Biography, Volume One: 1894–1939* (1973). These essays are the fruits of this new effort.

Aldous Huxley and the Novel of Ideas

by Frederick J. Hoffman

In his *Point Counter Point*, Aldous Huxley has Philip Quarles occasionally jot down in his notebook random observations on the craft of fiction. These may be considered a kind of handbook for a study of the "novel of ideas"—not the novel which incidentally *illustrates* ideas but the novel which uses them in default of characterization and other qualities of the traditional narrative. These passages from the notebook are, of course, immensely valuable for those who wish to investigate Huxley as artist and thinker, but their principal advantage is the way in which they illuminate an art form almost peculiar to twentieth-century literary history. This note, for example, is a "statement of principle" for such a novel:

> Novel of ideas. The character of each personage must be implied, as far as possible, in the ideas of which he is the mouthpiece. In so far as theories are rationalizations of sentiments, instincts, dispositions of soul, this is feasible. The chief defect of the novel of ideas is that you must write about people who have ideas to express—which excludes all but about .01 per cent. of the human race. Hence the real, the congenital novelists don't write such books. But then, I never pretended to be a congenital novelist.

At first glance, the notion that ideas might take precedence over characters in a novel seems no less than monstrous; and of this reaction Quarles is himself aware: "People who can reel off neatly formulated notions aren't quite real; they're slightly monstrous. Living with monsters becomes rather tiresome in the long run." But Huxley has often demonstrated in his novels the fact that ideas may possess qualities which are comparable with those which animate persons— and this particularly in a period of time when ideas are not fixed, calculated, or limited by canons of strict acceptance or rejection.

"Aldous Huxley and the Novel of Ideas" by Frederick J. Hoffman. From *College English* 8, no. 3 (1946): 129–39. Copyright © 1946 by the National Council of Teachers of English. Reprinted by permission of the publisher.

Ideas, as they are used in Huxley, possess, in other words, *dramatic* qualities. Dominating as they very often do the full sweep of his novels, they appropriate the fortunes and careers which ordinarily belong to persons.

I should like to draw further upon the ideas of Philip Quarles as they relate to this unusual and interesting adaptation of a respectable art form. To begin with, Philip is in a very special sense a "modern intellectual." He finds a much greater charm in ideas than in persons. For the ordinary, passive, "idea-less" men of the streets and tearooms—who, of course, exist on all levels of society—he cannot bring himself to command any respect or affection. In fact, in the world of human relationships he is "curiously like a foreigner, uneasily not at home among his fellows, finding it difficult or impossible to enter into communication with any but those who could speak his native intellectual language of ideas."

He meets each personal word, each expression of feeling or intimacy, with a generalization—one which includes his own circumstances and indicates understanding but is safely removed from the danger of immediate participation. His reaction to the personal circumstances which ordinarily demand intimate contact for their proper treatment is an understanding, bulwarked by such generalizations as make that understanding universally applicable. All of which distresses his wife Elinor, who is often hurt by his kind indifference and puzzled rather than made happy by his "occasional and laborious essays at emotional intimacy," but who is also attracted by his intelligence, "that quick, comprehensive, ubiquitous intelligence that could understand everything, including the emotions it could not feel and the instincts it took care not to be moved by."

Philip's unwillingness to be involved in the affairs of ordinary mortals has no small relevance for his attitude toward his art. For him, *persons* are either specimens, or statistics, or demonstrations—anything which can conveniently be lifted from the personal to the abstract. Thus, too, his humor, which takes the form of wit, of exaggeration, of caricature. To the unregenerate intellectual, persons are seldom if ever three-dimensional or actual; or, if they accidentally become so (as they do occasionally for Philip), the experience is a bit disagreeable, even shocking and disturbing. In consequence, his *idea* of personality is substituted for actual *evidence* of personality; ideas are acted out by characters, or demonstrated by them; and finally, a character often assumes the monstrous appearance of such a demonstration. He becomes a caricature which incorporates the furthest possible human demonstration of an attitude with certain grotesque inadequacies of person to which his whimsical creator condemns him. As if in compensation for not having given a character some personal symmetry and identity, he extends beyond credibility the one or few attributes which he does confer upon him.

Philip is a man of great sensitivity to philosophies and points of view. He is capable of accommodating each in its turn. This generosity toward influences is in essence a kind of ever-shifting eclecticism, as a result of which each form of thought may at one time attract him and then be deserted for some other.

> The essential character of the self consisted precisely in that liquid and undeformable ubiquity; in that capacity to espouse all contours and yet remain unfixed in any form; to take, and with an equal facility efface, impressions. To such moulds as his spirit might from time to time occupy, to such hard and burning obstacles as it might flow round, submerge, and, itself cold, penetrate to the fiery heart of, no permanent loyalty was owing. The moulds were emptied as easily as they had been filled, the obstacles were passed by. But the essential liquidness that flowed where it would, the cool indifferent flux of intellectual curiosity—that persisted and to that his loyalty was due.

Such a point of view is ideal—indeed, it is almost necessary—for the novelist of ideas. And at one time in Huxley's career, this it is which both Philip Quarles and his creator upheld. The true way of looking at things is "multiplicity," says Philip to his wife on one occasion. Each point of view differs from every other; and all are valid. A large and ample demonstration of the several approaches to morality and fact serves to bring one as close to truth as one may get. "Multiplicity of eyes and multiplicity of aspects seen," explains Philip. "For instance, one person interprets events in terms of bishops; another in terms of the price of flannel camisoles; another, like that young lady from Gulmberg," he nodded after the retreating group, "thinks of it in terms of good times. And then there's the biologist, the chemist, the physicist, the historian. Each sees, professionally, a different aspect of the event, a different layer of reality. What I want to do is to look with all those eyes at once."

II

This generous point of view is explained at some length in several of the essays published in the volume *Do What You Will*. They constitute the platform for the novelist of ideas. An idea, or large generalization about human behavior, when it is joined to a character in such a novel, is modified to become an attitude or mood. In the interests of narrative and dramatic movement, this attitude or mood leads to action—but it is always *typical* or *characteristic* action, the adventure not so much of a person as of an idea in its contemporary world. The formal essay proves; the novel of ideas demonstrates. Each is strongly dominated by the intellectual character of its author.

As explanation of this point of view, Huxley discusses, in *Do What You Will*, the psychological nature of truth. Truth, he says, is internal. A "psychological fact" is valid for the person who holds it, if for no other. This makes for a diversity of truths, for an infinite variety of interpretations, and for an emphasis upon *attitude* as the determinant of the quality of truth. Opposed to this point of view is the tendency toward unity—purely intellectual knowledge which secures a unity from diversity of experience and holds tenaciously to that unity. The weaknesses of Philip Quarles' kind of intellectual are admitted by Huxley in these essays. One must accept life in all its manifestations, he says in one place, condemning Swift for having failed in this regard; and, speaking of Wordsworth's "Handy Manual for Nature Lovers," he suggests that "it is fear of the labyrinthine flux and complexity of phenomena that has driven men to philosophy, to science, to theology—fear of the complex reality driving them to invent a simpler, more manageable, and therefore consoling fiction."

Each of us searches for his own way of accommodating himself to the universe. But we are frequently afraid of the reality we see and experience, and we hasten to impose upon it some form of order, original or borrowed. We are seldom hospitable toward mere diversity in itself; we are too often afraid of it. Huxley would have us accept the immediate first record of our senses, to be not affrighted but thrilled by their gift of disorder to our minds.

The principal defect in this philosophy of knowing is its marginless and limitless generosity to flux itself—so that one actually escapes the responsibility of *any* interpretation of life by accepting and entertaining momentarily *each* of them. Its value is great, however, for us who wish to apply it to our investigation of the twentieth-century novel of ideas. For it allows for a generous accommodation of all the currents of thought which have been influential in our times.

III

The novel of ideas is a narrative form peculiar to an "unstable" age—one in which standards are not fixed beyond removal or alteration. It assumes a diversity of mood and intention, but it is careful not merely to label its characters. They are not allegorical figures, for there is no single thing which the drama of their interaction is designed to illustrate. The novel which Philip Quarles wants to write is a novel of diversity in points of view, in each of which the intellectual nature is modified by the local circumstances governing it. Such a novel has a development which consists mainly of the demonstration in terms of human events of the effects of a point of view upon the person who holds it. The drama implicit in an idea becomes explicit when it is shown as a point of view which a *person* holds and upon which he acts. The comedy implicit in an idea is revealed in a concrete demonstration of its inherent untenability. But one cannot repeat too often that there is no "moral" to be drawn from the career and fate of ideas in such a novel. There is never any fixed contest between right and wrong, or between the true and the false, from which we are supposed to get what comfort or instruction we can.

One of the chief objectives of the novelist of ideas is to include men of varying temperaments and attitudes within the scope of one narrative and thus to dramatize the clash of these attitudes in his novel. Each character thus has given him (if little else!) a point of view drawn from the prevailing intellectual interests of his creator. On this point of view the character stands, wavers, or falls. Thus, implicit in this type of novel is the drama of ideas rather than of persons, or, rather, the drama of individualized ideas. The structural requirements of such a novel are perhaps simpler than they at first appear. One requirement is to get these people, or as many of them as is possible, together in one place where circumstances are favorable to a varied expression of intellectual diversity. The drawing room, the party, the dinner—these are all favorite points of structural focus. To supplement them, there are the notebooks (as in *Point Counter Point*), correspondence (which serves as a substitute for conversation and varies the narrative procedure), the casual or accidental meeting of two or three persons, who continue their discussions in one form or another, and the prolonged exposition, in essay form, of any given or chance suggestion which the narrative may allow.

The best examples of the novel of ideas are Huxley's novels of the 1920's. To be sure, he did not always use this form; nor is any of his novels purely a novel of ideas. In his shorter pieces, most notably in "Uncle Spencer," "Two or Three Graces," and "Young Archimedes," Huxley writes charmingly and sympathetically of persons and reveals a remarkable talent for a complete delineation of characters who are interesting almost exclusively as persons. But the works which mark the development of Huxley as a novelist—*Crome Yellow, Antic Hay, Those Barren Leaves,* and *Point Counter Point*—are, each in its own way, novels of ideas. Rarely does a Huxley character give himself away directly; rarely if ever does Huxley fail to give him away. The position, the point of view, of \ the Huxley character is usually revealed in the course of Huxley's discussion of his tastes, his intellectual preferences, his manner of behaving himself in the society of his fellows. Thus the *idea* which each is to demonstrate becomes in the novel the point of view he adopts—or, actually, *is*. There are varying shades of characterization, ranging from gross caricature to sympathetic exposition. There are degrees of the grotesque in the points of view described in Huxley's novels. Thus Lypiatt of *Antic Hay* is at times grotesque, at times pathetic, but almost always absurd. Gumbril Jr. is a pleasant enough grotesque, though his weaknesses at times make of him a pathetic figure. Other characters, like Mercaptan, are consistently and superbly themselves on all or almost all occasions.

These persons in *Antic Hay* have ample opportunity to express their individualities in an early gathering in a restaurant—a favorite setting, one in which points of view are given an opportunity for "free-lance" expression. Lypiatt's hostility to Mercaptan is one theme of the novel; it is an opposition of points of view much more than of wills. Lypiatt, the frustrated, would-be genius, is never a match for the genteelly cynical Mercaptan. The inequality reduces the conflict to an absurdity. Typically revealing examples of their conversation illustrate well their points of view and may help to show how the Huxley novel of ideas works:

> Lypiatt went on torrentially. "You're afraid of ideals, that's what it is. You daren't admit to having dreams. . . . Ideals—they're not sufficiently genteel for you civilised young men. You've quite outgrown that sort of thing. No dream, no religion, no morality." . . .
>
> "*What* there is to be ashamed of in being civilised, I *really* don't know," [Mercaptan] said, in a voice that was now the bull's, now the piping robin's. "No, if I glory in anything, it's in my little rococo

boudoir, and the conversations across the polished mahogany, and
the delicate, lascivious, *witty* little flirtations on ample sofas inhabited by the soul of Crébillon Fils. We needn't *all* be Russians, I
hope. These revolting Dostoievskys."

This clash between the vigorous but pathetically awkward and
mistaken artist and the mild but venomously precious esthete and
critic rises and subsides throughout the novel, until it issues in
physical violence. In the novel we also find the scientist, the incorri-
gibly self-sacrificing laboratory scientist, devoted to a ceaseless experimenting with endless demonstrations of a fragment of hypothesis. His point of view, consistent to the last lost shred of dignity, is
portrayed by Huxley as one of the more pathetic of the grotesques
in his fiction.

Perhaps because *Point Counter Point* is more deliberately
planned, that novel seems at least to have given each of its points of
view some discoverable beginning, middle, and end. By interweav-
ing these points of view, giving them a thematic structure, Huxley
has placed a large premium upon his view of supplementary ideas.
The interesting fact about this novel is that the several points of
view are acted out, tested as it were, in the modern world, and the
limitations of each are demonstrated in the individual fates of the
persons who hold them. Spandrell, in himself not concerned with
large social issues, lends courage to Illidge, scientist-Communist, so
that Webley, Fascist, comes to a violent end. Lord Edward's devotion to science is free, because he chooses it to be, of the embarrass-
ing complications which Illidge suffers through involvement in political action. He has instead what his assistant calls "a shameful and
adulterous passion for idealistic metaphysics." In each case, the
point of view, which becomes quite clear very early in the novel, is
so given as to form a core of responsibility for the action consequent
upon differences of opinion and opposing and clashing ideas.

IV

"Put a novelist into the novel" (that is, as one of the characters),
Philip Quarles advises himself in his notebook. "He justifies aesthetic generalizations, which may be interesting—at least to me. He
also justifies experiment. Specimens of his work may illustrate other
possible or impossible ways of telling a story. And if you have him
telling parts of the same story as you are, you can make a variation
on the theme." Philip is, of course, talking here of a novelist as one

of the characters, not of *the* novelist, not of himself. He does not consider it wise to set up the novelist in a place of authority, so that the other characters may consult him on occasion about what they are to do next, or how they are to feel about what they have just done.

But the author of a novel of ideas is a *person* of much greater stature in his own novel—and his presence is much more obvious, too. And, at least in the case of Huxley, there is a close interaction of the essayist with the novelist. They parallel each other for a time; they frequently supplement each other. The essayist is a sort of "supply station," to which the novelist has recourse. He is the "port of call" at which the novelist stops, to take on necessary and staple goods. The reputation of Huxley is chiefly that of the novelist. In another sense, however, he is the essayist-commentator upon twentieth-century morals and ideas. Just as his characters are often subordinate as persons to the ideas or points of view they express, so his novels as a whole are often mere carriers for the cargo of ideas which their author must retail.

The essayist's attempt to give animation to his ideas leads to the novel of ideas. In the course of Huxley's development as novelist, the characters of his creation stumble, swagger, or are carried through his novels, supported almost always by the essayist. Feelings, such as those mixed feelings with which Walter Bidlake contemplates both his mistresses, are freighted with ratiocination. The great difference between this kind of exposition and the *exempla* of medieval sermons is that in the former there is no fixed point of view to bring home to the reader. Rather, there are many points of view; and the reader is asked not so much to appraise as to enjoy them. To illustrate, Walter Bidlake's conquest of Lucy Tantamount proceeds by stages of speculation and comment, the essayist explaining and analyzing to the last detail of sentiment and caprice. Walter, says Huxley, "treated Lucy, not as the hard, ruthless amusement-hunter he had so clearly recognized her as being before he became her lover, but as an ideally gracious and sensitive being, to be adored as well as desired, a sort of combined child, mother, and mistress, whom one should maternally protect and be maternally protected by, as well as virilely and—yes!—faunishly make love to."

This much one wants, needs, by way of establishing the mood of the occasion. There follows an elaborate essay on sensuality and sentiment, based upon the relationship between Walter and Lucy, but a separate thing as well, an essay on the subject, broken occasionally to allow for a further demonstration of the points it is making. The commentator says: "This is a situation worthy of lengthy comment, because it illustrates what I have long thought to be true of modern moralities. Let me speak my mind, and in a short while I shall have these two characters back. In what they do you will see that I am right in my analysis." The essay begins: "Sensuality and sentiment, desire and tenderness are as often friends as they are enemies." A comment generalized from experience not real but imagined, projected upon the essayist's screen, to which he points in support of it. Some sentences further, the essayist permits Walter to assume his role as specific example, but the comment is itself a generalization: "Walter's desire to justify his longings by love was only, on final analysis, the articulately moral expression of his natural tendency to associate the act of sexual enjoyment with a feeling of tenderness, at once chivalrously protective and childishly self-abased."

Lucy and Walter—sensuality and sentiment, touching each other, embracing, and then separate, isolated points of view, their inherent conflict restored after a brief moment of self-indulgent union. "Living modernly's living quickly," says Lucy to Walter, as if to underline finally the fact that, in these times at any rate, sensuality and sentiment do not mix well. "You can't cart a wagonload of ideals and romanticisms about with you these days. When you travel by airplane, you must leave your heavy baggage behind. The good old-fashioned soul was all right when people lived slowly. But it's too ponderous nowadays. There's no room for it in the airplane."

In the novels of the 1920's, the essayist in Huxley strode along with the novelist. The essays he wrote for the *Athenaeum* and for *Vanity Fair* are matched by the conversation and contemplation recorded in the novels; and there is a supporting theory of composition to be found in certain of the essays. Beginning, perhaps, with *Eyeless in Gaza,* the essayist far exceeds the novelist. What has happened? The novel of ideas requires a poise, a balance, and most of all an eclectic faith in the democracy of ideas. Once the novelist deserts this position, his novels have only one of two ways to go: they may become novels not of ideas but of persons; this seldom occurs, because the conversion of a novelist of ideas is scarcely ever an esthetic conversion. Or they may become essays almost purely, and the narrative itself a setting for the *exposition* rather than the *dramatization* of ideas. This latter is what occurred in Huxley's later novels. He is alternately a caricaturist and an essayist; he is no longer a novelist of ideas, but a philosopher who knows not how gracefully to leave the house in which he has lived so graciously all his life. There are occasional delightful exceptions in *Eyeless in Gaza, After Many a Summer,* and *Time Must Have a Stop.* But in each case one feels that the essayist is impatient for the artist to finish building the platform, so that he may mount it for his "lesson." Anthony Beavis and Miller *of Eyeless in Gaza,* Propter of *After Many a Summer,* Bruno Rontini and his disciple, Sebastian Barnack, of *Time Must Have a Stop*—to these persons Huxley gives the responsibility for showing the development of the point of view which he himself presents at length in *Ends and Means.*

Huxley is no longer a novelist. His recent novels are lengthy essays, to which are added entertainments. But his novels of the 1920's *are* novels of ideas—ideas clothed, ideas given flesh and bone and sent out into a world in which they may test themselves. What is grotesque or pathetic or noble in each of them is revealed in various ways as the dramatic equivalent of its intellectual status. Compare the dialogue in any of Jane Austen's novels with that, let us say, in *Point Counter Point.* In the one, the larger morality of the day is taken for granted, and only the peculiarities of persons residing in a relatively fixed world receive treatment. In the other, nothing is taken for granted; everything is accepted, but only as it meets and clashes with everything else.

Huxley's novels of ideas are an expression of the tremendous vitality which ideas had in the 1920's; they are also a testimony of the intellectual confusion of that period. To record that confusion requires a tolerance of it and, above all, a willingness to grant for the moment at least that ideas may have a vitality and attraction quite apart from their more sober values, those values they possess when they remain confined within the limits of systematic philosophy or science. Most important of all, these novels are a brilliant portrait of the age, or at least of its intellectual interests and habits. Whatever defects of manner the novels of Huxley suffer, his vital interest in the intellectual concerns of his time has resulted in several dramatic portraits of contemporary life and thought.

A Critical Symposium
on Aldous Huxley
The London Magazine (1955)

YOUTH AT THE HELM AND PLEASURE AT THE PROW:
Antic Hay

by Evelyn Waugh

Not everyone in 1923, not I for one, knew without recourse to
the dictionary that a "hey" or "hay" was a country jig. As we sped
from Blackwell's with our eagerly awaited copies of Mr. Aldous
Huxley's second novel, its title suggested a neglected stable and,
strange to recall, as we read it in that fragrant age, the tale did
smack a little sour. To be quite accurate in reminiscence I got my
own copy second-hand from the present literary critic of the *Daily
Mail*—a young man already plainly destined for high position—and
he passed it to me (for a financial consideration) saying I should find
it "dreary." *Dreary!* Re-read now after all that has happened, after
all that has been written, after all Mr. Huxley has written, the book
has the lilt of Old Vienna.

It is placed in London in springtime. The weather, page after
page, is warm and airy and brilliant. Did we ever enjoy quite such
a delightful climate? We certainly do not find it in modern fiction.
And London is still in 1923 eminently habitable, a city of private
houses and private lives, leisurely, not too full even in the season,
all leafy squares and stucco façades and Piranesan mewses. The pave-
ments of Bond Street are "perfumed," the shops are full of desirable
goods. All one needs is a little money—not much; £300 a year is a
competence, £5,000 is wealth—and that little is easily acquired by
some whimsical invention such as a pair of pneumatic trousers. Re-
gent Street is doomed but Verrey's is still open, open after luncheon
until it is time to go out to tea. A few miles out in Surrey and Sussex

an arcadian countryside is opening to the never-failing sun. Although all the inhabitants of this delicious city have been everywhere and speak every language they are thoroughly English, at home in their own capital. No character in *Antic Hay* ever uses the telephone. They write letters, they telegraph, they call, and there are always suitable servants to say "not at home" to bores. It is Henry James's London possessed by carnival. A chain of brilliant young people linked and interlaced winds past the burnished frontdoors in pursuit of happiness. Happiness is growing wild for anyone to pick, only the perverse miss it. There has been the single unpredictable, inexplicable, unrepeatable calamity of "the Great War." It has left broken hearts—Mrs. Viveash's among them—but the other characters are newly liberated from their comfortable refuges of Conscientious Objection, to run wild through the streets.

The central theme of the book is the study of two falterers "more or less in" their "great task of happiness," Mrs. Viveash and Theodore Gumbril. Everyone else, if young, has a good time. Two clowns, Lypiatt and Shearwater, get knocked about, but that is the clown's *metier*. Rosie is happy in her pink underclothes and her daze of romantic fantasy, picked up, rolled over, passed on, giving and gaining pleasure and all the time astutely learning the *nuances* of cultural advancement. Coleman is happy, uproariously blaspheming. Men rather like him turn up later in Mr. Huxley's works, miserable men, haunted and damned. Coleman is boisterously happy, a sort of diabolic Belloc. And Mercaptan is happy, unambitious, sensual, accomplished, radiantly second-rate. He is a period piece, still in his twenties with the tastes and pretentions of ripe middle-age. They do not come like that today. Today one knows quite certainly that a young bachelor with a *penchant* for white satin sofas and *bibelots* would not be running after girls and, moreover, that though he might drop into idiomatic French, he would be quite incapable of writing grammatical English.

Mrs. Viveash and Gumbril are the falterers in the Great Task and their situation is not quite desperate. She has her classic, dignified bereavement. Promiscuous sexual relations bore her. But she has, we are told, almost limitless power, power which, I must confess, has never much impressed me. She was 25 when I was 20. She seemed then appallingly mature. The girls I knew did not whisper in "expiring" voices and "smile agonizingly" from their "death beds." They grinned from ear to ear and yelled one's head off. And now thirty years on, when women of 25 seem to me moody children, I still cannot weep for Mrs. Viveash's tragic emptiness.

Gumbril rejects the chance of a *Happy Hypocrite* idyll, of love, literally, in a cottage. But it would never have done. He is a clever, zestful cad. He would have been hideously bored in a week. He is off abroad to a wide, smiling continent full of wine and pictures and loose young women. He will be all right.

The story is told richly and elegantly with few of the interruptions which, despite their intrinsic interest, mar so much of Mr. Huxley's story-telling. The disquisition on Wren's London should be in a book of essays but the parody of the night-club play is so funny that one welcomes its intrusion. The "novel of ideas" raises its ugly head twice only, in the scenes with the tailor and the financier, crashing bores both of them but mere spectators at the dance. They do not hold up the fun for long.

And there is another delicious quality. The city is not always James's London. Sometimes it becomes Mediterranean, central to the live tradition. The dance winds through piazzas and alleys, under arches, round fountains and everywhere are the embellishments of the old religion. An ancient pagan feast, long christianized in name, is being celebrated in a christian city. The story begins in a school chapel, Domenichino's *Jerome* hangs by Rosie's bed, Coleman quotes the Fathers. There is an insistent undertone, audible through the carnival music, saying all the time, not in Mrs. Viveash's "expiring" voice, that happiness is a reality.

Since 1923 Mr. Huxley has travelled far. He has done more than change climate and diet. I miss that undertone in his later work. It was because he was then so near the essentials of the human condition that he could write a book that is frivolous and sentimental and perennially delightful.

THE HOUSE PARTY NOVELS: *Crome Yellow* and
Those Barren Leaves

by Angus Wilson

Aldous Huxley was already a considerable name to me when I was thirteen. My sophisticated, literary inclined elder brothers spoke of him with what they intended for familiarity. All that came over to me was the underlying awe. He alone, I imagined, could free me from the prison of family Philistinism and, at that time, I already felt like one born in the Bastille. On August 11, 1929, my fifteenth birthday, I was given *Antic Hay*. The revolutionary forces that released me were all and more than all that I expected. It seemed a revelation of emancipation and intellectual richness. To be precociously sophisticated, then, was indeed "very heaven." For many years *Antic Hay* and *Point Counter Point* were my favourites. Smart, intellectual and artistic London was after all just outside my door. The inmates of the Kensington hotels where I lived might talk as they would, but in every bus and tube on which I travelled to and from school there were brilliant, twisted Spandrells, blaspheming Colemans, or perhaps even "civilized" Mr. Mercaptan going home to read Crebillon fils's *Sofa*. A few years more and I, too, would be a Gumbril.

I read *Crome Yellow* and *Those Barren Leaves*, of course, but at that time they seemed less exciting—the world of country house weekend parties and of Italian villas lay too far away to give me the same thrill. In any case, like most adolescents, I was looking for a certain loucherie, a life of "fast" tempo. The strange, idyllic pastoral mood of *Crome Yellow* and *Those Barren Leaves* passed me by, or, if I noticed it, it rather bored me. Nevertheless, they ate deeper into my imagination than I realized. Nearly twenty years later when I wrote my first story, *Raspberry Jam*, I added to what came from the heat of my own fancy a character designed to give an element of wit and worldliness. I was proud of my creation. It was only afterwards that I realized that the addition was pure pastiche of Mr. Scogan or Mr. Cardan. Whatever our final verdict on Aldous Huxley's work, the debt of so many later authors to his work is extraordinary.

The appearance of *Decline and Fall* soon removed the creation of *Antic Hay* into another sphere. But the house party novels, *Crome Yellow* and *Those Barren Leaves*, remained alone. There were countless imitators, of course, in the late 'twenties and 'thirties, but only the novels of Richard Oke and a forgotten book, *They Winter Abroad*, can be called estimable. It was only when I had read more picaresque novels, and, above all, when I had read Peacock that I began to appreciate *Crome Yellow* and *Those Barren Leaves*. The influences were obvious, but the creation remained unique.

Those Barren Leaves (1925) follows exactly upon *Crome Yellow* (1921) though other books were to intervene. In his first novel, the pattern is a simple one: the young intellectually aspiring Denis visits the Wimbush household—a world of rich, witty, sophisticated, talkative people. He makes a fool of himself in word and in love. The destruction of youth's pretensions and illusions, particularly sexual ones, is a favourite theme of Aldous Huxley, but in these early novels the note is less shrill, more pleasing than in, for example, *Time Must Have a Stop*. The "philosophy" of sexual hedonism and the ideal of romantic love are mocked, but there is none of the pathological wallowing in physical disgust that began to darken the picture in *Point Counter Point* and *Eyeless in Gaza*, and has now become so tedious. Denis's intellectual aspirations are soon made absurd by contrast with Mr. Scogan's more mature cleverness, his love-making ends in farce when Ivor, with his genuine Byronic dash and his true sexual fervour, appears on the scene. Yet the author stands apart and mocks these mentors, too, with a nice irony, in which Denis's innocence plays a considerable part as a touchstone. In *Those Barren Leaves* the sexually competent, romantic Ivor returns in two roles: his speed, youth and energy, his "dashing" motor car appear in Lord Hovenden, a rare combination of absurdity and excellence in Huxley's work; his romantic prowess and heroic looks go to Calamy, the equivalent of Denis, the picaresque visitor hero with far more intellectual powers than either Denis or Ivor. Cynical, comfortable, sad, hedonistic old Mr. Scogan reappears in Mr. Cardan and is equally a mocked mentor. Most of the other characters reappear, but they are more formidable targets for Mr. Huxley's satire —the talk is better, the intellectual fireworks more astonishing, perhaps a little too much so. At the end of the novel Calamy retires to the mountains to meditate, whereas Denis just went back to London to his own social and intellectual uncertainty. The ending of *Those Barren Leaves*, in fact, brings us to that point of rejection of all material creeds, whether high or low minded, that search for spiritual truth to which all the author's later work is a coda. Whatever the validity of Mr. Huxley's religious creed, it has to be said at once that Calamy's spiritual doubts are artistically far more satisfying than the increasing dogma of the later novels.

Irony, wit, well described "humours," rejection of inadequate materialism and of spurious, popular spirituality—Mr. Barbecue-Smith of *Crome Yellow* is kin to the more sophisticated Burlap of *Point Counter Point*—are all there in as full measure as in the later, more ambitious works. Most of what was to be added later has not enriched Huxley's work. It is not, however, only a negative virtue that *Crome Yellow* and *Those Barren Leaves* possess; something that was in them has been lost. It is this quality, which I can only describe as the power to delight, that has made me value these two books with increasing affection. It is not, to my mind, present in *Antic Hay*, excellent though that is. The quality, I believe, is therefore connected with their country setting—the English country house, the farmyard of *Crome Yellow,* the Italian scene of *Those Barren Leaves.* Mr. Huxley has always made great sport of pantheism, nature worship or the transcendentalism of Daddy Wordsworth; yet there is in these two books an exultation, a sense of material pleasure in the natural world that irradiates the scene. They are, in a unique manner, idyllic, pastoral, bucolic. This does not mean that the satire is "kindly" or the approach sentimental, but only that, despite himself and his rejection of the world, Mr. Huxley communicates a satisfying acceptant quality which enchants. It shows itself most particularly, of course, in those two inserted episodes—the brilliant tale of the dwarf Sir Hercules in *Crome Yellow* and the touching story of Mr. Cardan's rescue of the feebleminded Miss Elver in *Those Barren Leaves.* It is present directly in the remarkable descriptive scenes. Its presence, however, is felt more subtly throughout both novels, and is not to be found anywhere else in modern literature.

THE TEACHER EMERGES: *Point Counter Point, Eyeless in Gaza, Mortal Coils*

by Francis Wyndham

Reading a book by Aldous Huxley is like being entertained by a host who is determined that one should not suffer a moment's boredom and works perhaps a bit too hard to ensure one's continual amusement. The fruit of his considerable erudition is lavished on his readers in flattering profusion: quotations from literature, references to art, history and science—if one takes the allusion, it is with a pleasant sense of sharing the author's culture, and if not one is privileged to learn a new fact or to hear an unusual and provocative point of view. For this reason Mr. Huxley is an ideal novelist for young men: remarkably intelligent, genuinely sophisticated, he takes for granted these enviable qualities in his readers. His first three novels, *Crome Yellow, Antic Hay* and *Those Barren Leaves,* and the stories, essays and poems of that period, represent a perfect form of undergraduate literature: elegant, informed, irreverent, ironic, as it seems amoral yet serious, they appeared at a time—the early 1920's—when the scene was set for brilliant young men and when to be a brilliant young man was the most rewarding thing to be. But brilliant young men must grow into brilliant middle-aged men; the undergraduate, though he may be sent down from one uni-

versity, eventually becomes a don at another. Mr. Huxley could not
forever maintain a position of gay and destructive criticism; a constructive remedy had to be proposed and the entertainer had to
make room for the teacher. In his later novels, the feast of diversion
spread before his readers is no less rich than before, but it has become slightly indigestible.

Point Counter Point, which was first published in 1928, brings his
earlier manner to a point of culmination and contains the germ of
his later development. Formidably long, it introduces a host of
representative characters (several of whom are clearly derived from
real people) and sets them talking at each other. A complexity of
design resulting from the large dramatis personae gives the novel's
construction a superficial resemblance to that of Gide's *Les Faux-
Monnayeurs,* which had appeared three years earlier; but neither
Point Counter Point nor *Eyeless in Gaza,* in which Mr. Huxley later
exploited a confusing time sequence, can lay claim to technical innovations. Mr. Huxley has never been an experimental writer; he is
rather an accomplished popularizer of experiments recently made
by others. *Point Counter Point* would be more amusing if it were
less exhaustive, if its gallery of rogues and fools were less definitive;
and *Eyeless in Gaza* might be easier to reread if its episodes were ar-
ranged in simple chronological order. The ideas of D. H. Lawrence
dominate *Point Counter Point,* expounded at second-hand through
the medium of a character called Mark Rampion. Rampion and his
wife are possibly the first figures in Mr. Huxley's novels to be treated
with a minimum of irony; yet the author's ironic attitude is infec-
tious and his readers catch it by mistake; Rampion emerges, unin-
tentionally, as a pretentious bore. However sympathetic to D. H.
Lawrence as an artist Mr. Huxley may be, his own talent is naturally resistant to Lawrence's influence; an impression is given by
Point Counter Point that the follies and vices of the time have been
condemned from a position that is not truly the author's own.

Brave New World may well prove to be Mr. Huxley's most lasting book. Purely satirical and brilliantly prophetic, it is the last
destructive work by an essentialy destructive writer. By the time
Eyeless in Gaza was published in 1935 Mr. Huxley had become a
disciple of Gerald Heard; and Anthony Beavis, the hero, hopes to
find balm for his disgust with life in the teachings of the mysterious Miller. From now on, an increasing concern with mysticism was
to take control of Mr. Huxley's life and work, and the final pages
of *Eyeless in Gaza,* which contain Anthony's spiritual meditation,

point the way to all his future writing, including his last book about mescalin. Why does this development, so boldly constructive and apparently so consistent, not entirely satisfy? A certain element in his treatment of what he thinks disgusting weakens, in his novels, the force of his striving towards what he thinks pure. In spite of the case made out for withdrawal Mr. Huxley, it seems, relishes life, and not at all in the way of which Mark Rampion would approve. In an early collection of slight but elegant stories, *Mortal Coils,* there is one about a nun whose lover rapes and abandons her, stealing her false teeth which he hopes to sell. This story, according to the blurb, has been described by Jocelyn Brooke as "admirably written in his best comic vein." Among the incidents in *Eyeless in Gaza* which drive Anthony to Miller's contemplative comfort are three, also written in Mr. Huxley's best comic vein, which are well known: a dead dog is dropped from an aeroplane to burst over Anthony while he makes love on a roof; a schoolboy is interrupted while masturbating by his friends who jeer and throw things at him; a young girl pointlessly steals raw meat from a butcher's shop. All these episodes *are* comic, but not straightforwardly so; one laughs less with the author than at him for having invented them, and one suspects that he (a witty but humourless writer) only thinks them funny to the extent that, in various ways, they are potentially shocking. He seems, in fact, to be perpetually trying to shock himself by emphasizing the inadequacies of physical life, by pointing out that lovers look ridiculous when copulating, that the food we enjoy eating is revolting when raw and makes us belch and so on, but the shock results in titillation rather than rejection and disgust. As the writer of pornography pays, in his fashion, a compliment to sex, so Mr. Huxley obliquely honours the sensual life; but this is done in a series of highly cerebral *divertissements* advocating discipline, control and meditation as the means towards spiritual peace and transcendent illumination. Yes, he is an excellent host; there is something here for everybody. The quality is high, the menu varied, but it is not, in the last analysis, a sustaining diet.

TRACTS AGAINST MATERIALISM: *After
Many a Summer* and *Brave New World*

by *John Wain*

Aldous Huxley, like George Orwell, W. H. Mallock, G. K. Ches-
terton and Charles Williams, is a pseudo-novelist; I use the expression not harshly, but merely to describe an author who finds himself using the form of the novel for some alien purpose. Mr. Huxley's
purpose is to write tracts. Both these books are tracts against materialism.

As *Brave New World* is complicated by its special form, let me
take the later book first. *After Many a Summer* concerns itself with
a group of characters who typify, in one way or another, the confusions and miseries of the materialistic outlook. This outlook is so
fruitful of confusions and miseries that Mr. Huxley can give us a
very large gallery of characters, ranging from Dr. Obispo, whose
personal character (as distinct, perhaps, from his work as a scientist)
is utterly repulsive, up to Mike, his laboratory assistant, who is just
a nice mixed-up kid. In between these two points on the graph lie
Mr. Stoyte, Jeremy Pordage, Virginia Maunciple, in all of whom
the author takes a protective interest, half tender and half repelled,
as one might in an idiot child.

These figures are not "characters," of course; they are Humours.
As such they would be more successful if they were not all facets
of the same Humour—highbrow Bloomsbury materialism, lowbrow
Hollywood materialism, clean-limbed bewildered materialism, and
so on. Over against them is set the figure of Mr. Propter (a most significant name—he is "proper" and a "prompter" and also *post hoc,
ergo propter hoc*) who knows all the answers, and is able to tell the
other characters why materialism is wrong. He it is who makes the
remark which sums up the effect on the reader of himself and his
fellow-characters.

> "They stand for certain things on the human level. But the things
> the writers force them to stand for when they describe events on the
> level of eternity are quite different. Hence the use of them merely
> confuses the issue. They just make it all but impossible for anyone
> to know what's being talked about."

He is actually referring, it will be remembered, to certain words in philosophical terminology, but his words apply startlingly well to this arid thesis untidily shovelled into the framework of a novel.

Apart from this artistic malaise, *After Many a Summer* is seriously damaging to its own cause. Its thesis is that materialism is to be abandoned and a version of mysticism ("on the level of eternity," as Mr. Propter is fond of saying) to be put in its place. But those who preach views of this kind should guard against giving the impression that to them, all human life is disgusting and wearisome, and all normal human emotions in themselves to be suspected. If the reader thinks that the book has been written by someone who just doesn't see the point of being human, the message will bounce off him. This impression has been enough to neutralize some of the very greatest satires, such as *Gulliver,* and it certainly neutralizes *After Many a Summer.* To turn to this book after reading, say, Chaucer, is to be struck by the difference between a wise and toleriant (however ironic) view of the human condition, and a mere foaming attack on it. In his eagerness to demonstrate that normal human pleasures are worthless and degrading, Mr. Huxley even repeats a situation he had already handled in an earlier novel; the scene in *Antic Hay* (chap. 20) where Coleman, preparatory to raping Rosie, tells her that it's a pity she is an agnostic, because she will miss half the fun of it by having no sense of sin, is a remarkable anticipation of the relationship between Obispo and Virginia:

> No romance, or anything; just that sniggering laugh and a lot of dirty cracks. Maybe it was sophisticated; but she didn't like it. She wanted Real romance, like in the pictures, with moonlight, and swing music, or perhaps a torch singer (because it was nice to feel sad when you were happy), and a boy saying lovely things to you, and a lot of kissing, and at the end of it, almost without your knowing it, almost as if it weren't happening to you, so that you never felt there was anything wrong, anything that Our Lady would really mind. . . .

But Obispo, like Coleman, enjoys making his victim feel that they are "honeying and making love over the nasty sty." And the only other sexual relationship described in the book (if we exclude Pordage's fortnightly visit to Maida Vale, where he apparently engages two women at once) is the monstrous sadism of the eighteenth-century nobleman, who keeps himself alive by swallowing fishes' guts, and is discovered at the end of the story, two or three centuries old and still finding his sole pleasure in inflicting pain on his mate, who "whimpers apprehensively" at his approach—recalling Virginia's "moaning and gibbering" under the attentions of the skilled

sex-mechanic Obispo. . . . What on earth has this got to do with
the life of a normally poised human being? Of course, it touches
the life of a normally poised person at this or that point; but my
submission is that the old mistake has, once again, been made; if
you set out to sermonize on the World, the Flesh and the Devil, and
reveal clearly by your writings that for you, personally, the ordinary
and attainable human joys are as tempting as a thumb in the eye,
the reader will simply shrug it off. We can all refuse to adopt the
methods of Coleman and Obispo without necessarily following the
example of Origen.

Brave New World is also an anti-materialist tract. It is a well-
understood convention that the Utopian kind of pseudo-novel,
though set in a remote position as to period or place, is always a
criticism of the author's own society. *Brave New World* is a criticism
of Western society in 1932, as *1984* is of the same society in the closing months of the Second World War; any discussion of such books
that sets out to assess their plausibility as *predictions* seems to me
hopeless off-centre. The citizens of the Brave New World are entirely conditioned to a life which ignores the possibility of any
values except those of pleasure and material well-being; they live
in great physical comfort which is paid for in terms of an appalling
spiritual dryness. As a criticism of the more prosperous Western
countries in the late 'twenties it could not be bettered; the "prophetic" framework is valuable largely because it allows free play
to the author's marvellous wit (the jokes about Ford, etc.).

The thrust against materialism had point in 1932, and has point
now; but in the actual future, I doubt if it will have any. People
who live very primitive and physically exhausting lives are never
materialistic; on the contrary, they are always deeply religious. And
it will, of course, be a primitive and laborious life that human
beings will live in a hundred years' time and indefinitely thereafter;
even if there are no World Wars, the increase of population, coupled
with the exhaustion of natural resources, will usher in an era of
famine and shortage. Our great-grandchildren will listen open-
mouthed to stories of the 1950's, when even quite ordinary people
had motor cars of their own, to go more or less where they liked,
and could buy petrol without a police permit; people who lived in
houses which could be warmed by merely switching on an electric
fire, and where hot water gushed out of the taps! I think, in short,
that humanity has already reached the most highly urbanized and
gadget-ridden state it is ever likely to reach; anyone who wants to
know how the peoples of the Western countries will be living in a

century's time could find out more from a tour of South-East Asia than anything else: that swarming, half-starved proletariat—*that* is our future, not a world in which ordinary citizens take trips by helicopter from London to New York.

It was the brave *old* world that Mr. Huxley was describing; the world with a tremendous material ascendancy, whose natural danger was sceptical materialism. In the world we are actually going to inhabit, the dangers will be devil-worship and witch-burning. But this fact does not, of course, diminish the value of Mr. Huxley's works.

ELECTRIFYING THE AUDIENCE: *Music at Night* and *Beyond the Mexique Bay*

by Peter Quennell

One of Mr. Aldous Huxley's Oxford contemporaries, who sometimes attended the same tutorials and heard him read his essays aloud, has described to me the admiration—the stupefaction almost —that they were apt to produce among his fellow undergraduates. His style was already fully fledged; he already displayed that breadth of reading, that gift of ranging rapidly to and fro across the fields of literature, art and science, discovering unexpected analogies between apparently diverse subjects which he has since revealed in a long series of novels, stories and critical essays. Few writers of the present age have combined greater facility with a larger share of erudition. But so much facility (as Mr. Huxley himself is well aware) has obvious disadvantages; and twenty-five years ago he published an admirable pamphlet entitled *Vulgarity in Literature,* which contains some incisive criticisms of the critic's own method. He is discussing the novels of Flaubert:

> The temptations (he writes) which Flaubert put aside are, by any man of lively fancy and active intellect, incredibly difficult to be resisted. . . . A phrase, a situation suggests a whole train of striking or amusing ideas that fly off at a tangent, so to speak, from the round world on which the creator is at work; what an opportunity for saying something witty or profound! . . . In goes the tangent—or rather, out into artistic irrelevancy. And in goes the effective phrase that is too effective, too highly coloured. . . .

The pamphlet was published in 1930. It was followed in 1931

by *Music at Night,* a book of miscellaneous essays, and three years
later by a collection of travel-sketches, which he called *Beyond the
Mexique Bay.* To re-read them is an interesting experience. Again
one marvels at the writer's dexterity; each of these essays and
sketches is the kind of production for which the editor of a weekly
or monthly journal is constantly looking and usually looks in vain
—adequately serious, sufficiently light, neatly fitted into the prescribed space, flavoured here and there with a paradoxical sense of
fun. They belong, of course, to that unregenerate period when Mr.
Huxley was still prepared to make irreverent jokes about "mysticism" and "misty schism." The Literature of mysticism, he then
assured us, "which is literature about the inexpressible, is for the
most part misty indeed—a London fog, but coloured pink." But
he had felt the heady influence of D. H. Lawrence, whose genius
is hailed, though not without some shrewd reservations, in
the last chapter of *Beyond the Mexique Bay*; and the sceptical
astringency of his early novels and stories, of *Crome Yellow* and
Mortal Coils, was slowly disappearing as the sceptic advanced on
middle age.

Yet, despite a gradual change in the author's outlook, he retained
many of his youthful foibles—his love of coining an effective phrase
and, regardless of the literary consequences, following up an irrelevant train of ideas. The result is diverting, but at times unsatisfying.
Many of the articles printed in *Music at Night* are surely a little too
slight to deserve republication? "The Beauty Industry," for example,
merely exhibits a number of ingenious variations on the familiar
journalistic problem as to whether feminine beauty is, or is not,
skin-deep; while others have the charm, but also the impermanence,
of entertaining table-talk. The essayist is repeatedly scoring points;
but the points he scores, and the flourish with which he advertises
them, are apt to seem more important than the convictions out of
which they rise. He is customarily on the side of the angels—"Fore-
heads Villainous Low" and "The New Romanticism" are timely ex-
posures of current literary fallacies; but by his glib manner of presentation he frequently weakens the angelic case.

More troublesome is what may perhaps best be described as the
lack of any *unifying* quality. It has often struck me that, while writing fiction and analysing the behaviour of his fictitious characters,
Mr. Huxley shows a strange inability to appreciate any type of experience that is not either ecstatic and spiritual or grossly and repul-

sively sensual. There is no intermediate stage. His characters must
either be exploring the heavens, opened by the great artists and the
great composers, or wallowing in the slime—which the novelist
describes with some relish—of their lowest physical appetites. There
is never a hint of a marriage between Heaven and Hell: never a suggestion that there might exist a whole range of experiences, available
to the ordinary human being, which never raise him to spiritual ecstasy yet, equally, never plunge him into the depths of moral squalor.
A similar limitation seems to afflict the essayist. If he is not—as
in *Music at Night* and *Meditations on El Greco*—writing of a subject by which he is deeply stirred and which inspires him to produce
his best prose, he is inclined to adopt an attitude of flippant distaste,
the flippancy sometimes degenerating into journalistic cleverness.
How marked the contrast with D. H. Lawrence, who, both as a
novelist and an essayist, often wrote very badly but, even at his
silliest and most perverse, seldom wrote insignificantly: whose peculiar vision of life pervaded all that he did and said, enlightening the
confusion and softening the contradictions! Lawrence was an intensely serious writer; and so, without a doubt, is Aldous Huxley.
But Mr. Huxley's work occasionally produces the impression that he
will only condescend to be serious upon the topics he has himself
selected.

Elsewhere he is content to display his virtuosity—a brilliant trick-
cyclist of the intellect, calculated to electrify the audience at any
literary music-hall. There are moments, indeed, when he simply
can't be bothered. Thus his travel-book consists of a series of essays
in which genuine feats of observation are interspersed with brisk
explosions of journalistic back-chat: "Jamaica (he informs us) is the
Pearl of the Caribbean—or is it the Clapham Junction of the West?
I can never remember." And Jamaica is thereupon dismissed in
three smart and skimpy paragraphs. Odd that he should have failed
to admire the island's exuberant natural beauty! But then, the essayist's mind is more readily excited by ideas encountered than by
things seen—and, among the things he sees and describes, he is generally less susceptible to Nature than to works of art. Sights, sounds
and scents leave his imagination comparatively unmoved; and, since
travel is primarily a *sensuous* experience, the effect made by his
travel-sketches is often rather bleak and arid. Like his essays, they
may instruct and entertain; but they arouse no sense of mystery,
open up no new perspectives, as did Lawrence in *Sea and Sardinia* or

in his book about the ancient Etruscans. The man who composed them, we feel, was always the prisoner of his own intelligence; and that intelligence, whether by accident or design, although it is splendidly equipped, in some of its essential features has remained severely circumscribed.

Aldous Huxley's Intellectual Zoo

by Sanford E. Marovitz

"Every human being is an amphibian," Aldous Huxley once wrote, "or, to be more accurate, every human being is five or six amphibians rolled into one. Simultaneously or alternately, we inhabit many different and even incommensurable universes." [1] This concept of man as a composite being is central throughout Huxley's novels and is apparent even in his early poetry,[2] but the manner in which the idea was conveyed altered according to the author's own gradually changing views of humanity as society, of the human being as an individual, and of the psyche as a largely unexplored cosmos in itself. As Huxley became increasingly aware of man's possibilities for self-improvement and psychic fulfillment, his emphasis shifted from "amphibian" man (mind/body) to "triphibian" [3] man (spirit/mind/body), and the tone with which he treated humanity in his novels was modified considerably from that of lightly ironic comedy to satire of a more serious, at times even grim, nature. The transformation is apparent with his use of animal imagery, a subtle and pervasive element in Huxley's novels that has not yet received adequate attention. Man "is at once an animal and a rational intellect," Huxley wrote, "a product of evolution closely related to the apes and a spirit capable of self-transcendence." [4] According to Hux-

"Aldous Huxley's Intellectual Zoo" by Sanford E. Marovitz. From *Philological Quarterly* 48 (1969): 495–507. Reprinted by permission of the author and the editor of *Philological Quarterly*.

1 "The Education of an Amphibian," *Tomorrow and Tomorrow and Tomorrow and other Essays* (New York, 1956), p. 1.

2 Charles M. Holmes, "The Early Poetry of Aldous Huxley," *TSLL*, VIII (1966), pp. 391–406. Professor Holmes's discussion is an enlightening and sometimes fascinating exploration of the apparent inconsistencies among Huxley's early poems; he suggests that these inconsistencies are evidence of "the highly complicated inner struggle which influenced, even determined the theme and the shape of [Huxley's] . . . fiction" (p. 391). [Mr. Holmes's essay is reprinted in this volume—ED.]

3 Humphrey Osmund, in *Aldous Huxley, 1894–1963: A Memorial Volume* ed. Julian Huxley (London, 1965), p. 122; hereafter cited as *Memorial Volume*.

4 "Education on the Nonverbal Level," *Perspective on Ideas and the Arts*, XI (September 1962), p. 18.

ley, then, we spend our waking hours as amphibians, inhabiting the
world of ideas and the world of experience, the world that we ap-
prehend through the senses and the world of speculation, in which—
as Emerson might have put it—we distill the empirical universe
through the alembic of Mind.

In a sense, each character in Huxley's fiction—like every human
being in the flesh—is "an ape that has learned to talk," [5] and in
view of the prevalent conversation that occurs in all of his novels, it
is not strange that considerably more critical attention has been
devoted to the ideas of his people than to the animal element of
their existence. The "ape" is disregarded for the "essence." But is
this one-sided critical view entirely justified? A careful rereading
suggests otherwise, for when we reconsider the fiction, particularly
the early work, with the author's "amphibian" view of humanity in
mind, we become aware that the characters in his novels are usually
more than simply "mouthpiece[s]"—as he himself feared they might
be[6]—voicing the divers facets of his remarkable intellect.

Indeed, only by relating Huxley's mystical and psychophysical
analysis of man to his fictionalized world of dilettantes and philo-
sophes, can we realize how necessary it is that his people live as well
as speak. To be sure, they often represent one distinct point of view
or another; nevertheless, they are—if not perfectly natural and
well-rounded—at least human enough to be organically alive. Were
they but voices from so many programed tape recorders, their ideas
—whether brilliant or ludicrous—could be directly associated neither with physical appearance nor action. And if we are to catch the
full charge of Huxley's irony and satire, we must recognize that no
matter how high their minds soar in the cosmic ether of philosophy
—be it pure speculation, morals, or aesthetics—his figures are still
lizard-like[7] or leonine,[8] dog-like,[9] ape-like,[10] "ferret-faced" [11] or aqui-
line[12] human animals who indulge in exactly the same fundamental
natural processes as the beasts called forth to represent them.

Alexander Henderson has noted that "Huxley [was] as fascinated

5 "The Education of an Amphibian," p. 2.

6 *Point Counter Point* (London, 1928), p. 409.

7 *Crome Yellow* (London, 1921), pp. 21–22.

8 *Crome Yellow,* p. 48; *Point Counter Point,* pp. 509–10; *Those Barren Leaves*
(London, 1925), p. 25.

9 *Time Must Have a Stop* (New York, 1944), p. 28.

10 *After Many a Summer* (London, 1939), pp. 311–14; *Ape and Essence* (New
York, 1948), pp. 34–53.

11 *Time Must Have a Stop,* p. 160.

12 *Those Barren Leaves,* p. 27.

by human beings as a zoologist at the sight of his first okapi or duck-billed platypus." [13] The comment is suggestive, for if the notebook of Philip Quarles in *Point Counter Point* (1928) reveals something of Huxley's own attitude toward living harmoniously, it also eluci-dates the underlying significance of his zoological interests as a writer of fiction. After speculating on a leading figure for a projected novel, Quarles decides that his character must be "a professional zoologist who is writing a novel in his spare time." [14] The reason for Quarles's seemingly peculiar choice of professionals is well-consid-ered: the broad-minded novelist with an intricate knowledge of zoology would be able to draw the necessary parallels between hu-man life and that of animals on lower levels; in this case the paral-lels would paradoxically bridge the gap between the several modes of existence, and the harmonious unity within nature would be clear. It was probably this fascination over human beings, then, that enabled Huxley to create recognizable characters rather than simply disembodied voices with names, such as the articulate shad-ows of Lucian or Fontenelle in their *Dialogues of the Dead*. His satire and discursive irony notwithstanding, the creatures who zip from ballroom to bedroom and back again in his novels do, indeed, wine, dine, and make love in a very human manner—although they often partake in these activities, it is true, to the rhythm of seem-ingly interminable conversations.

Huxley, who was granted the aesthetic sensibility of an artist (though his talent and desire to draw were necessarily checked by his deteriorating eyesight),[15] portrayed his people with precise words and images that enable us to see them functioning bodily, and usu-ally comically, before us. "If I could paint and had the necessary time," Huxley wrote, "I should devote myself for a few years to mak-ing pictures only of olive trees. What a wealth of variations upon a single theme!" [16] He did after all produce his "variations upon a single theme," not by transposing olive trees onto canvas, however, but by transforming London's gadabout intellectual elite, with

13 Alexander Henderson, *Aldous Huxley* (London, 1935), p. 130.
14 *Point Counter Point*, p. 438.
15 According to Juliette Huxley, Julian's wife, Aldous was a capable artist; she wrote: "He used to draw, with a sure and loving touch, outlines of female nudes"; and she recalled his "drawings of bosoms and rounded thighs" (*Memorial Volume*, pp. 41–42, 47). Also, in a very informative essay, Gerald Heard has pointed out that "As a boy, [Huxley] was determined to become an artist" ("The Poignant Prophet," *Kenyon Review*, XXVII [1965], p. 52).
16 "The Olive Tree," *The Olive Tree and Other Essays* (London, 1936), p. 297.

whose foibles he was most familiar, into the diversified "human animals" [17] that he often described in terms more suitable for the zoological gardens than the drawing room. This technique provides the basis for much of his early satire.

In *Crome Yellow* (1921), Huxley's first novel, the author employed this animalistic method of description to introduce Mr. Scogan, Crome's self-assessed man of reason: "In appearance Mr. Scogan was like one of those extinct bird-lizards of the Tertiary. His nose was beaked, his dark eye had the shining quickness of a robin's. But there was nothing soft or gracious or feathery about him. The skin of his wrinkled brown face had a dry and scaly look; his hands were the hands of a crocodile. His movements were marked by the lizard's disconcertingly abrupt clockwork speed; his speech was thin, fluty, and dry" (pp. 21–22). Through animal imagery the highly intellectual man—here probably modeled largely from Bertrand Russell and yet partially a self-portrait, too—has been depicted characteristically as a hard, cold-blooded individual, an observer with a quick eye for detail. A moment after the portrait was presented, Huxley drew a comparison between Scogan and Gombauld, a hedonistic artist at Crome, who is described as being "altogether and essentially human" (p. 22). But later, when Gombauld reappears dancing with Anne, the interlocked couple shuffling across the floor resemble "a single creature, two-headed and four-legged. . . . The beast with two backs" (pp. 92, 94). Throughout the novel Anne is charming, intelligent, and unmoved by passion; yet she and Gombauld are parts of the beast. This implicit contrast pulls together the dual elements apparent in nearly all of Huxley's early cast of characters and illustrates one of his most effective satirical methods, whereby irony is achieved through the intimate juxtaposition of high intellect and low animal.

The continued emphatic association of these contrasting elements through imagery, metaphor, and analogy was one result of Huxley's recognizing the type of fiction he wrote, that is, the "novel of ideas," [18] in which the character might be simply a "mouthpiece" for the views he expresses. Again the notebook of Philip Quarles (in *Point Counter Point*) is revealing, for it discloses Huxley's awareness that ideas rather than men dominate his own fiction and that the result of subordinating Man to Mind is the inevitable loss of reality. "The great defect of the novel of ideas," Quarles wrote, "is

---

[17] *Those Barren Leaves*, p. 294.
[18] *Point Counter Point*, p. 409.

that it's a made-up affair. Necessarily; for people who can reel off neatly formulated notions aren't quite real; they're slightly monstrous. Living with monsters becomes rather tiresome in the long run" (p. 410). Huxley's method of dealing with these "monsters" was to stress the animalistic features of their appearances and actions, while he allowed them as speakers to give their ideas full play. The result of this method of portrayal is a gamut of egocentric personages who are either largely or entirely unconcerned with humanity but are contented riding their own hobby horses with great volubility and fervor wherever they appear.

It is not difficult, then, to see why few of Huxley's characters enjoy matrimonial bliss; his chattering innocents, egoists, and idealists are either unhappily married or not married at all. (The Rampions in *Point Counter Point,* modeled from D. H. Lawrence and his wife, are notable exceptions.) Most of them are busily engaged— with varying degrees of competence—in the art of seduction, an activity which sometimes leads them to sexual gratification but seldom to extended periods of happiness. Often intellectuals, they are usually inadequate lovers because they are more concerned with themselves or their ideas than their love-making; whereupon Huxley converts their egocentric foibles into light comedy through the application of ironic animal imagery.

Shearwater, for example, in *Antic Hay* (1923), is considerably more interested in kidneys than in his wife, who therefore becomes the likely, if accidental, object of Gumbril's seductive powers. A sometimes timid friend of Gumbril's, Shearwater is too blind to realize that Rosie has begun to give herself away to his companions; his *in*sight is as defective as the *eye*sight of the rabbits on which a "doggy" [19] young colleague has been experimenting—and Huxley clearly wanted us to make this association. He described Shearwater's suppressed passion for Myra Viveash in term of rabbits: Gumbril speaks with his over-anxious friend and notes that before long "the particulars began to peep, alive and individual, out of the vagueness, like rabbits"; he waits for the rabbits "to come out into the open"; and when Myra's name is finally uttered, "it amused [Gumbril] to see the rabbits scampering about at last" (pp. 165–66). An additional animal reference evolves through Shearwater's name, which as well as suggesting his preoccupation with perspiration and kidneys, has probably been taken from a gull-like bird with the same

---

[19] *Antic Hay* (London, 1923), p. 140.

appellation: the shearwater is usually seen skimming the waves on long flapping wings far out at sea. The name is appropriate for Shearwater because he, like the bird, is always on the way to somewhere else, escaping, as it were, from a full life to a preoccupation with kidneys, from his wife to an unattainable mistress, from the outside world to a sweat box in which he becomes his own guinea pig or rabbit pedaling his way to nowhere.

Other characters in *Antic Hay* are described in similar terms. Mr. Boldero, "like a bird in appearance" but "like a caterpillar" (p. 145). in mind, is able to consume and regurgitate ideas so quickly and completely that they appear to be his own; and Shearwater's promiscuous wife, Rosie, recalling her recent seduction, sensually caresses her body, hidden "like a warm serpent" (p. 144) beneath her pink kimono. Perhaps the most amusing animalistic description to be found in all of Huxley's fiction appears not in *Antic Hay,* however, but in the author's third novel, *Those Barren Leaves* (1925), with the extended portrait of Cardan's moronic fiancée. At first she and her "spidery" (p. 225) brother strike Cardan, the "parasite," (p. 31) as being "interesting specimens" (p. 223); but as soon as he learns of the pathetic girl's wealth, she becomes a ludicrous target for matrimony. Huxley described her through bird images in a manner suggestive of the animated cartoons that still enliven television and the Saturday matinées:

> Ungainly as a diving-bird on land, Miss Elver scuttled into the house. . . . Uttering shrill little cries and laughing, she ran towards him. Mr. Cardan watched her as she came on. He had seen frightened cormorants bobbing their heads in a ludicrous anxiety from side to side. He had seen penguins waving their little flappers, scuttling along, undignified, on their short legs. He had seen vultures with trailing wings hobbling and hopping, ungainly, over the ground. Memories of all these sights appeared before his mind's eye as he watched Miss Elver's approach. . . . [L]ike a diver out of water, like a soaring bird reduced to walk the earth, Miss Elver trotted along at his side, rolling and hopping as she walked, as though she were mounted, not on feet, but on a set of eccentric wheels of different diameters. (pp. 242, 245, 249)

How clearly one can see the unfortunate Miss Elver clumsily trundling across the screen of his imagination! Yet this absurd conjunction of cumbersome bird with moronic woman has a more serious purpose than the successfully comic image it creates, for Miss Elver's ungainly presence allows us to compare a physically uncoordinated and intellectually incapable person with Cardan, who has the wherewithal to function normally in body and mind but lacks the initiative to be a "genuine," [20] or "full-blown" [21] human being. Each figure makes the other appear ridiculous and pathetic. Hence, by over-emphasizing one element of human life at the expense of another, Huxley illustrated through contrast and comedy how necessary it is that man dwell harmoniously among "many different . . . universes" in order to achieve a satisfactory balance in his existence as an "amphibian."

The author's increasing seriousness of purpose, evident in the fiction published after *Those Barren Leaves,* largely precluded a further abundance of humorous animal imagery. *Point Counter Point* offers a few exceptions—such as Burlap's secretary pecking like a woodpecker at Walter, and Webley "doing the lion" as he dictates[22]—but it is *Time Must Have a Stop* (1944) that includes Huxley's last examples of the sharply drawn comical animal images prevalent in *Crome Yellow* and *Antic Hay.* The aged Mrs. Gamble, for instance, speaks sharply, and "on its withered tortoise's neck, the old head turned questioningly from side to side in a succession of quick blind movements" (p. 196); and Uncle Eustace, the Epicurean, becomes appropriately elephantine: "In that expanse of flabby face the little eyes . . . were like an elephant's. An elegant little elephant in a double-breasted black coat and pale gray check trousers" (p. 41). Again the figures are accurately and succinctly characterized through quick comparisons with well-chosen animals. But *Time Must Have a Stop* was clearly a weightier effort than those delightful bantering *romans à clef* of the early 1920's, for Huxley was already conjecturing over the powers of the living mind after the body's death. His parapsychological explorations suggest that in writing this novel, the author was taking long thought-strides forward while still occasionally glancing at the once-favored technical method that his new, more vital interests had made obsolescent.

It should be clear that Huxley's animal images were effective not only because they were so sharply focused but because they were so strikingly appropriate to reveal and display with immediate force the idiosyncracies of the characters and character types being portrayed. How was this quality of suggestive *vraisemblance* achieved? The natural animal first was made image, and the image then be-

---

20 *Those Barren Leaves,* p. 294.
21 *Island* (New York, 1962), p. 236.
22 *Point Counter Point,* pp. 221, 509–10.

came symbol. Admittedly a "poor visualizer," [23] Huxley—like all men (he wrote)—could symbolize clearly in his imagination, where he was not hindered in the least by defective vision. "Spiders can't help making flytraps, and men can't help making symbols," he wrote in *Island* (1962); "That's what the human brain is there for—to turn the chaos of given experience into a set of manageable symbols" (p. 208). The idea behind this probably unintentional restatement of Susanne K. Langer's "new key" to philosophy—that "man's basic need [is] the *need of symbolization*" [24]—underlies Huxley's creation of well-defined if often ludicrous types of "human animals."

That his assorted beasts symbolized human *types* as well as caricatured individuals is also brought out in *Island,* where children are taught "in terms of analogies with familiar animals": "Cats like to be by themselves. Sheep like being together. Martens are fierce and can't be tamed. Guinea pigs are gentle and friendly. Are you a cat person or a sheep person, a guinea-pig person or a marten person? Talk about it in animal parables, and even very small children can understand the fact of human diversity and the need for mutual forbearance, mutual forgivness" (p. 241). This passage can be taken as a key to all of the animal imagery in Huxley's fiction, for the animal as symbol adds another dimension to his portrait of the lizard-like Scogan in his first novel as well as revealing the method of Palanese schooling in his last. Huxley simply described as appropriate animals the characteristic human types he saw around him, and the result was a travesty of his own society, the chattering men and women of what might be called his "intellectual zoo."

As early as *Point Counter Point,* Huxley had begun to employ animals more seriously than he had in his previous work. Although he did occasionally use them here, as before, to accentuate comical physical characteristics or peculiarities of individual figures, in *Point Counter Point* animals also took on the more essential purpose of representing man's bestial nature. A striking example of Huxley's newer method appears in the drawings of Mark Rampion, an artist striving to achieve a well-balanced life. Rampion condemns excessive intellectualism and specialization of all kinds; he regards these excesses as forms of brutality, and several of his drawings manifest

[23] *The Doors of Perception* (New York, 1954), p. 15; Huxley confessed here that he was a "poor visualizer" and that "even the pregnant words of poets, do not evoke pictures in my mind."

[24] Susanne K. Langer, *Philosophy in a New Key: A Study in the Symbolism of Reason, Rite, and Art* (Harvard University Press, 1942), p. 41; Mrs. Langer's italics.

his scorn for the lopsided modes of existence that he finds characteristic of his age. One drawing, entitled "Fossils of the Past and Fossils
of the Future," depicts a variety of prehistoric beasts marching in a
procession led by "human monsters, huge-headed creatures, without
limbs or bodies, creeping slug-like on vaguely slimy extensions of
chin and neck. The faces were mostly those of eminent contemporaries," including G. B. Shaw and a clergyman named Dr. Crane.[25]
On another sheet Rampion displays a pair of drawings which he
calls "Outlines of History" according to H. G. Wells and himself.
Wells's "Outline" portrays the ancestry of man, commencing with a
small monkey and graduating to contemporary giants, including
Wells himself. Rampion's own "Outline" depicts man at his peak
during the Periclean Age of Athens and decreasing in size and stature since that time until he "had begun to be dwarfish and mis-
shapen" during the Victorian Age. "Their twentieth century succes-
sors were abortions. Through the mists of the future one could see
a diminishing company of little gargoyles and foetuses with heads
too large for their squelchy bodies, the tails of apes and the faces of
our most eminent contemporaries, all biting and scratching and dis-
embowelling one another with that methodical and systematic energy which belongs only to the very highly civilized." [26] The drawings reveal humanity and civilization as seen by the broad-minded
artist, who has observed that the liberty, harmony, and balance enjoyed by the Classical Greeks have never been restored to any major
culture since their day. From a vantage point in the "Roaring Twenties," Huxley prognosticated through Rampion's drawings the violence and horror that would culminate in *Ape and Essence* (1948)
two decades later.

Generally, Huxley's use of animals in fiction transformed from
brightly ironic to sardonic and pessimistic, and ultimately to mystical as he grew increasingly preoccupied with social concerns. The
gradual conversion can be partially telescoped and traced through
his assorted ape images and figures, for the anthropoid seemed to
hold a manifest fascination for Huxley from the time he wrote some
of his earliest poems—in which Charles M. Holmes already recognized the ape as a "familiar Huxley motif" [27]—to his placid analo-
gizing of man with gorilla in *The Genius and the Goddess* (1955).

25 *Point Counter Point*, p. 289.
26 *Ibid.*, p. 291.
27 "The Early Poetry of Aldous Huxley," p. 398; see particularly the poems of
Jonah (1917) and "First Philosopher's Song" in *Leda* (1920).

An illustration of his earlier manner is provided in *Antic Hay,* where he offered a glimpse of a "rejuvenated" fifteen-year-old monkey in Shearwater's laboratory. Mrs. Viveash and Gumbril watch the creature "shaking the bars that separated him from the green-furred, bald-rumped, bearded young beauty in the next cage. He was gnashing his teeth with thwarted passion" (p. 326). If the caged monkey partially represents Shearwater and, perhaps, Gumbril himself, he also anticipates the "rejuvenated" Fifth Earl of Gonister in *After Many a Summer* (1939), Huxley's most ingenious exploitation of the macabre. Unlike the frustrated monkey of *Antic Hay,* however, the Fifth Earl enjoys the company of his whimpering apish mistress, locked with him in the same cage; but he has degenerated in mind and body almost to the pathetic idiocy of the "simian" elevator man (an Epsilon-Minus Semi-Moron) of *Brave New World* (1932).[28] To be sure, the foetal ape theory by which a deathless man becomes a mature anthropoid is as imaginative as it is implausible; nevertheless, it points up the inevitable tie that links humankind to beast and suggests what man descends to when he overreaches himself.

It was but a step from the ape-like creatures of *After Many a Summer* to the baboon society of *Ape and Essence,* a peculiarly neglected novel published nearly ten years later. *Ape and Essence* was written in the form of a motion-picture script within a narrative frame, having for its setting a Hollywood studio on the day of Mahatma Gandhi's assassination in 1948, the year in which the book was published. Obviously Huxley wrote it quickly and probably in a kind of fervor. The novel opens with a description of a sick society; the author narrates as himself and reproduces several conversations in which he has taken part, commonplace chatter that exemplifies a culture dominated by bestial and materialistic desires. The topics shift from Gandhi's murder (violence) to adultery and divorce (unlimited sexual gratification) to a needed raise in salary (material wealth) to commercial art (munificence and artificiality rather than aesthetic quality) to a religious movie (sex and sentimentality). As Huxley and his companion walk, the script of *Ape and Essence* drops into their hands from the bed of a passing garbage truck, and Huxley becomes interested enough in it to trace its author, a Jew who has recently died and whose family in Germany, the curious narrator is told, "passed on" during the war. "I don't have anything

[28] *Brave New World* (London, 1932), p. 69.

against Jews," his informant assures him, "but all the same. . . . Maybe Hitler wasn't so dumb after all" (p. 27). Meanwhile, in the kitchen, Huxley's Hollywood companion, already committing adultery and preparing for a divorce, is attempting to entice an adventuresome young school girl to the thrills of stardom.

With these natural views of our everyday world, the reader is subtly introduced to the horrors of *Ape and Essence* before the actual script begins, for the motion picture simply abstracts and symbolizes what should be evident to us all in the society around us. It is not merely appearance, therefore, but reality with which we are confronted when we observe the first few brief scenes in the script itself. They depict a society of baboons—warlike, egocentric, sensual, and materialistic—that is a duplicate of our own but for the physical features of its members. There are baboon technicians, baboon financiers, baboon soldiers wearing polished leather boots, and even "a bosomy young female baboon, in a shell-pink evening gown, her mouth painted purple, her muzzle powdered mauve, her fiery red eyes ringed with mascara. Swaying as voluptuously as the shortness of her hind legs will permit her to do, she walks onto the brightly illuminated stage of a night club and, to the clapping of two or three hundred pairs of hairy hands, approaches the Louis XV microphone" (p. 35). There is no mention, obviously, of baboon novelists or artists. The baboons live as we live and keep their human scientists—Michael Faraday and several Louis Pasteurs and Albert Einsteins—on chains, much as we do, forcing them to construct missiles and bombs that will ultimately lead to their own destruction. Unwilling to create the weapons, the scientists are unable to defend themselves against their baboon masters; hence the missiles are manufactured and fired, and the baboon culture is annihilated. It knows no better than to expunge itself. "Today," the narrator states, "thanks to that Higher Ignorance which is our knowledge, man's stature has increased to such an extent that the least among us is now a baboon, the greatest an orangutan or even, if he takes rank as a Saviour of Society, a true Gorilla" (p. 36). Not only do the baboons destroy themselves, but the extent of the radiation damage they cause makes it unlikely that a healthy society will be regenerated on the grounds which have been bombed.

Two groups of people remain in existence after the baboons and their scientists have been slain: one is comprised of New Zealanders not killed off in the war; and the other is a group of mutants in California, whose sexual needs and desires have become seasonal—as they are in animals. Mutants beget mutants, and the babies that are too horribly deformed are exterminated in a mass sacrificial slaughter on Belial Day—vaguely reminiscent of a bleating priest and his bawling flock in *Those Barren Leaves*[29]—which commences a two-week period of orgiastic activity among all members of the society except the Arch Vicar and his clergymen, who are voluntary eunuchs. *Ape and Essence* is an unrelieved series of horrors, a nightmare, grotesque and sardonic, and the title alone of the novel suggests the profound gap that exists between the bestial men who comprise and control the bulk of society and the few truly good men—epitomized in Gandhi—whom they assassinate. *Brave New World* was by no means Huxley's most pessimistic anti-Utopian novel.

The unity of body, mind, and spirit which Huxley regarded as essential for a satisfactory "amphibious" existence, was often paradoxically discussed in his fiction with reference to the excretory organs and excretion. As his progression toward the Palanese ideals of *attention* and *compassion* ("*karuna*") gained momentum—particularly, it seems with his new knowledge of hallucinatory agents—Huxley did not neglect that essential unity, but the tone with which he treated it changed considerably. The gross part of our animal nature was not to be disregarded. Coleman, for example, in the early *Antic Hay*, speculates on whether or not "God ha[s] a pair of kidneys" and decides, on the basis of their "miraculous [and] positively divine precision" (pp. 62–63), that not even the Lord should be ashamed of owning them. In *Point Counter Point*, published five years later, Spandrell points out to Illidge, in language reminiscent of Swift[30] and the young Schiller,[31] that "the heart's a curious sort of manure-heap; dung calls to dung, and the great charm of vice consists in its stupidity and sordidness" (p. 395). And, finally, in *Island*, the book which Huxley attempted to make his *chef-d'oeuvre*,[32] Will Farnaby laughs under the influence of the psychedelic Moksha medicine when he finally decides—after long finding it impossible

29 *Those Barren Leaves*, p. 337.

30 See Huxley's essay on Swift in *Do What You Will* (London, 1929), pp. 93–106.

31 I am thinking here specifically of *Die Räuber*, in which the villainous Francis (*Franz*), ranting about "the filthy cycle of human fate," says: "Man is made of filth, and for a time wades in filth, and produces filth, till at last he fouls the boots of his own posterity" (*The Robbers*, translated by H. G. Bohn, *Schiller's Complete Works*, edited by Charles J. Hempel [Philadelphia, 1861], I, p. 187).

32 See Julian Huxley, *Memorial Volume*, pp. 23–24. Unfortunately, few reviewers seem to have grasped Huxley's aim and fewer, still, to have recognized his achievement in *Island*.

to see "turds as gentians" (p. 100)—that "Eternity . . . [is] as real as shit" (p. 313). The views expressed by Huxley's characters do not, of course, necessarily represent those which the author himself held in favor at the time they were written; but they do reflect, through manner and tone, his gradual shift in thought from his early period through the phase of disillusionment and pessimism manifest in *Point Counter Point* and *Brave New World,* and finally into *Eyeless in Gaza* (1936) and the last half of his life, nearly three decades characterized by his devotion to pacifism and semi-mystical self-fulfillment. After passing through stages of satire and cynicism, the uneven mixture of body, mind, and spirit is finally declared solute in terms that link animal waste metaphysically with the ineffable Ultimate of existence. The "ape that has learned to talk" has nearly become a "full-blown human being" at last.

Aldous Huxley's Quest for Values:
A Study in Religious Syncretism

by Milton Birnbaum

> Given the nature of spiders, webs are inevitable. And given the
> nature of human beings, so are religions. Spiders can't help
> making flytraps, and men can't help making symbols. That's
> what the human brain is there for—to turn the chaos of given
> experience into a set of fairly manageable symbols. Sometimes
> the symbols correspond fairly closely to some of the aspects of
> the external reality behind our experience; then you have sci-
> ence and common sense. Sometimes, on the contrary, the sym-
> bols have almost no connection with external reality; then you
> have paranoia and delirium. More often there's a mixture, part
> realistic and part fantastic; that's religion. Good religion or bad
> religion—it depends on the blending of the cocktail.
>
> —Aldous Huxley, *Island*

Aldous Huxley's first comments on religion indicate that he
began as a sardonic skeptic. In one of his earliest novels, for example, we find a character comment on God as follows:

> I am that I am. . . . But I have with me . . . a physiologue, a peda-
> gogue and a priapagogue; for I leave out of account mere artists and
> journalists whose titles do not end with the magic syllable. And
> finally . . . plain Dog, which being interpreted kabalistically back-
> wards signifies God. All at your service.[1]

In *Jesting Pilate,* published in 1926, he writes that it may be true
that "religion is a device employed by the Life Force for the promo-

"Aldous Huxley's Quest for Values: A Study in Religious Syncretism" by Milton
Birnbaum. From George A. Panichas, ed., *Mansions of the Spirit* (New York:
Hawthorn Books, Inc.), pp. 239–58. Copyright © 1967 by the University of Mary-
land. Reprinted by permission of the author and publishers. [An expanded version
of this essay appears as chapter ten of his *Aldous Huxley's Quest for Values*
(Knoxville, 1971)—ED.]

[1] *Antic Hay* (New York, 1923), p. 79.

tion of its evolutionary designs. But they would be justified in adding that religion is also a device employed by the Devil for the dis-
semination of idiocy, intolerance, and servile abjection." [2] In his
essay "One and Many," found in *Do What You Will*, published in
1929, he declares himself "officially an agnostic." He develops the
theory that God is simply a projection of the human personality:
". . . men make Gods in their own likeness. To talk about religion
except in terms of human psychology is an irrelevance." [3] He ridi-
cules the anthropomorphic conception of God because it reflects the
weaknesses and aspirations of the society in which a particular god
is worshiped. Using himself as an example, he writes that when he
is enjoying good health and when the weather is propitious, then he
can well believe that "God's in his heaven and all's right with the
world." "On other occasions, skies and destiny being inclement, I
am no less immediately certain of the malignant impersonality of
an uncaring universe." [4] In a poem he wrote in 1925 called "Philosophy," he says that it is difficult to hear what God is saying because
"God stutters." He would prefer to believe in the sanctity of what he
calls the "Human Personality" than in the "myth" of God. "We do
at least know something of Human Personality, whereas of God we
know nothing and, knowing nothing, are at liberty to invent as
freely as we like." [5] The reason that people believe in this "theological game" is that they find it much more psychologically satisfying
to conform to habit than to be subjected to the discomfort of rebellious skepticism.

The vacuum created by Huxley's rejection of an anthropomorphic
conception of religion was filled in the 1920's by his espousal of the
Lawrentian doctrine of the instinctive life. Man should not favor
what is felt to be a false spirituality but should live passionately and
instinctively. In *Point Counter Point* Mark Rampion (who is supposed to represent D. H. Lawrence) speaks of the three diseases
plaguing mankind: "Jesus' and Newton's and Henry Ford's disease." All three "diseases" could be eliminated, both Lawrence and
Huxley felt, by the rejection of science, technology, and traditional
Christianity. In *Do What You Will*, published the same year as
Point Counter Point, Huxley makes the same points. He writes that
the world is faced with three dangers: (1) monotheism and the men-

---

2 *Jesting Pilate: An Intellectual Holiday* (New York, 1926), p. 58.
3 *Do What You Will: Essays* (New York, 1931), p. 1.
4 *Ibid.*, p. 2.
5 *Ibid.*, p. 141 ("Fashions in Love").

ace of the "super-humanist" ideal; (2) "the worship of success and efficiency"; (3) "the machine." Monotheism and the "super-humanist" ideal constitute a danger because they are not based on any foundation in reality and thus do not allow the living of the fully instinctive life. "The worship of success and efficiency constitutes another menace to our world. What our ancestors sacrificed on the altars of Spirituality, we sacrificed on those of the Bitch Goddess and Taylorism." [6] "The machine" is a menace because it robs man of his creativity and makes him merely a passively efficient robot. These three menaces have killed people's instinctive love of the fully integrated life, and "the result is that they lose their sense of values, their taste and judgment become corrupted, and they have an irresistible tendency to love the lowest when they see it." [7]

When we analyze Huxley's comments on Judaism and Christianity, we can readily appreciate why the Nazi propagandists used some of his statements in their attacks on Western democracies.[8] In 1929, for example, he made the following attack on Jews:

> Their mission, in a word, was to infect the rest of humanity with a belief which . . . prevented them from having any art, any philosophy, any political life, any breadth or diversity of vision, any progress. We may be pardoned for wishing that the Jews had remained, not forty, but four thousand years in their repulsive wilderness.[9]

Similarly, in *Along the Road* he sympathizes with those who have to work "eight hours a day in an office for the greater enrichment of the Jews." In *Antic Hay* a stranger whom Gumbril meets on the train complains: "Hideous red cities pullulating with Jews, sir. Pullulating with prosperous Jews. Am I right in being indignant, sir?" [10] He blames the monotheistic religion of the Jews for the emphasis given by other peoples to wealth and materialism, for the sentimentality current in music, and for the inculcation of other false values in our civilization. It should be pointed out, however, that Huxley's blatant anti-Semitism disappeared after the advent of Hitler. In his later books he deprecates the savagery of the Nazis;

6 *Ibid.*, p. 83 ("Spinoza's Worm").

7 *Ibid.*, p. 88.

8 See, for example, Wilhelm Poschmann, *Das Kritische Weltbild bei Aldous Huxley: Eine Untersuchung über Bedeutung, Grenzen und Mittel Seiner Kritik,* Doctoral Dissertation (Bonn, 1937). See especially pp. 39–40, 42–48, 60–63.

9 *Do What You Will*, p. 18.

10 *Antic Hay*, p. 263.

in one of his novels, *After Many a Summer,* one of the minor characters is a sympathetic Jew who falls victim to the ruthless business cunning of Jo Stoyte, a non-Jew.

The kind of misfired generalization that characterizes his attack on the Jews also characterizes his castigation of what, at different times, he calls "Christianity," "Puritanism," "Calvinism," and "organized religion." His objections to "Christianity" are several: first of all, he attacks the cruel persecutions by the more fanatical Christians. Although in the following excerpt he is singling out the Puritans, he makes similar attacks on other Christian groups in many of his other works as well:

> The puritan was free to range the world, blighting and persecuting as he went, free to make life poisonous, not only for himself, but for all who came near him. The puritan was and is a social danger, a public and private nuisance of the most odious kind. Baudelaire was a puritan inside out. Instead of asceticism and respectability he practised debauchery. The means he used were the opposite of those employed by the puritans; but his motives and theirs, the ends that he and they achieved, were the same. He hated life as much as they did, and was as successful in destroying it.[11]

The cruelty which Huxley finds so distasteful in the Puritans is like the cruelty which he discovers among the Catholics in the centuries during the Inquisition. "In medieval and early modern Christendom the situation of sorcerers and their clients was almost precisely analogous to that of Jews under Hitler, capitalists under Stalin, Communists and fellow travelers in the United States. . . ."[12] In *The Devils of Loudun* he describes the brutality of the Roman Catholic hierarchy toward one of their own priests who refused to admit that he was inhabited by a devil. Their cruelty did not stem from their alleged hatred of heresy alone; it arose, according to Huxley, because their entire religion was motivated by hatred:

> Ecclesiastical history exhibits a hierarchy of hatreds, descending by orderly degrees from the Church's official and ecumenical hatred of heretics and infidels to the particular hatreds of Order for Order, school for school, province for province and theologian for theologian.[13]

In addition to attacking the extreme cruelty of both the Puritans

---

[11] *Do What You Will,* pp. 192–193.
[12] *The Devils of Loudun* (New York, 1952), p. 122.
[13] *Ibid.,* pp. 19–20.

and the Catholics, Huxley also blames them for making people believe that this world is but a gloomy interlude between earthly pain
and celestial euphoria. "Christianity has always found a certain
difficulty in fitting the unfatigued, healthy and energetic person into
its philosophical scheme." [14] If perchance Christianity does come
upon a person who says that he is quite happy for the moment, then
it reminds him that this state of well-being is but illusory and certainly temporary; every silver lining is but hiding an imminent
cloudburst. The Greeks, Huxley avers, were far wiser in being realistically pessimistic and in using this pessimism to justify their epicurean and instinctive way of life. Huxley here seems either to be unaware of or else ignorant of the fact that the same society which gave
rise to the Epicureans also gave rise to the Stoics.

There are other features which Huxley attacks in Christianity. He
seems to take unusual delight in pointing out that often its priests
themselves do not practice the austerity which they so unctuously
preach. In *The Devils of Loudun* he points out that essentially
there were two Urbain Grandiers: Grandier the sensualist and
Grandier the sermonizing priest. He describes how between Grandier's weekly debaucheries he was preparing sermons filled with
"what eloquence, what choice and profound learning, what subtle,
but eminently sound theology!" [15] When Grandier hears the discom-
forting news from one of his female parishioners that he is the father
of her unborn child, Huxley describes his hypocritical reaction as
follows:

> Shifting his hand from the bosom to the bowed head and changing
> his tone, without any transition, from the bawdy to the clerical, the
> parson told her that she must learn to bear her cross with Christian
> resignation. Then, remembering the visit he had promised to pay to
> poor Mme. de Brou, who had a cancer of the womb and needed all
> the spiritual consolation he could give her, he took his leave.[16]

In his essay "Variations of a Philosopher," published in *Themes
and Variations,* Huxley analyzes the term "shepherd" to demonstrate
how, like sheep, people never stop to consider that "a shepherd is
'not in business for his health,' still less for the health of his sheep."
If a shepherd takes good care of his flock, it is only to fatten them

---

[14] *Texts & Pretexts: An Anthology with Commentaries* (New York, 1933), p. 287.
[15] *The Devils of Loudun,* pp. 26–27.
[16] *Ibid.,* p. 35.

for the eventual slaughter. People should consider the meaning of the term "shepherd" before they proceed to talk sentimentally about their pastors:

> Applied to most of the States and Churches of the last two or three thousand years, this pastoral metaphor is seen to be exceedingly apt —so apt, indeed, that one wonders why the civil and ecclesiastical herders of men should ever have allowed it to gain currency. From the point of view of the individual lambs, rams and ewes there is, of course, no such thing as a *good* shepherd; their problem is to find means whereby they may enjoy the benefits of a well-ordered social life without being exposed to the shearings, milkings, geldings and butcheries which have always been associated with the pastoral office.[17]

There are still other serious faults that Huxley has found with "most of the States and Churches of the last two or three thousand years." He complains that "compared with that of the Taoists and Far Eastern Buddhists, the Christian attitude towards Nature has been curiously insensitive and often downright domineering and violent." [18] Encouraged by "an unfortunate remark in Genesis," Christians have treated animals as things to be exploited for their own benefits. Furthermore, Huxley is very bitter against the Church because it has not offered any kind of opposition to the waging of wars. In *Ape and Essence,* where his bitterness has perhaps reached its most intense pitch, he writes:

> The brass bands give place to the most glutinous of Wurlitzers, "Land of Hope and Glory" to "Onward, Christian Soldiers." Followed by his very Reverend Dean and Chapter, the Right Reverend, the Baboon-Bishop of the Bronx advances majestic, his crozier in his jeweled paw, to pronounce benediction upon the two Field Marshalissimos and their patriotic proceedings.[19]

If we look at the ministers in Huxley's novels, we find that they are all satirically drawn. In *Crome Yellow* we have the Reverend Bodinham, who is much disturbed because his prediction of the coming of the Lord ("He'll sneak around like a thief") has not been realized. In *Antic Hay* we have the Reverend Pelvey, whose ineffectiveness as a preacher is satirically demonstrated: while the Reverend Pelvey is preaching, one of the audience to whom his religious

17 *Themes and Variations* (New York, 1950), p. 57.
18 *The Perennial Philosophy* (New York, 1945), p. 77.
19 *Ape and Essence* (New York, 1948), pp. 45–46.

message is directed is thinking of "trousers with pneumatic seats."
In *Eyeless in Gaza* Mr. Thursley, a minister, is successful in his sermons and in the publication of his articles in the *Guardian,* but he
becomes uncontrollably angry when his wife fails to fill up his ink-
well. In *Time Must Have a Stop* Huxley pictures the minister-father
of Mrs. Thwale as a completely futile man: while the minister is
trying to reform the world, he does not realize that his daughter is
becoming bitterly opposed to religion; ironically enough, it is the
minister's daughter who worships material comfort and commits
adultery.[20]

Of all the Christian faiths, Huxley seems to have the greatest respect for Catholicism and the greatest admiration for Quakerism
and those early Christians in whom he found mystic strains. The
Quakers he admires for their opposition to war and for their contributions in alleviating some of the world's ecological problems. As
for his attitude toward Catholicism, he writes:

> Catholicism is probably the most realistic of all Western religions.
> Its practice is based on a profound knowledge of human nature in
> all its varieties and gradations. From the fetish-worshipper to the
> metaphysician, from the tired business man to the mystic, from the
> sentimentalist and the sensualist to the intellectual, every type of
> human being can find in Catholicism the spiritual nourishment
> which he or she requires. For the sociable, unspiritual man Catholi-
> cism is duly sociable and unspiritual. For the solitary and the spirit-
> ual it provides a hermitage and the most exquisite, the profoundest
> models of religious meditation; it gives the silence of monasteries
> and the bareness of the Carthusian church; it offers the devotional
> introspection of À Kempis and St. Theresa, the subtleties of Pascal
> and Newman, the poetry of Crashaw and St. John of the Cross and
> a hundred others. The only people for whom it does not cater are
> those possessed by that rare, dangerous, and uneasy passion, the pas-
> sion for liberty.[21]

20 The satire of ministers is not confined to the novels. In his essays he also
minimizes the effectiveness of churchmen when they attempt to practice their
"Christian ideals":
   In the lounge, waiting for the coffee, we got into conversation with the clergyman. Or rather, he got into conversation with us. He felt it his duty, I suppose,
as a Christian, as a temporary chaplain in the Anglican diocese of Southern Europe, to welcome the newcomers, to put them at their ease. "Beautiful evening,"
he said, in his too richly cultured voice. (But I loved him for his trousers.) "Beautiful," we agreed, and that the place was charming. "Staying long?" he asked. We
looked at one another, then round the crowded hall, then again at one another.
I shook my head. "Tomorrow," I said, "we have to make a very early start." (*Do
What You Will,* pp. 111–112 ["Paradise"].)
   21 *Proper Studies* (London, 1927), pp. 186–187 ("The Essence of Religion").

Presumably it is Huxley's "passion for liberty" which constitutes one of the reasons for his objection to Catholicism. But there are other reasons. I have already spoken of his attacks on Christianity because of its failure to oppose wars and its encouragement of materialistic success even to the extent of treating animals as mere property; Huxley does not exculpate Catholicism from his generalized attack on Christianity. He also objects to Catholicism (at least to Catholicism as it is practiced in England) because it stresses the ritual at the expense of the more meaningful "mental prayer." In *Eyeless in Gaza* we note the following extract from the diary of Anthony Beavis: "For English Catholics, sacraments are the psychological equivalents of tractors in Russia." [22]

It is not the ritual in Catholicism alone to which he objects; he seems to find little value in the ritual of any religion. In *Eyeless in Gaza* he describes a funeral in which he satirizes the significance of the accompanying ritual. After describing the playing of the organ, the "little procession of surplices," the flowers, the singing, and the intoning of the funeral prayer, he points out the ineffectiveness of all this ritual on Anthony Beavis: "But Anthony hardly heard, because he could think of nothing except those germs that were still there in spite of the smell of the flowers, and of the spittle that kept flowing into his mouth. . . ." [23] Similarly, in *Ape and Essence* he describes the procession in honor of Belial and refers to "the collective imbecility" which is one of the products of ceremonial religion.

Having found little cause for admiration in either Judaism or Christianity, Huxley turned to the East to find the answer to his religious quest.[24] It should be emphasized at this point that Huxley's apparent rejection of the Judeo-Christian tradition did not

22 *Eyeless in Gaza* (New York, 1954; copyright 1936), p. 386.
23 *Ibid.*, p. 25.
24 It should be pointed out that his few references to Mohammedanism indicate a dislike for that religion also. In "In a Tunisian Oasis," published in *The Olive Tree* in 1937, he writes that "Too much insistence on the fatalism inherent in their [Arabs'] religion has reduced them to the condition of static lethargy and supine incuriousness in which they now find themselves." He blames the Arabs' religion for the fact that "half their babies die, and that, politically, they are not their own masters." This "static lethargy and supine incuriousness" which he attributes to the Mohammedan religion sounds rather incongruous when juxtaposed with the comment he made about Mohammedanism some eight years later in *The Perennial Philosophy* (p. 158): "And in Mohammedanism we find a system which incorporates strongly somatotonic elements. Hence Islam's black record of holy wars and persecutions—a record comparable to that of later Christianity, after that religion had so far compromised with unregenerate somatotonia as to call its ecclesiastical organization 'the Church Militant.' "

mean his denial of either the worth of religion or of the existence of
God. As early as 1926 we find him writing: "The fact that men have
had stupid and obviously incorrect ideas about God does not justify
us in trying to eliminate God from out of the universe. Men have
had stupid and incorrect ideas on almost every subject that can be
thought about." [25]

Whenever Huxley found elements of mysticism, as he did in the
Book of Ecclesiastes; in the writings of such mystic Christians as St.
Augustine, St. Bernard of Clairvaux, Meister Eckhart, Walter Hil-
ton, William Law, St. François de Sales, Thomas Traherne, and
others; and in the Sufi books of Islam, he accepted their teachings of
contemplation, renunciation of worldly preoccupation, and the
practice of love. It is, therefore, not so much religion itself that he
was rejecting but what he felt was the perversion of the religious
essence.

Myticism is not an easy concept to define. As Huxley himself
wrote, there are elements of mysticism common to nearly all religions. Inasmuch as he embraced not the mysticism of any particular
religion (although he leaned more toward Buddhism than to any
other) but rather mysticism itself as a kind of philosophical concept,
perhaps the definition given by Evelyn Underhill, two of whose
books he includes in the bibliography in *The Perennial Philosophy,*
most clearly explains mysticism in the sense in which Huxley uses it:
"I . . . understand it to be the expression of the innate tendency
of the human spirit towards complete harmony with the transcendental order, whatever be the theological formula under which that
order is understood." [26] It is significant that the one book of Huxley's entirely devoted to a survey of mysticism as it has appeared in
all religions in all ages is called *The Perennial Philosophy,* not *The*

[25] *Jesting Pilate,* p. 219.
[26] *Mysticism: A Study in the Nature and Development of Man's Spiritual
Consciousness* (New York, 1911), p. x. Christopher Isherwood, who espouses the
Vedanta type of mysticism, writes: "Vedanta also teaches the practice of mysticism;
it claims, that is to say, that man may directly know and be united with his
eternal Nature, the Atman, through meditation and spiritual discipline, without
the aid of any church or delegated minister." This quotation is taken from pp.
xii–xiii of the Introduction to *Vedanta for Modern Man* (New York, 1951), a
collection of various writings on Vedanta, edited by Isherwood. To this anthology
Huxley contributed several essays. To Huxley mysticism is one of the two
branches of spirituality: "Spirituality is—asceticism and mysticism, the mortification of the self and ultimate Reality." See his "Readings in Mysticism," *Vedanta
for the Western World,* ed. Christopher Isherwood (Hollywood, 1945), pp. 376–
382. It should be noted, however, that Huxley elsewhere speaks out against the
"mortification of the self."

Perennial Religion. Huxley himself declares both his incompetence and his lack of desire to note the differences among the various modes of mysticism as manifested in the different religions. He says, for example, "I am not competent, nor is this the place to discuss the doctrinal differences between Buddhism and Hinduism." [27] Although *The Perennial Philosophy* is his only book devoted entirely to a critical interpretation of selections from mystical writings, his comments on this subject go back much further.

Huxley's first comments on mysticism were hostile. In 1929 he was writing: ". . . the mystics are never tired of affirming that their direct perceptions of unity are intenser, of finer quality and intrinsically more convincing, more self-evident, than their direct perceptions of diversity. But they can only speak for themselves. Other people's direct intuitions of diverse 'appearances' may be just as intensely self-evident as *their* intuition of unique 'reality.' " [28] But in another essay of the book from which the previous quotation is taken, he admits that "it is also true that, in certain circumstances, we can actually *feel,* as a direct intuition, the existence of the all-comprehending unity, can intimately realize in a single flash of insight the illusoriness of the quotidian world of distinctions and relations." [29] Even in his earlier novels we detect some elements of mysticism—the urge for a contemplative life, the distrust of a life of action. Thus in *Those Barren Leaves,* Calamy (who at the end retires to the hills to start a life of pure contemplation) says: "The mind must be open, unperturbed, empty of irrelevant things, quiet. There's no room for thoughts in a half-shut, cluttered mind." [30] Later he comes out even more strongly for the contemplative life:

> No, it's not fools who turn mystics. It takes a certain amount of intelligence and imagination to realize the extra-ordinary queerness and mysteriousness of the world in which we live. The fools, the innumerable fools, take it all for granted, skate about cheerfully on the surface and never think of inquiring what's underneath. They're content with appearances, such as your Harrow Road or Café de la Rotonde, call them realities and proceed to abuse any one who takes an interest in what lies underneath these superficial symbols, as a romantic imbecile.[31]

27 *The Perennial Philosophy,* p. 9.
28 *Do What You Will,* p. 38 ("One and Many").
29 *Ibid.,* p. 63 ("Spinoza's Worm").
30 *Those Barren Leaves* (London, 1925), p. 347.
31 *Ibid.,* p. 370.

It should not be assumed that Huxley completely believed in mysticism back in the 1920's; but even when he denies the claim of the mystics that they achieve a unity with God, he qualifies this denial by writing that "That does not in any way detract from the value of mysticism as a way to perfect health." [32] Similarly, in *Brave New World,* published in 1932, he is more against the tendency of the world to drift into a technological "utopia" than he is for mysticism; but in this book, also, we detect unmistakable signs of his eventual conversion to mysticism. Thus, as Mustapha Mond is signing the papers banning a work on "A New Theory of Biology," one of the reasons for his proscription of the book is that people might begin to think that "the goal was somewhere beyond, somewhere outside the present human sphere; but the purpose of life was not maintenance of well-being, but some intensification and refining of consciousness, some enlargement of knowledge." [33]

Eyeless in Gaza, published in 1936, contains Huxley's first complete endorsement of mysticism. In it he outlines the details of his mysticism which he was to elaborate in his subsequent works. It is in this book that he first advocates the achievement of a union with God. Evil is that which separates man from man; manifestations of evil, such as hatred, greed, and lust, should be avoided. Good is that which unites; love, compassion, and understanding are demonstrations of unity. Huxley admits that this unity is difficult to achieve, but man should at least attempt to achieve it through meditation and inner serenity. Through the attainment of inner peace, he will be better able to withstand the external evil which is the condition of the world. From the notebook of Anthony Beavis we take the following expression of Huxley's mysticism at this time:

Empirical facts:

One. We are all capable of love for other human beings.

Two. We impose limitations on that love.

Three. We can transcend all these limitations—*if we choose to.* (It is a matter of observation that anyone who so desires can overcome personal dislike, class feeling, national hatred, colour prejudice. Not easy; but it can be done, if we have the will and know how to carry out our good intentions.)

---

[32] *Jesting Pilate,* pp. 217–218.
[33] *Brave New World* (New York, 1950; copyright 1932), p. 211.

Four. Love expressing itself in good treatment breeds love. Hate expressing itself in bad treatment breeds hate.

In the light of these facts, it's obvious what inter-personal, inter-class and inter-national policies should be. But, again, knowledge cuts little ice. We all know; we almost all fail to do. It is a question, as usual, of the best methods of implementing intentions. Among other things, peace propaganda must be a set of instructions in the art of modifying character.[34]

In *Ends and Means* Huxley repeats some of the thoughts concerning mysticism which he expressed in *Eyeless in Gaza,* but he adds some new features. Thus he again writes that "Meditation . . . is the technique of mysticism." [35] But he emphasizes the necessity of intuition in attaining this detachment from the world of animality. He again stresses the importance of will power in helping the individual to achieve the intuitive experience which will bring him into the mystical state: "What we perceive and understand depends upon what we are; and what we are depends partly on circumstances, partly, and more profoundly, on the nature of the efforts we have made to realize our ideal and the nature of the ideal we have tried to realize." [36] Since the will is so important in achieving the mystical experience, Huxley particularly urges the reader to remember Irving Babbitt's statement that meditation produces a "super-rational concentration of will." Huxley concedes that all of us have animal instincts which cannot be ignored, but he does not want us to devote our entire attention to the satisfaction of these instincts. "Goodness is the method by which we divert our attention from this singularly wearisome topic of our animality and our individual separateness." [37] This loss of preoccupation with bodily needs may cause some physical suffering, but it is more than adequately compensated by the knowledge and the inner serenity which accompany the mystical experience. The nonattachment of mysticism is infinitely preferable to the attachment of the individual to the pursuit of the life of meaningless action.

In his next novel, *After Many a Summer,* Huxley further elaborates his theories of mysticism. His espousal of the life of self-

34 *Eyeless in Gaza,* p. 156.
35 *Ends and Means: An Inquiry into the Nature of Ideas and into the Methods Employed for Their Realization* (New York, 1937), p. 332 ("Beliefs").
36 *Ibid.,* p. 333.
37 *Ibid.,* p. 346.

transcendence is thus expressed in the answer which Mr. Propter gives to Pete's question as to what good is and where it is to be found:

> On the level below the human and on the level above. On the animal level and on the level . . . well, you can take your choice of names: the level of eternity; the level, if you don't object, of God; the level of the spirit—only that happens to be about the most ambiguous word in the language. On the lower level, good exists as the proper functioning of the organism in accordance with the laws of its own being. On the higher level, it exists in the form of a knowledge of the world without desire or aversion; it exists as the experience of eternity, as the transcendence of personality, the extension of consciousness beyond the limits imposed by the ego. Strictly human activities are the activities that prevent the manifestations of good on the other two levels. . . . Directly or indirectly, most of our physical ailments and disabilities are due to worry and craving. We worry and crave ourselves into high blood pressure, heart disease, tuberculosis, peptic ulcer, low resistance to infection, neurasthenia, sexual aberrations, insanity, suicide. Not to mention all the rest.[38]

In addition to craving liberation from the fetters of the ego, Mr. Propter wants liberation from time, which he describes as "a pretty bothersome thing." Furthermore, the cultivation of virtues is not sufficient; it must be the cultivation of the right virtues—specifically, understanding and compassion. The possession of the other virtues is no guarantee of virtuous conduct: "Indeed, you can't be really bad unless you *do* have most of the virtues. Look at Milton's Satan for example. Brave, strong, generous, loyal, prudent, temperate, self-sacrificing." [39] But because Milton's Satan lacked the qualities of understanding and compassion, he could not be a virtuous leader.

In *Grey Eminence,* published in 1941, Huxley gives two additional suggestions to those who would embrace mysticism: First, the good achieved by a practice of mysticism "is a product of the ethical and spiritual artistry of individuals; it cannot be mass-produced." [40] Secondly, people should beware of "only false, ersatz mysticisms— the nature-mysticism of Wordsworth; the sublimated sexual mysticism of Whitman; the nationality-mysticisms of all the patriotic

38 *After Many a Summer* (New York, 1954; copyright 1939), pp. 99–100.
39 *Ibid.,* p. 95.
40 *Grey Eminence: A Study in Religion and Politics* (New York, 1937), p. 303.

poets and philosophers of every race and culture, from Fichte at the beginning of the period [the nineteenth century] to Kipling and Barrès at the end." [41] The only valid manifestation of mysticism is the intuitive knowledge and love of God.

It is in *The Perennial Philosophy* that Huxley gives the fullest expression to his espousal of mysticism. Technically it is an anthology of selections from the utterances of many of the religious writers from previous centuries who have espoused mysticism, or what he calls the "Perennial Philosophy": "This book . . . is an anthology of the Perennial Philosophy; but, though an anthology, it contains but few extracts from the writings of professional men of letters and, though illustrating a philosophy, hardly anything from the professional philosophers." [42] Only those who have made themselves "loving, pure in heart, and poor in spirit" are capable of apprehending the nature of this perennial philosophy, which, he says, "is primarily concerned with the one, divine Reality substantial to the manifold world of things and lives and minds." [43] The book is divided into twenty-seven chapters dealing with various aspects of human and divine experience. The importance of the book, however, lies not in the selection of excerpts from the writings of others (excellent though they may be) but rather in the ample comments which Huxley makes on these excerpts. His views can be summarized as follows: every phase of human activity must be judged in terms of its hindering or facilitating the achievement of the ultimate purpose of life: "In all the historic formulations of the Perennial Philosophy it is axiomatic that the end of human life is contemplation, or the direct and intuitive awareness of God." [44] That society is good which does not emphasize technological advances but makes possible and desirable the pursuit of contemplation. The love which is released by the exercise of this intuitive contemplation will cure many of the evils that are plaguing mankind. Thus this love will lead to the treating of nature kindly: the earth's resources will no longer be ravaged by people motivated only by self-interest. Similarly, this love will restore man's creativity in work so that he will no longer be a slave to the machine. This love will also make it impossible for political rulers to oppress their peoples. Above all, it will release the individual from bondage to selfhood and from the

41 *Ibid.*, p. 77.
42 *The Perennial Philosophy*, p. viii.
43 *Ibid.*
44 *Ibid.*, p. 294.

fetters of time and sensual demands. The liberation from these fetters will even rid us of the ailments of "most of the degenerative diseases": our heart, kidneys, pancreas, intestines, and arteries are now subject to deterioration because we do not live in harmony with "the divine Nature of Things." Self-denial will not only bring us into union with the essence of the Godhead, but will, in so doing, relieve us of all our physical pain.

Man should not be troubled by such problems as the origin of the Divine Ground or the seeming injustice of seeing evil people prosperous and good people impoverished. God *is* because He *is:* "Only when the individual also 'simply is,' by reason of his union through love-knowledge with the Ground, can there be any question of complete and eternal liberation." [45] As for the seeming injustice of the "bad" man enjoying prosperity and the "good" man afflicted with poverty, Huxley offers the following explanation: "The bad man in prosperity may, all unknown to himself, be darkened and corroded with inward rust, while the good man under afflictions may be in the rewarding process of spiritual growth." [46]

Until the Perennial Philosophy is adopted and recognized as "the highest factor common to all the world religions," until the worshipers of every religion renounce their egocentric, time-based, and false idolatries, then "no amount of political planning, no economic blueprints however ingeniously drawn, can prevent the recrudescence of war and revolution." [47] What is the way to achieve this ideal state? To answer this question, Huxley recommends Buddha's "Eight-fold Path":

> Complete deliverance is conditional on the following: first, Right Belief in the all too obvious truth that the cause of pain and evil is craving for separative, egocentred existence, with its corollary that there can be no deliverance from evil, whether personal or collective, except by getting rid of such craving and the obsession of "I," "me," "mine"; second, Right Will, the will to deliver oneself and others; third, Right Speech, directed by compassion and charity towards all sentient beings; fourth, Right Action, with the aim of creating and maintaining peace and good will; fifth, Right Means of Livelihood, or the choice only of such professions as are not harmful, in their exercise, to any human being or, if possible, any living creature;

45 *Ibid.*, p. 238. (See also his essays "Seven Meditations" and "Reflections on the Lord's Prayer," *Vedanta for the Western World*, pp. 163–170 and 298–312.)
46 *Ibid.*, p. 239.
47 *Ibid.*, p. 200.

sixth, Right Effort towards Self-control; seventh, Right Attention or Recollectedness, to be practised in all the circumstances of life, so that we may never do evil by mere thoughtlessness, because "we know not what we do"; and, eighth, Right Contemplation, the unitive knowledge of the Ground, to which recollectedness and the ethical self-naughting prescribed in the first six branches of the Path give access. Such then are the means which it is within the power of the human being to employ in order to achieve man's final end and be "saved." [48]

Huxley is not excessively optimistic that these prescriptions will be followed by most people. "But then no saint or founder of a religion, no exponent of the Perennial Philosophy, has ever been optimistic." [49]

It would seem that Huxley's search for the "ideal" religion would end in the place where religion began—in the East. Huxley's insatiable intellectual thirst, however, refused to be permanently quenched. It should be remembered that Huxley was the grandson of Thomas Henry Huxley, the scientist, and the grandnephew of Matthew Arnold. Huxley's soul was always the battleground between the challenging barks of "Darwin's bulldog" (Thomas Henry Huxley's sobriquet) and the melancholy promptings for withdrawal of his maternal granduncle. The urgings for self-transcendence gave way to a continued scientific probing. And so in his essay entitled "The Double Crisis," published in *Themes and Variations* in 1950, Huxley again calls upon technological science to help solve the world's problems. It is somewhat difficult to reconcile the advocacy of self-mortification found in *The Perennial Philosophy* with the advice given in the following excerpt:

> Man cannot live by bread alone; but still less can he live exclusively by idealism. To talk about the Rights of Man and the Four Freedoms in connection, for example, with India is merely a cruel joke. In a country where two thirds of the people succumb to the consequences of malnutrition before they reach the age of thirty, but where, nonetheless, the population increases by fifty millions every decade, most men possess neither rights nor any kind of freedom. The "giant misery of the world" is only aggravated by mass violence and cannot be mitigated by inspirational twaddle. Misery will yield only to an intelligent attack upon the causes of misery.[50]

48 *Ibid.*, pp. 202–203.
49 *Ibid.*, p. 211.
50 *Themes and Variations*, p. 257 ("The Double Crisis").

In the last ten years of his life Huxley continued to turn to science, both to help solve the world's problems of feeding its excessive population and settling its economic difficulties and to provide the means to increase his own aesthetic and religious perceptions. All the books published in his last decade—*The Doors of Perception, Heaven and Hell, Tomorrow and Tomorrow and Tomorrow, Brave New World Revisited, Island,* and, finally, *Literature and Science*—indicate Huxley's return to his first love—science. He himself experimented with several drugs—mescalin, LSD (lysergic acid diethylamide), etc.—to help increase his aesthetic and spiritual awareness. His intention was to utilize science to facilitate the achievement of a beatific union with the Godhead, but one wonders whether in his metaphysical edifice the temple did not become the waiting room to the laboratory.

In his last published novel, *Island* (1962), Huxley no longer offers man the choice he offered him in *Brave New World* (1932)—the meaningless diversions of a mechanized Utopia or the almost equally barren existence of the primitive. In his last Utopia Huxley attempts to make the best of both worlds. He had always realized—his attacks on the Judeo-Christian tradition notwithstanding—that "the ethical doctrines taught in the Tao Te Ching, by Gotama Buddha and his followers of the Lesser and above all the Greater Vehicle, in the Sermon on the Mount and by the best of the Christian saints, are not dissimilar." [51] What Huxley actually wanted was a kind of fusion of the mystical contributions of the East with the technological improvements of the West. What had happened, unfortunately, was that East and West had borrowed not the best but the worst features of each other's cultures; in *Ape and Essence* he comments on how Belial "persuaded each side to take only the worst the other had to offer. So the East takes Western nationalism, Western armaments, Western movies and Western Marxism; the West takes Eastern despotism, Eastern superstitions and Eastern indifference to individual life. In a word, He [Belial] saw to it that mankind should make the worst of both worlds." [52] In *Island* Huxley found the perfect solution: "Our recipe is rather different: Take twenty sexually satisfied couples and their offsprings; add science, intuition and humor in equal quantities; steep in Tantrik Buddhism and simmer indefinitely in an open pan in the open air over a brisk flame of

[51] *Ends and Means,* p. 327 ("Beliefs").
[52] *Ape and Essence,* p. 184.

affection." [53] The marriage of science and religion does not seem to work very well in his fictional island of Pala, for at the end of the book the greedy and the vulgar are about to smash the *moksha*-induced beatitudes of the fortunate ones. The insects at the end of the book are still vulgarly copulating—to the background music of Bach's "Fourth Brandenburg Concerto"—and the female insect still devours the male after the sexual consummation. It is quite true that Will Farnaby, the central character, has learned *karuma* (compassion) and has achieved an inner strength to help him withstand the inevitable onrush of idiocy, materialism, and war. But one wonders whether this inner illumination is the result of wisdom and free will or of the *moksha*-medicine, "the reality revealer, the truth-and-beauty pill." Curiously enough, *moksha*, as the Indian scholar Nagarajan relates,[54] means "freedom for evermore." A freedom induced by a mushroom-produced drug seems hardly different from the euphoria resulting from the taking of *soma* in *Brave New World*.

Essentially, then, Huxley's religious quest was a paradoxically tortuous one. He began by mocking and rejecting the Judeo-Christian tradition (though accepting its occasional manifestations of mysticism), flirted temporarily with the Lawrentian doctrine of instinctive living and "blood consciousness," changed to contemplative investigation, turned to the East for further illumination, and died in the West trying to balance in an uneasy syncretism the Caliban of Western science with the Ariel of Buddhist mysticism. One speculates whether it was a consummation devoutly to be wished. The religious syncretism turned out to be a synthetic product; the metaphysical quest ended with a pharmacological solution.

53 *Island* (New York, 1962), p. 103.
54 See S. Nagarajan's article "Religion in Three Recent Novels of Aldous Huxley," *Modern Fiction Studies*, V (Summer 1959), pp. 153–165.

The Early Poetry of Aldous Huxley

by Charles M. Holmes

When Basil Blackell in 1916 published *The Burning Wheel*, the first volume of poems by Aldous Huxley, he was hoping to check "the enervating influence of the novel." [1] He seemed for a while to have succeeded, for Huxley was soon placed "among the most promising" of the younger poets of the period.[2] In retrospect, however, we can see that Blackwell was helping, not weakening, the cause of fiction. Huxley's poetry turned out to be unconscious preparation for *Point Counter Point, Brave New World,* and the other novels which made his name so widely known. He was to learn that only with the "formidable and lovely freedom" of the novel [3] could he project in something like its true complexity the curious, almost baffling structure of his mind and soul. His early poetry is a record of the highly complicated inner struggle which influenced, even determined the theme and the shape of his much more popular, much more successful fiction. After *The Burning Wheel* he quickly produced *Jonah* (Oxford, 1917), *The Defeat of Youth* (Oxford, 1918) and *Leda* (London, 1920), and he appeared several times in the annuals *Oxford Poetry* and *Wheels*. Although this work shows some development in technique, some improvement in quality, it illustrates more clearly Huxley's shifting and ambivalent attitude toward the very practice of literary art. Like his fiction, Huxley's verse embodies his need to express himself entangled inextricably with the problem of how to do so. From the earliest poems the crucial inner conflict appears; Huxley tries various styles to express it; the need to choose a style then intensifies the conflict as Huxley is forced to choose between

"The Early Poetry of Aldous Huxley" by Charles M. Holmes. From *Texas Studies in Literature and Language,* 8 (1966): pp. 391–406. Reprinted by permission of the author and the editor of *Texas Studies in Literature and Language.*

[1] Adverisement in *The Burning Wheel* (Oxford, 1916), p. [52].

[2] Harold Monro, *Some Contemporary Poets* (London, 1920), p. 124.

[3] In his Preface to *This Way to Paradise* (London, 1930), Campbell Dixon's dramatization of *Point Counter Point,* p. [iv].

sincere expression and effective poetry. It is this dilemma I have attempted to follow, up to the point where Huxley virtually abandoned verse for fiction.

I

The first sign of inner conflict is a startling inconsistency between poems expressing a rebellious desire to shock and other poems voicing merely conventional sentiment. Huxley's first published poem, "Home-Sickness . . . From the Town," [4] is as obviously anti-Victorian as anything he ever was to write. He is disgusted by the "debile virgins talking Keats" and the disguised prurience of an "arch" and "artful" widow. Shouting "No Social Contract," the poet rejects "the whole crowd," and urges us to lead most un-Victorian lives:

> From the teats
> Of our old wolfish mother nature drink
> Sweet unrestraint and lust and savagery.

He wants to "Feel goat-hair growing thick and redolent/On loin and thigh," to watch his nymph girl's "moony floating flanks and haunches white." As in so many of the novels, a deliberately shocking frankness about sex is combined with the makings of a new poetic style forged of knowing allusions and esoteric words. Yet in *The Burning Wheel* a few months later we find verses in the very manner Huxley seemed to have attacked, poems almost shockingly banal and stale where conventional phrases and worn-out notions abound. "Escape" begins like inferior Tennyson:

> I seek the quietude of stones
> Or of great oxen, dewlap-deep
> In meadows of lush grass, where sleep
> Drifts, tufted, on the air or drones
> On flowery traffic. . . .

"Philoclea in the Forest," an even staler poem, is set amidst Arcadian wood-moths, flowers, and lutes. "Sentimental Summer" is a maudlin poem of love:

> The West has plucked its flowers and has thrown
> Them fading on the night. Out of the sky's
> Black depths there smiles a greeting from those eyes,

---

4 *Oxford Poetry,* edited by G.[eorge] D.[ouglas] H.[oward] C.[ole] and T.[homas] W.[ade] E.[arp] (Oxford, 1915). Huxley helped to edit the 1916 volume.

Where all the Real, all I have ever known
Of the divine is held. And not alone
Do I stand here now . . . a presence seems to rise:
Your voice sounds near across my memories,
And answering fingers brush against my own.

Although there is something typically youthful in this inconsistency, in Huxley's case it was a most important symptom, not
just the sign of an inevitable but temporary stage. His inconsistency
in poetic attitude and style was rooted in deep and lasting inner
conflict, a conflict destined to increase, to plague him for years, to
become and remain the most important force in all his work.[5]
"Home-Sickness . . ." is an exaggerated recognition of the real,
"Escape" and "Sentimental Summer" a sincere gesture toward the
ideal. Like Shelley and other romantics of the century before, Huxley saw a clash between the two. He presented the ideal as beauty,
as love, or as spirit, and the real as the disappearance or transcience
of beauty, the loss of love, sometimes replaced by lust, or the ugly
facts of the surrounding material world. Most important, not only
is his own soul affected by this clash; it is also both a part and an
illustration of it. Shelley could separate the unhappy details of his
personal life from his idealized visions of a reformed and better
world; Huxley, on the contrary, finds both the ideal and the real
within himself. Only occasionally could he project a vision of the
ideal untarnished by unpleasant actuality, seen residing outside, in
others, or within. Though he has been called a "frustrated romantic," [6] he was inwardly split as most of the romantics never were.
As he put it himself in one of his poems, "Contrary to Nature and
Aristotle," his soul was an "amphisbaena," a two-headed serpent
looking in both directions at once. He visualized a purer love, a
permanent beauty, a world deserving nothing but our devotion and
his praise. But he recognized his own tendency toward such romantic
flights of fancy, and he also understood the frequent sordidness of
actuality, in the world, in others, but—most disturbingly—in himself.

Inconsistency is a result as well as evidence of Huxley's split.
"Sentimental Summer" finds harmony and divinity in love, but

[5] See my article, "Aldous Huxley's Struggle with Art," *Western Humanities Review*, XV (Spring, 1961), pp. 149–156.
[6] David Daiches, *The Novel and the Modern World* (Chicago, 1939), p. 192.
Daiches' chapter on Huxley, eliminated in the revised version of his book (Chicago, 1960) remains one of the most provocative essays on Huxley's work.

"Escape" shows the poet wanting to forget his fleshly sin. One head of his soul's amphisbaena "Turns to the daytime's dust and sweat" while the other creeps toward solace in the ideal world of books. Sometimes books are not a true solution, for they can produce, in "Vision," the "black disease" of doubt. Their opposite, the bustling world, may even be the answer; were he to die, says Huxley in "The Choice," he would deliberately pick a noisy place to lie in where the world's activity would shake his "sluggish being."

But more surprising than these contradictions is his own reaction to them. His inconsistencies apparently leave him unperturbed. He can be disturbed, of course, by what he finds in the world and himself, but not by the pattern of contradictions in his response. Yeats, who was at least as sharply split as Huxley, began to search for "Unity of Being" and regularly found his art a way to resolve his inner tensions. Huxley was not so much trying to dissolve his inner conflict as attempting to express or project it in his verse. Though he may have been searching for inner harmony, he seems to have been more interested in something theoretically external—a usable, original, aesthetically pleasing style. *The Burning Wheel* not only shows that inner conflict exists, it shows Huxley trying several different poetic styles, several different ways of putting the conflict into words.

In the title poem, "The Burning Wheel," an obviously symbolist style is used. The wheel of life, "Wearied of its own turning," painfully spinning "dizzy with speed," agonizingly yearns to rest. But even with its will thus fulfilled "in fixity," the "yearning atoms"

> . . . beget
> A flaming fire upward leaping,
> Billowing out in a burning,
> Passionate, fierce desire to find
> The infinite calm of the mother's breast.

Here, somehow becoming the Christ-child, the flame loses its "bitterness" until death arrives to wake it and "once again" beget the yearning wheel, which again will search for "that vast oblivious peace." The real-ideal conflict is seen here not through the specific emotions of the poet, but rather as symbolically generalized and abstract, as the opposition of life and death, the tension between activity and calm. The theme will find new symbols in the novels: the crystal of quiet described with such intensity in *Antic Hay*, and the connected pair of cones in *Eyeless in Gaza*, symbolizing the same quiet along with the flux of tortured lives. But Huxley immediately abandoned this kind of symbolism in his verse. Three other styles dominate the early poems.

"Escape," "Sentimental Summer," and their ilk are written in a "romantic" style, a diluted version of the manner perfected a century before, now superannuated though still so frequently used. It is easily recognized, in Huxley's early poems, by the direct, unguarded expression of emotion, by supposedly "poetic" phrases and words, by imprecise and worn-out metaphors. We find it, of course, when Huxley can believe in his ideal—when, for example, he can see love as untarnished by lust:

> . . . evening holds those strands
> Of fire and darkness twined in one to make
> Your loveliness a web of magic mesh, . . .
> [A] cross-weft harmony of soul and flesh . . .
> ("Sentimental Summer")

But just as frequently it expresses his disillusionment; his sense of the real, the unpleasant, the actual, victorious over the imagined, the ideal:

> . . . all the heaven that one time dwelt in me
> Has fled, leaving the body triumphing.
> Dead flesh it seems, with not a dream to bring
> Visions that better warm immediacy.
> (Sonnet, "If that a sparkle . . .")

Most of the poetry in this romantic style is buncombe, soon to be parodied by Huxley himself in *Crome Yellow* when Denis Stone idealizes the older Anne in the lyric he calls "The Woman who was a Tree." [7] Yet Huxley never abandoned either the romantic attitude or the corresponding style. They are important in almost all of his novels, from *Antic Hay* and its visions of young Gumbril to the synthesized utopia of Huxley's final statement, *Island*.

Huxley also tried a simple dialectic, a style embodying versified argument or discussion. Yeats had already begun to use it for expressing inner conflict, for presenting artistically his battles with himself. But Huxley was attracted by a curious potential unappealing to Yeats—the fact that two sides of his conflict could be expressed in dialectic with no demand that the conflict be resolved. In "The Walk," the long, often awkward last poem in *The Burning Wheel*, "He" and "She" engage in a conversational struggle, a bat-

---

[7] Chapter II. In Chapter XXII he writes an "elegant quatrain" on "brooding love."

tle over the significance of routine suburban life. The argument is not about what they see and hear on their stroll—meat and vegetables time and again and mumblings of people engaged in weekly prayer. They disagree about the nature and possible presence of God. To the man the pitiful old Infinite is dead; to the woman the divine, though in another dimension, still exists. There is no way of telling what Huxley really thinks. In his dialectic poems in *The Burning Wheel* and later, all Huxley had to do was argue with himself, as Yeats did with Hic and Ille, or with Michael Robartes and Owen Aherne. But Yeats was likely to award the victory, to let the side of himself which he really favored win after a vigorous and dramatic battle in the poem. Huxley's conversation poems are more objective, more explorative. For Huxley had as yet none of Yeats' will to believe. He frequently seems to be nurturing his conflict, almost preserving it as a subject for his poems.

Huxley was to transform his dialectic style into the sparkling conversations of the novels, the house party discussions of *Crome Yellow* and *Those Barren Leaves*. But his fourth, "ironic" style was an even more congenial voice, destined to be the one his public wanted to hear and most frequently heard. It became the characteristic trademark of his fiction, the tone of *Point Counter Point*, the very conception of *Brave New World*. Suggested as early as "Home-Sickness . . . From the Town," with its "debile" women and allusions to Rousseau and Keats, the style depends on the ironic contrast provided by the unexpected, in the form of such learned allusions and esoteric words. Its irony also involves another favorite Huxley strategy, setting the real against the ideal by putting human beings into a zoo. The two-headed serpent of Huxley's soul lives there; so does the creature of "The Ideal Found Wanting," the unromantic, weird, tailless apteryx bird. "Mole" uses that smallish animal to allegorize the life of man, while "The Two Realities" transforms the soul into another beast, the largest creature of the earth. When an idealist sees as "splendid" a blazing yellow-and-scarlet wagon, the realist supplies that adjective to a child kicking a turd. A grotesque, zoological pair of stanzas follows:

> Our souls are elephants, thought I
>   Remote behind a prisoning grill,
> With trunks thrust out to peer and pry
> And pounce upon reality:
>   And each at his own sweet will

Seizes the bun that he likes best
And passes over all the rest.

In such verses does the family gene of biologist appear.

II

When Huxley shifts in a single volume from one style to another,
juxtaposing "treasured things" and "golden memories" with turd-
kicking children and souls as elephants' snouts, he is obviously un-
settled, perhaps thoroughly confused. Yet his experiments, his vacil-
lations in style seem to have made his conflict even more severe.
Faced with the dilemma, the conflict posed by the real and the ideal,
Huxley had tried four different styles in attempts to express himself, to put the conflict into words. He found that sincerity asked for
the use of one of his styles but poetic effectiveness called for the use
of another. To be candid about his state of mind, dialectic was the
obvious choice, and it dominates his contributions, a year after *The
Burning Wheel,* to the 1917 volume of *Wheels.*[8] In "The Life
Theoretic," for example, the poet sets his way of life against another.
While he has been "fumbling over books/And thinking about God
and the Devil and all," others have been actually struggling in the
world, or with their "brazen faces like battering-rams" have actually
"been kissing the beautiful women." "God knows," he ends in in-
conclusive and ineffective fashion, "perhaps after all the battering-
rams are right." [9] "Retrospect," a longer poem, carries dialectic to a
more complicated extreme. Walking on Leicester Square, the poet is
plagued by emotions soon to be felt by the anti-heroes of the novels,
from Denis Stone and Gumbril and Chelifer to young John Rivers
of *The Genius and the Goddess:*

> . . . those fears and jealousies and doubts,
> Those rages and the aguish trembling bouts
> Of overmastering desire, when she
> Was absent. . . .

His strategy is to discuss with himself his future view of "the present
me." He tries to predict his opinion, at forty, "Of all the odd gri-
maces" he knows he is making now. He sees himself possibly as the

8 *Wheels: A Second Cycle* (Oxford, 1917).
9 Denis Stone, in Chapter X of *Crome Yellow,* envies Gombauld his "face of
brass—one of those old, brazen rams. . . ."

first Grave-Digger, "tipsily priapic," combined "comically" with a hating, disdainful, smiling Hamlet observing the vulgarities of a vile, fleshly world, which cannot "understand the pain of doubting . . . doubting whether anything's worth while." His questions also explore the future view of his past, the time when he found the poets lied by idealizing passion. Like "The Life Theoretic," the poem ends in unresolved and formless fashion. "Oh yes, decidedly," he concludes, "One will amuse oneself, decidedly . . . !"

Huxley seems gradually to have realized that his dialectic style, burdened by such complexities and awkwardnesses as these, could never be as effective as his ironic style and its amusing human zoo. But the greater aesthetic discipline the ironic style imposed either inhibited or made impossible sincere and frank expression. As a result a new element of inner conflict appeared; the clash between sincerity and the desire to develop effective style became another dominant motif of his career. In a later essay, "Sincerity and Art," Huxley tried to escape from the dilemma. Being sincere, he claimed, is not "a moral choice between honesty and dishonesty," but rather "mainly an affair of talent," a matter of "possessing the gifts of psychological understanding and expression." [10] It demands only a side step in logic to assume that talent is the result of sincerity, or at least that talent is the more important to show. The writer does not have to expose his feelings, to explore his deeper self, to heed the cries of his truest inner voice. He merely needs to use his talent, to compose the most skillful, the most carefully polished poems.

The slim, rare volume *Jonah* (1917) seems to demonstrate this conclusion in the craft so evident in the dozen poems it includes. The idealistic Huxley of the romantic style, the split Huxley of dialectic have all but disappeared. Instead of the self-conscious involutions of "Retrospect," we find Huxley's ironic style prevailing again, this time reinforced by the influence of other poets. "The Oxford Volunteers" reflects the bitter manner of Wilfred Owen, but more frequently the poems echo the work of Arthur Rimbaud, whose startling imagination helped Huxley to fill his weird, ironical zoo. "Behemoth," for example, is a Rimbaldien kind of fantasy:

> Basking his belly, fast asleep
> He sprawls on the warm shingle bank;
> And the bold Ethiops come and creep
> Along his polished heaving flank,

[10] *Essays New and Old* (London, 1926), pp. 303–304.

> And in his navel brew their wine
> And drink vast strength and grow divine.

Even more Rimbaldien is "Zoo Celeste," one of the four *Jonah* poems actually composed in French.[11] A familiar Huxley motif has been transformed: the "Ideal" in this fantastic, supernatural garden is an ape who flaunts the "dazzling azure" of his rump. Other inhabitants of Huxley's zoo also appear. Elephants get drunk from the black milk they suck from a negress; whales dream on the flower-filled water, their crystal spray falling on lotus blossoms bathed in perfume; Behemoth, this time, walks on the golden shore, and whole new universes are produced from time to time, each equipped with a conceited little Almighty. The world of Rimbaud's famous "Après le Déluge," where a hare prays through a spider's web to the rainbow and "Madame***sets up her piano in the Alps," is larger, more dazzling, more varied than Huxley's zoo, and his poem a more remarkable imaginative achievement. But "Zoo Celeste" is hardly less fantastic and less odd.

Rimbaud suggested motifs and subjects, and ways of rendering ironically the imagined and the ideal. Another Frenchman, Jules Laforgue, helped Huxley to find a congenial tone and to apply his ironic style to himself. Temperamentally and stylistically the converse of the older symbolist, Laforgue developed a bored, self-deprecating irony as evident in *Jonah* as the fantastic imagery so clearly drawn from Rimbaud. When the woman in Laforgue's "Autre Complainte" advances toward Lord Pierrot with love, he plans to answer with irrelevant and unromantic comment: "The sum of the angles of a triangle, dear soul, is equal to two squares." When the lady of Huxley's "The Betrothal of Priapus" intoxicates the poet with the smell of her clothes and hair, he claims he would like to swoon in pleasant languor. The Moselle he has drunk, however, leads to hideous belching instead. The same spirit, though the structure differs, appears in "Sententious Song." Here the wish for escape, handled so tritely in *The Burning Wheel,* is, to say the least, hardly romantic:

> Beauty for some provides escape,
>> Who gain a happiness in eyeing
> The gorgeous buttocks of the ape
>> Or Autumn sunsets exquisitely dying.

---

[11] The others are "Sonnet à L' Ingénue," "Dix-Huitième Siècle," and "Hommage à Jules Laforgue."

> Some swoon before the uplifted Host,
>   Or gazing on their navels find
> Both Father, Son and Holy Ghost
>   On that small Ark of Ecstasy confined.

"Minoan Porcelain," reprinted from an earlier story,[12] combines a hint of Rimbaldien fantasy with Laforgue's ironic attitude toward love—in a vocabulary easily recognizable as Huxley's. It is a tightly written description of an uninhibited pagan princess:

> Her eyes of bright unwinking glaze
> All imperturbable do not
> Even make pretences to regard
> The jutting absence of her stays,
> Where many a Tyrian gallipot
> Excites desire with spilth of nard.

A small jar, for Huxley, is a "gallipot"; overflow is "spilth"; ointment is "nard"; and rouge, a line later, is "fard." "Jonah" itself is an even more remarkable example of this peculiar, efficient, distinctive style, as Laforgue's ironic use of scientific and medical words is merged with the spirit of fantasy of Rimbaud. Seated on a kidney in the inside of the whale, Jonah can see

> Many a pendulous stalactite
> Of naked mucus, whorls and wreaths
> And huge festoons of mottled tripes
> And smaller palpitating pipes
> Through which a yeasty liquor seethes.

While the great whale swims through the water,

>   Jonah prays
> And sings his canticles and hymns,
> Making the hollow vault resound
> God's goodness and mysterious ways. . . .

These unusual poems were produced by subjugating at least a degree of sincerity to talent. They do not represent, as Huxley's romanticism proves, the attitude he consistently really felt, nor do they even hint at the struggle raging within. But they involved or suggested a kind of compromise procedure, a strategy allowing Huxley to write effectively without completely stifling the voice of

[12] "Eupompus Gave Splendour to Art by Numbers," *The Palatine Review*, No. 4 (October, 1916), pp. 5–13.

inner conflict. He could use his clever, ironical, exaggerated style
as an inverse kind of "sincere" poetic mask. The poet, to a degree, is
there for all to see. But his deeper concerns, his sensitivities are hidden; he is protected even in self-expression by the masking effect
of his style. Only one direct confession of inner conflict appears in
Jonah, the poem entitled "Hommage à Jules Laforgue." Addressing
the Frenchman as a brother also split by his search for the ideal,
Huxley admits that in living ambivalently—contrary, as before, "to
Nature and to father Aristotle"—he has made himself rather ridiculous. Even this apparent frankness, however, is disguised; the poem
to Laforgue was published only in French. *Jonah* shows Huxley
grappling with the sincerity-art dilemma by developing a style that
would serve him as a mask. Wearing it, he could make gestures toward the sincere while composing his best ironic poems.

Huxley never transformed his need for a mask into a theory, as
Yeats was soon to do as part of his system in *A Vision.* His problem
was too personal for such objective treatment, too elusive and complex for any highly organized plan. He preferred persenting himself
in verses like "The Contemplative Soul" as a weird, deeply sub-
merged, ship-inhabiting fish:

> Fathoms from sight and hearing,
> Where seas are blind and deaf,
> My soul like a fish goes steering
> Her fabulous gargoyle nef:
>
> Her nef of silver and mouldering
> Mother-of-pearl with eyes
> Of bulging coral smouldering
> Down dim green galleries.

Since a danger awaits if the soul-fish comes to the surface, it decides
to remain far down below:

> To climb the brightening ladder
> Of layer on layer of the sea
> She dare not; her swimming-bladder
> Would burst in the ecstasy
>
> Of sunlight and windy motion,
> White moons and the sky's red gates.
> Still in the depth of ocean
> She sits and contemplates.

Perhaps Huxley is already aware of his future: the final images hint at the mysticism he will eventually pursue. But the secret, whatever it is, is only barely suggested beneath the comical, self-deprecating mask.

III

Though Huxley had formed a style useful for deceptively partial self-expression, he did not employ even it with any consistency. It was a limited, temporary resolution of his dilemma, even though it produced the best of his early poems. The style of his next group, for the 1918 cycle of *Wheels*, is merely the purest, clearest expression of the impact on him of Rimbaud. T. S. Eliot, a friend of Huxley during these years, had faced and projected his own sense of alienation in "Prufrock," a poem heavily indebted to Laforgue. Spotting the influence of Laforgue on Huxley's work, Eliot diagnosed it as a "serious attack." [13] But the "disease" of the 1918 poems for *Wheels* was obviously transmitted by Rimbaud.[14] Unlike the *Wheels*, 1917, selections they are not in dialectic, nor are they in any other previous Huxley style; they are prose poems in the manner of *Illuminations*, with something of the energy of Rimbaud's imagination. "Gothic" describes rattling bright green copper leaves shaking over an ape, a knight, a manticore, and a friar, four "gargoyles" engaged in a game of dice. The Huxley zoo reappears in the zodiac beasts of "The Merry-Go-Round," although these animals are driven, to the poet's alarm, by "a slobbering cretin grinding at a wheel."

Rimbaud the visionary, who saw beyond sordid actuality to an ideal, inspired the most important of these poems. "Beauty" is a glowing, lyrical disquisition, and—for Huxley—a surprising autobiographical admission. The search narrated in the poem is not really for beauty itself but for a way of living in the world with minimum conflict, and at the same time for a posture that will help him to create. Like the Rimbaud of "Being Beauteous," Huxley sees a dazzling female image, a "perpetual miracle, beauty endlessly born." But whereas Rimbaud will fall "à traverse la mêlée," Huxley's much longer poetic search continues. After a questioning glance

13 As Apteryx, "Verse Pleasant and Unpleasant," *The Egoist,* V (March, 1918), p. 44.
14 See Ruth Temple's analysis, "Aldous Huxley et la littérature française," *Revue de littérature comparée,* XIX (January–March, 1939), esp. pp. 66–89 *passim.* She cites (p. 87) a letter from Huxley of October 9, 1937, recalling his "imitations de Rimbaud dans sa poésie de jeunesse."

at commercial ocean steamers, moving mechanically and unknow-
ingly over the water, he eventually finds himself in ancient Troy.
Here beauty is incarnate in the fabulous but paradoxical Helen,
who gives eternity to Paris while at the same time robbing him of his
life. Rejecting the Greek escape from this dilemma, the Heraclitean
theory of opposites, the poet yet admits his strong connection with
Troy and searches for a better answer to resolve the paradox. Reason, one possibility, unfortunately depends on the abolition of nature: the patterns of geometry, unable to account for the curves of
Helen's body, are possible only where trees are absent and rivers are
made of steel. Huxley decides to "take the world as it is, but meta-
phorically, informing the chaos of nature with a soul, qualifying
transcience with eternity." Permanent beauty will be found only
"when even Helen's white voluptuousness matches some candour of
the soul." The only true poets are centaurs, he concludes; their bel-
lies travel close to the ground but their heads are in the air.

As this final image hints, though "Beauty" is an idealistic, visionary poem, it is the vision of an idealism severely challenged by actuality—so severely that it may corrode away. No mask, no ironical
pose appears in the poem. The poet instead suggests that he is
tempted to be a cynic—not to hide his idealism underneath a comic
mask, but to flaunt his discovery that the ideal is mocked by the real.
Well before the final poet-as-centaur image, when Huxley finds not
only Helen but Cressida in Troy, he admits knowing all about the
"damning Theory of woman." And the brotherly world he imagines
after the discovery of permanent beauty will involve, he tells us,
not only eating and drinking, "marrying and giving in marriage,"
but also "taking and taken in adultery."

The idealist-turned-cynic accounts for Huxley's next book title,
the volume he called *The Defeat of Youth and Other Poems.* The
title refers to the volume's opening sonnet sequence, a group of
poems directly avowing the cynical view. They redescribe Huxley's
earlier idyllic view of love; reaffirm his idealized vision of true
beauty; trace the change of love to lust in consummation; and leave
the weary poet disillusioned, now in sight of a very different truth.
The quest for the ideal, it appears, has been forsaken; the strategy
of hiding conflict behind a mask has been abandoned; the poet has
no choice but the cynical, tired view, and his earliest and least effective style, the romantic.

Yet the poems which follow "The Defeat of Youth" demonstrate that nothing could be farther from the truth. Cynicism is another alternative, another temporary phase. In "Stanzas" and "Poem" Huxley *is* the sentimental romantic, guilty of the triteness so common in *The Burning Wheel*. Yet, more frequently the grotesque, ironic style reappears—in esoteric words like "quotidian" and "crapulous," in a lady who has "charnel beauty" and is a "tainted well," in another whose soul has "a slabby-bellied sound," which rubs itself upon "the rind of things." The ironies of "Topiary" not only apply to the nature of men, who are given fantastic shapes by God-as-expert-clipper of shrubs. The poem also includes a reminder of Huxley's earlier mask: he sees himself again as "remote and happy, a great goggling fish." As if to reassert his interest in and need for the ironic style, Huxley again reprints "Minoan Porcelain," perhaps the best ironic poem in *Jonah*.

The Defeat of Youth is a more bewildering set of contradictions, of contrasts in attitude and of the various Huxley styles, even than those in Huxley's first book, *The Burning Wheel*. Yet this great variety apparently served as a kind of creative catharsis, a test which isolated the worst and the best and helped the vacillating poet to make his ultimate choice. In *Leda*, Huxley's last collection of early verse, and in the handful of poems for the last three collections of *Wheels*, the ironic style becomes once and for all Huxley's most frequent, most characteristic voice, and he regularly appears exposed and hidden with his mask. "Frascati's" [15] finds poet and lady watching the "human bears"; rhetorical questions parody Keats' elegant "Ode on a Grecian Urn":

> What negroid holiday makes free
> With such priapic revelry?
> What songs? What gongs? What nameless rites?
> What gods like wooden stalagmites?

When the ragtime "swoons" to a waltz, the poet takes his lady's hand,

> And there . . . [they] sit in blissful calm,
> Quietly sweating palm to palm.

"Male and Female Created He Them" [16] again recalls the bored, medicinal irony of Jules Laforgue. When Huxley's heroine,

---

[15] In *Wheels, 1919* (Oxford, 1919), p. 15.
[16] In *Leda*. Reprinted in Aldous Huxley, *Verses & A Comedy* (London, 1946), pp. 52–53.

> drunk with sleep, . . .
> Feels her Corydon's fingers creep . . .
> Strummingly over the smooth sleek drum
> Of her thorax . . . ,

and thrills to his supposedly "God-like" passion, he is really calcu-
lating the cost of lunch, and the total expense she will put him to
in a year. But the best and most typical are the four "Philosopher's
Songs," [17] the self-deprecating lyrics of a bard who continues to find
the ridiculous or the grotesque in life and love. In the First, he sees
himself "a poor degenerate" inferior to the ape—able, however, to
be better than apelike with his mind:

> a nimble beast
> Possessing a thousand sinewy tails,
> A thousand hands, with which it scales,
> Greedy of luscious truth, the greased
>
> Poles and the coco palms of thought . . .

In the Fifth, he is the one sperm who happened to survive:

> And among that million minus one
>   Might have chanced to be
> Shakespeare, another Newton, a new Donne—
>   But the One was Me.

And in the Second he tells his Lesbia that if he should ever take his
life, his body "Would drift face upwards on the oily tide/ With the
other garbage, till it purified." Since hers, surely, would float face
down modestly, exposing only its buttocks, it is obvious that this
"best of worlds" has been carefully planned.

The conflict masked in the grotesquerie of poems such as these,
Huxley's increasingly obsessive concern for love and lust, is a little
more obvious in "Morning Scene" and "From the Pillar." [18] In the
first the poet sees, poised above Goya's image of scattered hair and
tempting bosom, "a red face/ Fixed in the imbecile earnestness of
lust." In the other he seems to project an exaggerated version of
himself. As Simeon, the withered ascetic, he observes the "human
beasts" shattering the quiet with their orgies. "The steam of fetid
vices" climbs "From a thousand lupanars." Watching this behavior
from his high, detached position, Simeon is split by a mixture of
hatred and envy. Huxley's desire both to accept and reject the flesh

---

[17] In *Leda*. Reprinted in *Verses & A Comedy*, pp. 56–60.
[18] Both in *Leda*. Reprinted in *Verses & A Comedy*, p. 60, p. 53.

may account for yet another experiment, the final one before he virtually abandoned writing poems. All his poems before *Leda* had been short ones. He needed a more flexible, more extended mode of expression, especially to explore the continuing problem of the flesh. The temporary answer appears in the two poems which begin and end the volume, poetry in the form of narrative.

"Leda," which has found many critical admirers,[19] is a long, elaborate treatment of the myth so powerfully compressed in Yeats' sonnet "Leda and the Swan." Expansively and elegantly, Huxley's blank verse follows Leda talking and swimming with her maidens, Jove observing the world from his sumptuous bed on Mount Olympus, planning his approach to Leda in debate with Aphrodite, then descending to the rape as a "proud-arching opulent" swan. The poem is not only a polished handling of the myth, it is also an allegory of Huxley's plaguing concern. Leda is the ideal, another vision of "perfect loveliness." Jove, embodying superhuman, transcendent power, is driven like mere mortals by restlessness and an irresistible sensual itch. His possession of Leda is the rape of "almost spiritual grace." Like the parade of women who soon will people Huxley's novels, Leda is unable, unwilling to resist. Feeling pity for the swan—the emotion which is here, as later, "the mother of voluptuousness"—Leda feels "a quick, involuntary thrill," and utters a sound of "utmost pleasure or of utmost pain." Even centuries ago, the implication is, the gross forces of life destroyed the virginal ideal.

"Soles Occidere et Redire Possunt" (Suns are able to set and to return) is a narrative in a less traditional, more flexible medium. In loosely rhymed stanzas with a line of varying length, Huxley traces a day in the life of a friend killed in the War. Yet just as the friend sounds very much like Huxley, the style combines the elements Huxley had already used before. John Ridley, the supposed subject of the poem, lies in bed engaging in dialectic with himself, an idealized dream battling with an approaching "quotidian" task. Later he reads a letter from his Helen, who though she is a "heavenly vision" of his temple is also a "votary of the copulative cult." Ridley himself composes a poem about the difficulty of catching truth, abandons it for a session of the reading he prefers, then heads for his quotidian visit with insentitive Aunt Loo. Walking through the city

---

[19] For example, Douglas Bush, *Mythology and the Romantic Tradition* (New York, 1963), p. 478: "*Leda* is hardly an important work, yet it is an original combination of conventional mythological romanticism with animal and tropical heat and exotic color."

and its "lumps of human meat," his thoughts are of the cesspool in himself and the "mounds of flesh and harlotry" outside. Thought, he feels, is only a blind alley; action, only beating water that goes back to rest. The poem ends shortly after another meaningless rapprochement with a woman, another Laforgue-like encounter without love. Through Ridley, Huxley seems to project his own life once again, but at greater length than in any earlier poem.

"Soles" and "Leda" both were abortive efforts, however; neither was a final answer, a proper mode for self-projection. Blank verse, however well he could employ it, was obviously a style wedded to a remote past. The contrasting jerky, cacophanous rhythms of "Soles" were the work of a poet really out of his element, who seems to be writing for the first time all over again. Earlier, his work in dialectic had allowed him the freest self-expression, yet his self was often what he most deeply wanted to mask. The ironic style had provided the mask and produced his most effective poems, yet its very indirectness, with the brevity it encouraged, inhibited full expression of his themes. The long narrative poems had at least helped to suggest an answer. If no style of poetry would work, perhaps the combination of prose and narrative would. Huxley was not quite yet ready to publish his first novel, but he was more than ready to try to master the short story. Before 1920, the year of *Leda,* was over, he had in the stories of *Limbo* most auspiciously begun.

The Counterpoint of Flight: Huxley's Early Novels

by Jerome Meckier

Despite the fact that their tone perceptively darkens, Aldous Huxley's first three novels—and for freshness and exuberance they may be his finest comic achievement—seem at first glance much too similar. The same characters appear from one novel to the next under different names that one tends to regard as aliases; and the situations, though never repetitious, seem ultimately to support a basic repertoire of themes. Thus an examination of *Crome Yellow* (1921) leaves one as thrilled with Huxley's first novel as his original audience was. But if a perusal of *Antic Hay* (1923) and *Those Barren Leaves* (1925) follows immediately, one may conclude that Huxley has written the same novel three times. This is not a thoroughly misguided judgment, but rather an imprecise one and therefore it states negatively what is actually a positive accomplishment.

What Huxley has done, however, is to go over and over the same themes but never from precisely the same angle and never with the same results. The heroes of the first two novels are defeated in different ways by similar problems whereas the third protagonist enjoys a tentative, modified, perhaps only temporary success. Each time his hero confronts the central problems and fails, Huxley has someone similar to him, but also different, try over again from a slightly different approach.

When these three novels are looked at as a sort of trilogy, they remain infinitely readable in themselves but also take on an added significance in that the thematic alterations they catalogue reveal in microcosm the direction in which Huxley will develop in terms of

"The Counterpoint of Flight: Huxley's Early Novels" by Jerome Meckier. From *Aldous Huxley: Satire and Structure,* chapter 3 (originally "The Counterpoint of Flight"). (London: Chatto & Windus Ltd. 1969). Copyright © 1969 by Jerome Meckier. Reprinted by permission of the author, Chatto & Windus, Ltd. and Barnes and Noble Books, U.S. distributors.

ideas as well as craftsmanship. The changes the three novels exhibit
in their handling of the same set of themes show Huxley doing
between 1921 and 1925 what he would only permanently accomplish and accept by 1934 with the appearance, in *Eyeless in Gaza*,
of his first full-fledged mystic-hero. At the same time, the increasing
mastery of structure and technique from novel to novel and the
sense one has that all three novels are really one book with three
complementary, perhaps even contrapuntal, sets of characters and
events make the many-layered complexity of *Point Counter Point*
(1928) inevitable.

I

Crome Yellow, Huxley's first novel, is the love song of its hero,
Denis Stone. The young poet has come to Crome[1] to tell Anne
Wimbush he loves her. What the novel's thirty chapters actually record, however, is his failure to deliver the message. The theme of
ineffectual communication spans the novel while permeating the
majority of scenes. The direction of these scenes is towards a sort of
awakening wherein Denis, who has concluded that people are un-
crossing parallel lines, is suddenly forced to look at himself as he
appears to others.

Hercules the Dwarf is a grotesque figure in a satiric parable that
Henry Wimbush presents as a piece of straight history from the book
he is writing on Crome (XIII). Denis, on the other hand, appears as
the hero of a supposedly realistic story. Yet the pair actually belong
to the same species of eccentric in trying to make reality conform to
their expectations. Like the dwarf, who reduced life to his own pro-
portions, Denis has a fund of patterns to impose on events but is seldom prepared for experience itself. To him, life is a rehearsable
play. He blocks out scenes with himself in the central role and
attempts to stage them. The missed cues and unexpected replies that
follow as the interpretation of Pharaoh's dream that is written and
directed by Denis Stone falls apart provide excellent comedy. Denis
plans, for example, to tell Anne how adorable she is, but the scene

[1] In *Aldous Huxley: A Memorial Volume*, p. 30, T. S. Eliot informs us that
Crome is patterned on the house of Lady Ottoline Morrell at Garsington. Some
of Lady Ottoline's guests, Eliot claims, appear in *Crome Yellow*. The guest-list
at Garsington often included Bertrand Russell, Lytton Strachey, D. H. and Frieda
Lawrence, Katherine Mansfield, and John Middleton Murry. Priscilla Wimbush is
Lady Ottoline, Mr. Scogan is either H. G. Wells or Norman Douglas, Mary is
Dora Carrington, Gombauld is Mark Gertler, and Jenny is Dorothy Brett.

collapses when she comments on the attractiveness of his white flannel trousers. The conversation takes "a preposterous and unexpected turn" (IV) in which the heroine usurps the hero's opening line and addresses him as though he were a little boy and not a contender for her love.

Language, a perennial problem for Huxley characters, even for the artificially stabilized society of *Brave New World,* stands between Denis and reality the way Keats' sensuous richness threatened his involvement with society. Denis regards words as though they were things. They become his substitute for reality and his conversation deteriorates into one long fallacy of misplaced concreteness. As a Procrustean, Denis wants the meaning of *carminative* to correspond with its beautiful sound. Although he feels it should illustrate his theory that the artist creates something out of nothing through the power of words, *carminative* nevertheless means *windtreibend.* Denis' mind, Huxley notes, "wandered down echoing corridors of assonance and alliteration ever further and further from the point" (I). Denis' centrifugal use of language takes him away from reality and into a private world.

Whenever Denis supplies the literary touch, it is simultaneously the embalmer's. His neatly-turned observations transform an object into a frozen scene for some Grecian Urn. Anne looks at the sunflowers and finds them magnificent, but Denis must observe that their dark faces and golden crowns make them "kings in Ethiopia" (IV), an apt description but ultimately a substitute for seeing things as they are. If he lacks a fine phrase of his own, Denis quotes another poet, for an object becomes "more real" to him if he can employ "somebody else's ready made phrase" (IV). In Denis' propensity for quotes and for the continual transformation of life into art, Huxley satirizes his own tendency to be too precious, overly multisyllabic, and, at times, esoterically erudite. Rehearsed scenes, ready-made phrases, words instead of things—these are the barriers Denis imposes between himself and life. He is the first in a series of Huxley characters who personify a paradoxical union of egotism and shyness. Jeremy Pordage of *After Many a Summer* (1939) is an example of Denis in middle-age. He has the young poet's penchant for apt quotation and for books over experience. In the scene in which Anne comments on his trousers, Denis had hoped to work up to the old romantic stand-by, the pregnant silence. But he fails to impregnate the silence, just as the boxes containing the unedited Hauberk papers Pordage must sort out are "Twenty-seven crates of still unravished brides of quietness" (Part 1, v) and the only brides the ineffectual Pordage will ever know. Denis is also a forerunner of Philip Quarles. He agrees with Quarles that one should live first and then make one's philosophy fit life, but Denis says this with arms outstretched "in an attitude of crucifixion." He is once again playing a role, whereas Anne says she has "always taken things as they come" (IV). Thus if Denis and Anne married, they would become Philip and Elinor Quarles. In the course of the novel, Denis discovers he is a split-man. His responses are purely mental, for although he shouts his love for Anne "mentally," "not a sound issues from his lips" (IV). His emotions, like Quarles', remain "theoretical" (XVII).

Denis is basically an escapist. But the barriers he puts up are also moulds that re-shape the world of experience into forms his ego can manage. He has elected himself life's playwright and he expects the portion of life treated in the novel to be handled from his point of view. In choosing art over life and translating the latter into the former, he also personifies Huxley's suspicion that the entire process by which life becomes art makes the artist as much of a theme-bending egotist as any of the speakers in a *Point Counter Point* discussion scene. The artist who imposes patterns on experience, Huxley fears, produces works that embody his own limitations. Philip Quarles' novels provide an all-too-obvious example. Denis, Gumbril Jr. of *Antic Hay,* and Calamy in *Those Barren Leaves,* the heroes of Huxley's first three novels, are three of the author's fictional versions of himself and his own limitations. The first two heroes fail to get out of themselves. They do not achieve a viewpoint broad enough to protect them from their egos. Calamy, however, is a potential success; and it is Calamy's method Huxley tries, first as a novelist in *Point Counter Point,* and later as a mystic in both novels and non-fiction prose.

Jenny Mullion, whose deafness stands between her and the other characters in the novel, is, ironically, the person who penetrates Denis' barriers. All through the novel she functions as a comical sphinx whose riddle Denis tries to read. Her "enigmatic remoteness" unsettles him as she periodically emerges from her interior world "like a cuckoo from a clock." It is after an abortive conversation with her that Denis decides the world consists of parallel lines (IV). This is a quasi-philosophical theory made from his own vantage point and with the tacit assumption that he, at least, is striving for contacts. An accidental glance into Jenny's notebook, however, confronts Denis with his own egotism: he discovers a cutting caricature sketch of himself (xxiv). The phenomenon of other people, the existence of points of view different from and unsympathetic to his own is made plain to him. He finds it "inconceivable that he should appear to other people as they appeared to him."

Denis' egotism is threatened, his way of looking at himself and the world comically overturned. The validity of one's personal viewpoint—to be questioned technically and structurally in *Point Counter Point* and politically but perhaps more naively in *Ends and Means*[2]—is effectively challenged. in Denis, Keats' way with language exists without Keats' ability to become the people and things he described. The red notebook forces Denis to see himself with Jenny's eyes. Cast as a nonentity in Denis's play, Jenny suddenly appears in the role of Max Beerbohm.

The possibility of realizing the intricateness of other people to the same extent one is aware of complexity in oneself frightens Denis and intrigues Huxley. Denis must come to terms with "the vast conscious world outside himself." In so doing, he can no longer imagine himself the world's sole intelligent being, nor ignore the fact that others are "in their way as elaborate and complete as he is in his . . ." (xxiv).[3] He must live with the fact that he seems as ridiculous and secondary to others as they do to him. His first move, however, is a retreat as he contrives his immediate departure from Crome. Jenny's cartoon has exploded his barriers, but the phony telegram he sends himself provides him with a new means of escape. He plays his leave-taking as a funeral scene and makes the reader wonder if his epiphany has taught him anything. His bad habits continue as he aptly quotes Landor (xxx), but so does his ineffectualness, since nobody notices. Henry Wimbush and Crome's other inhabitants remain self-absorbed. Despite his epiphanic experience with Jenny's notebook, Denis' departure constitutes escapism, a flight *from* rather than *to*. The confrontation of a Huxley hero with the phenomenon of other people must be tried again in the author's next novel.

2 See *Ends and Means*, p. 44, where Huxley argues that international chaos results because egoistic nations plan their policies solely from their own point of view.

3 In *The Devils of Loudun* (New York, 1965), p. 102 (first published 1952), Huxley notes that "other people can see through us just as easily as we can see through them. The discovery of this fact is apt to be exceedingly disconcerting."

II

Huxley's second novel, *Antic Hay,* is organized around images of futility. It ends with Myra Viveash and Theodore Gumbril Jr. taxiing back and forth across London while Shearwater, scientist and kidney expert, pedals a stationary bicycle. The essayist Mercaptan's "delicious middles" (essays meant for publication neither at the start nor end of a journal) are thus the perfect art form for a novel of futility whose characters have little sense of their origins and no ends to pursue. Though Gumbril Jr. is practically Denis Stone and Prufrock all over again, the novel draws its atmosphere from T. S. Eliot's *The Waste Land.* Myra Viveash, who resembles Ernest Hemingway's Brett Ashley in *The Sun Also Rises* and Evelyn Waugh's Margot Beste-Chetwynd in *Decline and Fall,*[4] epitomizes the ennui of modern life when she insists "tomorrow will be as awful as today" (xxiii). In a novel full of tag names, Mrs. Viveash's suggests light without heat. She kindles love for herself in every male in the novel, but can offer no answering warmth of her own. Her voice, the articulation of society, seems to come from a deathbed and is "always on the point of expiring" (v).

The influence of T. S. Eliot's poetry on satiric novels of the 1920s and 30s has never been sufficiently stressed. In Waugh's *A Handful of Dust* (1934), the title of which comes from *The Waste Land,* F. Scott Fitzgerald's *The Great Gatsby* (1925), and in *Antic Hay* (1923), past and present are ludicrously contrasted and characters are dwarfed by roles their ancestors played with ease. Gumbril Sr. seems a weak version of Christopher Wren, as is Gumbril Jr. of the Rabelaisian man, and Coleman makes a ridiculous Satan. Casmir Lypiatt wishes to fill Michelangelo's shoes, but is clearly patterned on the bragging, unsuccessful Romantic painter, Benjamin Haydon.[5] In art, in life, even in their capacity for evil, Huxley's characters in *Antic Hay* are a shrivelled lot. Like Denis Stone, they all

[4] Not only does Myra resemble Brett and Margot, two *femmes fatales* of the 1920s, but she also contrasts satirically with E. M. Forster's Mrs. Wilcox and Mrs. Moore, two highly sensitive, mystical women, and with Mrs. Woolf's Clarissa Dalloway and Mrs. Ramsay.

[5] For similarities between Lypiatt and Haydon, compare Casmir with the Haydon who appears in Huxley's introduction to *The Autobiography and Memoirs of Benjamin Haydon* (New York, 1926). Reprinted in *The Olive Tree* as "B. R. Haydon." To compare Gumbril Sr. and Wren, see the essay written for Wren's bi-centenary in *On the Margin* (1923). Wren is praised as a master of "proportion," a quality Huxley's characters lack.

play roles; they are all escapists trying to be something they are not. The extent to which each inhabits a private world is further emphasized by the different role each chooses in an attempt to increase his stature. What Christopher Wren, Satan, the Complete Man, and a bombastic Romantic painter could say to each other is hard to determine.

In conversation with the diabolist, Coleman, Shearwater confesses that the kidneys are his only interest in life. "You hold the key to everything," Coleman mockingly replies, "The key, I tell you, the key" (IV). Coleman has read T. S. Eliot: "We think of the key," T. S. Eliot wrote in *The Waste Land* (414–415), "each in his prison. Thinking of the key, each confirms a prison." Shearwater has made kidneys into an imprisoning private world on the assumption that they are talismanic. The old roles absurdly revived by Gumbril Jr. and Lypiatt no longer work, nor does the new science, as personified by Shearwater, seem any more successful. Yet Shearwater holds the key to everything in a real sense, inasmuch as what he has done, like the saga of Hercules and the autobiography of Chelifer, explains the eccentricity of many of Huxley's characters.

Between Denis and Gumbril Jr., however, one important difference exists. Gumbril seems more aware both of his own inadequacy and of egos other than his own. He even has a dream-self in which he succeeds where Denis failed. Like Gaveston in Marlowe's *Edward II* (1, i, 59–60), he prefers "men, like satyrs [who] . . . with their goat-feet dance an antic hay." In his dream, chance encounters and plotted opportunities occur and recur as they never did for Denis. Reality fulfills Gumbril's expectations and, in his dream life, he combines Keatsian power with breadth of vision comparable to Huxley's in *Point Counter Point*: he can "understand all points of view" and is able to "identify himself" with such unfamiliar types as mill girls and engine drivers (I).

Unfortunately, Gumbril is really the victim of a plot full of more outrageous coincidences than any Waugh or Dickens novel contains. He masquerades as Toto, the Rabelaisian man, but the first woman he conquers is Rosie Shearwater, his wife's friend. The theme of missed opportunity, so prevalent in *Crome Yellow*, recurs as a coincidental meeting with Myra Viveash prevents Gumbril from joining Emily. His disguise as Toto, an attempt at actualizing his dream-self, has led to Emily and a happiness Gumbril can only fatalistically describe as "unreal, impossible" (XII). Emily scarcely functions in the novel as a developed character, but she symbolizes the possibility of mystical union with the mysterious presence the sleepless Gumbril often feels approaching but never dares to face. She not only represents Gumbril's final opportunity to transcend himself but is also an intimation of the fusion of the sexual and the mystical (in which the first leads to the second) that Huxley will return to in *The Genius and the Goddess* (1955) and, most explicitly, in *Island* (1962). The mysterious presence is something, says Gumbril (xii), "inexpressibly lovely and wonderful" yet "inexpressibly terrifying," for should it "engulf you, you'd die." The death he has in mind is death to the self, the catastrophe all of Huxley's egotists fear most.

The central irony in the novel is that in a moment of crisis, when the opportunity to control events occurs, Gumbril Jr. chooses contrivance and coincidence over a chance for genuine contact. Despite his masquerade as Toto, Gumbril remains the parasite of events, and thus the genuine heir of Gaveston in a less flattering sense. Instead of goat-feet, he has cold ones. Although a rational theology where God is $2 + 2 = 4$ dismays him (i) and he hungers for something more physical and emotional, Gumbril cannot confront what Eliot calls "The awful daring of a moment's surrender/Which an age of prudence can never retract" (404–405). His pose as Complete Man could always be dropped, but his commitment to Emily would have to be permanent. In an atmosphere of withered values, Gumbril lacks sufficient faith. The chance to be Keats rather than a parallel line comes, but he retreats. He sends Emily a telegram—just as Denis sent himself one—saying he will join her a day late because of a slight accident. The slight accident is Myra Viveash, the novel's siren, whose desire for company lures Gumbril from his intended visit to Emily. Gumbril also telegrams Rosie to arrange a rendezvous, but purposely gives her Mercaptan's address and Coleman's name. As she proceeds to have affairs with each of them, the futility of Gumbril's affair with her is underlined. Through connivance, Gumbril equates the genuine contact he has made with Emily with its farcical counterpart in Rosie and strips himself of both.

As Myra and Gumbril dance, the band, parodying *Hamlet*, blares "What's he to Hecuba?/Nothing at all" (xv). Prufrock protested he was no Hamlet, nor is Gumbril. He feigns an accident; like Hamlet, he procrastinates; but it leads to missed opportunity rather than climactic confrontation. The relevant play he watches in the nightclub with Myra after the band has finished (xvi) does not catch his conscience as Hamlet's did the king's. He is not shaken by the lines: "Somewhere there must be love like music. Love harmonious and

ordered: two spirits, two bodies moving contrapuntally together."
For Gumbril, as well as Huxley, love is never sufficiently aesthetic.
Gumbril accepts the band's song as a summary of his relations with
both Myra and Emily. When her letter arrives next morning to put
off his trip forever, Emily describes Gumbril's accident as a warning
sent *by Providence* to show her hope for happiness was "hopelessly
impractical" (xvi). Gumbril's failure to confront the situation and
Myra's ability to disrupt it cast them both in the role of Providence.
That Gumbril should be described as the controller of events he has
always desired to be at the moment he is most disloyal to his dream
is exquisite irony. Had he come, Emily writes, "I'd have twisted myself into the threads of your life." Instead, Gumbril realizes, he has
forsaken the one person with whom "he might have learned to await
in quietness the final coming of that lovely terrible thing": from
which "ignobly he had fled" so many times. Like Denis, Gumbril
remains an escapist, a separatist. In the last chapter, he plans to flee
to the continent to sell the pneumatic trousers he has invented.
These and not Emily, comprise the threads of his life. He invented
them to put cushioned material between humanity's posteriors and
hard wooden benches and they signify his willingness to place some
barrier between himself and the hard surfaces of reality.[6]

III

In *Those Barren Leaves,* his third novel, Huxley moves Crome to
Vezza, Italy. The characters in the book seem to succeed where those
in Huxley's previous novels failed. The novelist Calamy, whose
arrival at Vezza seems to be a return from a flight-journey similar to
that undertaken by Gumbril at the end of *Antic Hay,* has more
success with women than his two male predecessors combined. So
too, Francis Chelifer, instead of living in a private world, at first
seems completely identified with his environment. Even Mary
Thriplow, though a flourishing novelist and a woman of many pre-
tences, does not always put art before life. She does regard most
experiences as material for her novels, but she has the experiences

---

6 Another barrier Gumbril erects against life—and it too is a sign of his inability to make connections—is the stream of unrelated facts he can set flowing
any time. Philip Quarles also has this encyclopedic facility (vi), as does Uncle
Spencer in the story named after him in *Little Mexican and Other Stories* (London, 1924). Here again Huxley has himself in mind. In *Along the Road,* p. 71,
he professes his fondness for reading a volume of *Encyclopaedia Britannica* while
on his travels.

first, and then arranges them into patterns. Though Huxley severely
satirizes her, her novels do not keep her from life as thoroughly as
Quarles' do. Like Calamy, however, Huxley is dissatisfied with these
"successes." Whereas Denis and Gumbril Jr. were satirized for rais-
ing shields against reality, Calamy's final retreat into solitude and
speculation is favourably counterpointed against their flights.

Huxley's first three novels thus contain in miniature one of the
major movements of his career: from a desire for involvement and
unity to a later preference for properly motivated escape. The burden of inadequacy shifts in the course of these three novels until it
rests less on the Prufrockian heroes and more on the society in which
they live. In *Those Barren Leaves,* Huxley seems at times to suspect,
perhaps even to discredit, the very things *Crome Yellow* and *Antic
Hay* pursued.

Unlike Gumbril Jr., Calamy regards passion and its fulfilment as
the barrier between himself and higher things (Part 1, IV). As the
novel and his routine affair with Mary proceed, Calamy's dissatisfac-
tion increases. He "couldn't at the same time lean out into the silence beyond the futile noise and bustle—into the mental silence
that lies beyond the body . . . and himself partake in the tumult"
(Part 3, XIII). If one compares Calamy's statements with some of the
more basic advice to the yogi contained in the *Bhagavad-Gita,* it
becomes clear that Calamy is discussing a few fairly fundamental
contemplation procedures. He concludes that in "thinking really
hard about one thing—this hand, for example— . . . one might be
able to burrow one's way right through the mystery and really get
at something . . ." (Part 5, 1). (The yogi is supposed to sit in some
isolated spot and, while holding the senses and imagination in check,
to keep the mind focussed on its object. The yogi's heart will then
become pure.) For as Calamy realizes, his hand exists simultaneously
in a dozen parallel worlds. He resolves to search for relationships between "different modes of being," for what exists in common between life and chemistry, a collection of cells and the consciousness
of a caress. Like many Huxley heroes, Calamy is after a vision part
Keatsian, part Blakean, in which staring at one object in all its aspects with sufficient intensity can lead to an explanation of all
things. Quarles' notebook in *Point Counter Point* insists "the medi-
tative eye can look through any single object and see, as through a
window, the entire cosmos" (XIX). Even something insignificant, such
as "the smell of roast duck" can furnish "a glimpse of everything,
from the spiral nebulae to Mozart's music and the stigmata of St.

Francis of Assisi," Quarles writes, purposely exaggerating his point. Like the author of *Point Counter Point,* and unlike the parallel-line-characters in that novel, Calamy desires to see a dozen worlds simultaneously and to discover the relationships between them. Both elements in Huxley—that which inclines towards the ideal of completeness and that which prefers mysticism, or, in other words, the extrovert and the introvert—encourage him and Calamy to search for links between different modes of being. But where Denis and Gumbril failed to resuscitate the romantic imagination and its capacity for sympathetic projection, Calamy initiates a new approach to the problem of how to transcend one's personal limitations: he opens gulfs between people and between things. To discover relationships, he dissociates his mind from his body and resolves to rely solely on the former.

In his flight to the mountains and in his hermit's existence there, however, Calamy seems to leave half of himself, the physical half, behind. Huxley is reluctant to sanction such a move and Calamy himself dreams of a "graceful Latin compromise" featuring "cultivation of mind and body" (Part 3, xiii). Then D. H. Lawrence appears (he and Huxley became friends in 1926, a year after *Those Barren Leaves* was published), and possibly seems to be that compromise personified. The shift from Gumbril and Denis' attempts at involvement to Calamy's exaltation of the contemplative life is arrested. The ideal of the whole man, fleetingly personified by Gumbril as Toto, enjoys a triumphant resurgence. But the Huxley novels from the mid-1930s onwards have their origins in the intentionally celibate Calamy. After his Lawrencian interlude, Huxley returns to Calamy's mountain top and the rudimentary outline of the perennial philosophy Calamy has already formulated. Calamy insists the axes "chosen by the best observers have always been startlingly like one another. Gotama, Jesus and Lao-tze, for example; they lived sufficiently far from one another in space, time and social position. But their pictures of reality resemble one another very closely" (Part 5, iv). This is clearly a foreshadowing of the perennial philosophy's contention that "Thou art That" is at the base of all religious experience and that mystics in all eras have enjoyed the same basic vision.

The chapter entitled "Escape" in *Texts and Pretexts,* Huxley's attempts to combine the explication of poetry with the personal essay, seems written from Calamy's point of view: "The world in which our bodies are condemned to live is really too squalid, too vulgar, too malignant to be borne. There is no remedy save in flight. But whither?" [7] Chelifer flees to the world's navel or Gog's Court, Gumbril Jr. departs for France, and Calamy climbs to a mountain top. Denis Stone returns to London and Shearwater pedals his bicycle in a perspiration experiment that is really a futile attempt to escape his desire for Myra Viveash. The novels present three major encounters with the phenomenon of other people, but none of the three main heroes, each patterned on Huxley himself, comes to terms with his world. Each hero seems to start where his predecessor left off: Denis never makes contact; Gumbril has a more than golden opportunity, but fails; Calamy, finding the encounters modern society provides unsatisfactory, tries to make contact with higher things.

Crome Yellow, Antic Hay, and *Those Barren Leaves* thus form a natural trilogy containing Huxley's initial explorations of egotism and alienation within the self. Each of the three main heroes reacts differently to the chasms that separate people. In their different responses and their variant forms of flight, the heroes encourage a reading of Huxley's first three novels as an exercise in counterpoint in which, as Quarles' notebook in *Point Counter Point* was later to prescribe (xxii), similar themes are pushed into different shapes from one novel to the next. In 1928, these three novels might have been written as one.

IV

Huxley's first three novels thus show him becoming increasingly ambitious in his use of counterpoint. He begins to exploit his themes in terms of a multiplicity of similar situations and to view these situations as simultaneously as possible. In *Crome Yellow,* Mary Bracegirdle's often disastrous search for a meaningful relationship is a simple variation on Denis' attempts to make contact with Anne and Jenny. The novel, with its many caricatures and exuberant inset tales from the history of Crome that Henry Wimbush is writing, stands as Huxley's freshest and possibly most amusing work. *Antic Hay,* a more serious comic novel than many critics suppose, is more complex in its use of variation. As Rosie proceeds from her self-absorbed husband to Gumbril, Mercaptan, and Coleman, she brings out their variant forms of egotism and one-sidedness. Like

[7] *Texts and Pretexts,* p. 296.

Grace Peddley of "Two or Three Graces," [8] Rosie has no substantial character of her own and is transformed into the ideas of each successive male she sleeps with. The collapse of traditional values is made apparent by the various roles the characters assume but cannot fill. The unreal happiness Gumbril continually desires is what Shearwater, at the start of the novel, is never aware of and what every act of Coleman, the inverted idealist, tries to violate and refute.

Though still technically distant from *Point Counter Point, Those Barren Leaves* constitutes a decisive move in the direction of that novel. Calamy and the intentionally non-sapient Chelifer are obvious counterparts, while Irene's indecision over whether to make her own underclothing ("illicit love and rebellious reason") or write poetry ("spirit, duty, and religion") (Part 1, VI) parodies Calamy's dilemma when he must choose between Mary Thriplow and spiritual progress. Part 3 of the novel, entitled "The Loves of the Parallels," tries for similarity in situation and simultaneity in action (Part 3, II). The use of what Quarles later calls "parallel, contrapuntal plots" or situations (XXII) re-enforces Huxley's opinion that the characters themselves are parallel lines. On different terraces, one above the other, Huxley presents Calamy and Mary Thriplow, Mrs. Aldwinkle and Chelifer, Mr. Cardan and Mr. Falx. The chiefly physical love of the first pair is compared with Mrs. Aldwinkle's possessiveness. Cardan and Falx are in love with ideas and learned discussions, but their inability to converse without arguing reveals them both as parallel lines. The terrace effect is meant as a rather rudimentary schematic statement of theme. The final variation is provided by Irene and Lord Hovenden who are in the country, but seated "at the edge of a little terrace" (Part 3, IV) scooped out of the slope. Their love affair, a mixture of the comic and the idyllic, is handled with sympathy as a positive though only faintly reassuring counterpoint to the loves already mentioned. If one imagines all these events occurring at once, something resembling the effect produced by related but different melodies in a musical composition begins to emerge.

All three novels move towards or stem from moments of insight. The themes of missed opportunity and bungled epiphany seem closely related. Denis has his experience with Jenny's notebook,

---

[8] "Two or Three Graces" is really a long short story or a novella. It was published along with three other stories in New York and London as *Two or Three Graces* in 1926.

while Chelifer sees his whole life as a series of negative epiphanies in which he discovers the banal nature of reality. His recognition of Barbara's true character, of the extent to which, despite her physical allurements, she personifies the stupidity of modern life (Part 2, v), is a prime example. Gumbril Jr. never has sufficient courage to wait for the mysterious presence whose coming he often senses. He and Denis never take the chances they are offered, whereas Shearwater unearths the value of proportion but applies what he has learned about the need for physical and emotional contacts to a fruitless pursuit of Mrs. Viveash. When he finally realizes the epiphany may have relevance for himself and his wife, Rosie has too many liaisons on hand to notice him. By pedalling his stationary bicycle as part of a perspiration experiment, he tries to reduce himself to sheer water, to his former unknowing one-sidedness.

Crome Yellow is largely a high-spirited Peacockian novel, whereas the waste land atmosphere of futility and ennui in *Antic Hay* makes it a less exuberant work. *Those Barren Leaves,* in the barrenness of its characters and in Calamy's renunciation of them, seems darker yet. It remains a comic novel, but much of its comedy comes from parodies of Dickensian situations, parodies as effective as Evelyn Waugh's in *A Handful of Dust* (vi).[9]

In a lengthy critique of Dickens, Chelifer accuses him of being one of "the jolly optimistic fellows" (Part 2, 1) who become "chronically tearful" when they find virtue in the midst of squalor. But these virtues, Chelifer argues, are only of the animal variety and men inherit them from their animal forefathers. They are not the "peculiarly human virtues," such as open-mindedness, complete tolerance, reasonable pursuit of social goods, and they are therefore not worth celebrating, according to Chelifer. The animal virtues Dickens lavishly praises reveal not merely his vulgar sentimentalism, Chelifer implies, but, more important, his basic escapism. The squalor, Chelifer argues, is the result of a lack of *human* virtues. Thus when Dickens condescends to look at reality, Chelifer says, he seizes on the purely animal virtues in order to avoid the real picture. The antiescapist Chelifer must discredit Dickens lest it appear he himself has chosen to live in Gog's Court for sentimental reasons. In *Those Barren Leaves,* Dickensian scenes are re-done in an anti-sentimental manner, the way Chelifer would agree they ought to have been written. Barbara, for example, whom he pursues but never permanently

9 This entire chapter, "Du Côté de Chez Todd," suggests Dickens has a purely emotional effect on his readers, never a practical or permanent one.

attains, is Chelifer's Estelle, but for him there is no revised ending (Part 2, v).

The scenes at Miss Carruthers's boarding house are patterned after those at Mrs. Todgers's in *Martin Chuzzlewit.* Dickens' novels often present, within the larger world of the novel itself, a little world in which a ludicrous figure struts as cock of the walk. Mr. Lillyvick, the collector of water-rates in *Nicholas Nickleby,* is one such figure, as is Mr. Jinkins, that "man of superior talents," at Mrs. Todgers's in *Martin Chuzzlewit.* Similarly, the witty sallies of the "Inimitable Brimstone" make him the oracle of Miss Carruthers's table. The pretentiousness and egotism of a little world such as this is immediately apparent in both Dickens and Huxley, good-humouredly in the first and more satirically in the second. Huxley takes Brimstone and his domain as a microcosm for society's breakup into countless private worlds. In addition, the squalor in Gog's Court produces vulgarity, not virtue. Mrs. Cloudsley Shove is permitted to darken the doorway with her widowhood, but Mr. Dutt's black skin deprives him of the right to an opinion.

Miss Elver, a comic blend of Oliver Twist, Smike, and Little Nell, is not the waif who merits a fortune; in fact, she already has one. Instead of Mr. Brownlow, Cardan turns up to rescue her from her brother's plots. Miss Elver, despite her clumsiness, is named "Grace," and to Cardan, she and her £25,000 seem sent from heaven to stave off his poverty. The wooing of this unattractive idiot child, who is actually thirty years old, by the cynical realist Cardan becomes the most memorable episode in the book. Their courtship is appropriately included as another variation in the section entitled "The Loves of the Parallels." Grace's death from food poisoning is intentionally "disgusting," though no less amusing than some of the grotesque deaths in Waugh. In killing Grace off, Huxley makes a premeditated attack on the "consoling serenities" (Part 4, IX) that palliate the deaths of Paul Dombey and Little Nell.[10] Though disgusting, Grace's death is not without pathos, and Cardan seems, at one point, genuinely moved. "Blessed are the fools . . . for they shall see nothing," he reflects, possibly having two sets of fools in mind: those whose concern with consoling serenities blinds them to the real nature of an event, and those who see the real nature (disgust plus pathos) but miss the irony. Miss Elver's brother wished to kill

---

10 As frequently happens in Huxley, a subject treated in the novels also appears in the essays, or *vice versa.* For more on Huxley's criticism of Dickens, see "Vulgarity in Literature" in *Music at Night and Other Essays* (London, 1931).

her for her money. After rescuing her, Cardan unwittingly accomplishes her brother's design and Philip Elver becomes Grace's heir.

Huxley may share Chelifer's unfair views of Dickens, but not Chelifer's view of himself. As Calamy perceives, Chelifer is also a fool who sees nothing, the type who vanishes into the mess rather than have to cope with it. Ultimately, though he does not escape from reality, Chelifer flees from responsibility. He becomes, as Calamy charges, Dickens inside out and that is his form of escapism. Calamy's withdrawal, unlike the other retreats, is not a renunciation of responsibility. One can neither put a jolly face on reality nor merge into it, Huxley decides. In Denis, Gumbril Jr., Chelifer, and Dickens, Huxley considers alternative responses to reality and different escapes from it. Although at the end of *Those Barren Leaves* it seems by no means certain that Calamy will remain an isolated hermit until and beyond Cardan's next visit some six months hence, Huxley finds Calamy's act the only justifiable one. Huxley's development towards mysticism follows *Eyeless in Gaza*. Yet Anthony Beavis, the hero of that novel, is clearly a modified version of Calamy and Huxley's development from 1936 on is partially a return to elements already present in his novels of the 1920s. In between, there is Huxley's Lawrencian interlude, in which the theme of completeness has its apotheosis.

The Music of Humanity:

Point Counter Point

by Peter Firchow

Point Counter Point is probably Huxley's most imporant and most controversial novel.* It has been variously and savagely denounced as inept, puerile, misanthropic, mechanical, raw, unreadable, false, purposeless, inorganic, unorginal, journalistic, and inartistic.[1] It has also, but far less frequently and much less impassionedly, been defended as a successful work of art. At the same time it has continued to be widely and generally read, and is even taught in some universities. In the collected works edition alone, *Point Counter Point* has been reprinted at least four times since 1947, and a number of other editions (both hard-cover and paperback) have appeared. Its importance remains undeniable, despite the regrets of the majority of the critics.

Of course, popular and artistic success are not necessarily synonymous. The mass of Huxley's readers may, it is possible, simply be

"The Music of Humanity: *Point Counter Point*" by Peter Firchow. From *Aldous Huxley Satirist and Novelist* (Minneapolis: University of Minnesota Press, 1972), chapter 4. Copyright © 1972 by Peter Firchow. Reprinted by permission of the author and publisher.

* Huxley had thought of changing the title to *Diverse Laws,* a phrase from the Fulke Greville epigraph to the novel *Letters,* 296). However, as a letter dated June 19, 1928 (in the Stanford Manuscript Collection), from C. H. C. Prentice of Chatto and Windus to Huxley's agent, Ralph Pinker, indicates, the change, already made in the English proofs was finally decided against because of objections from G. H. Doran, Huxley's American publisher. Earlier, because Doran had felt nothing with Mexico in the title would sell in America, Huxley's collection of short stories *Little Mexican* (1924) was called *Young Archimedes* in the American edition.

1 See John Atkins, *Aldous Huxley: A Literary Study* (London, 1956), p. 103; Ludwig Borniski, *Meister des modernen englischen Romans* (Heidelberg, 1963), pp. 236–237; David Daiches, *The Novel and the Modern World* (Chicago, 1939), p. 209; André Gide, *Journal 1889–1939* (Paris, 1948), p. 1037; Wyndham Lewis, *Men without Art* (London, 1934), p. 302; D. S. Savage, *The Withered Branch: Six Studies in the Modern Novel* (London, 1950), p. 141; and Virginia Woolf, *A Writer's Diary,* ed. Leonard Woolf (London, 1954), p. 238.

a vulgar, tasteless lot. Huxley himself once implied as much in one
of his more autobiographical short stories, "After the Fireworks,"
(*Brief Candles,* pages 170–172). Still, if a considerable number of
readers did not turn to him primarily for aesthetic reasons, one can
certainly infer from the well-publicized subject matter of *The Sun
Also Rises* and from the equally well-publicized *Ulysses* obscenity
trial that the same could be said of many readers of Hemingway and
Joyce. To be sure, Hemingway and Joyce have received a favorable
critical and academic press. They are officially recognized "classics,"
though perhaps not yet, in Huxley's phrase, "fossilized classics."
Point Counter Point on the other hand, has not received any such
official stamp of approval—fortunately, perhaps, or so Huxley would
think, declaiming any desire to be fossilized. But decidedly unfortunate in that this has prevented a truly open-minded reading of the
work, thereby perpetuating its misinterpretation.*

Much has been written about the narrative method of this novel,
a method to which its title explicitly calls attention, and which is
in part outlined by the novelist within the novel, Philip Quarles.
Quarles calls this method the "musicalization of fiction," and a
number of critics have gone to the trouble of attempting to read
the score with varying degrees of success. The substance of most of
their criticisms, with some important exceptions, is that the complex structure and the musical analogy of this novel serve no dis-
cernible purpose, and are therefore gratuitous and pretentious. David Daiches, for example writes: "The musical analogy in *Point
Counter Point* is quite false and the tampering with chronology
there is quite purposeless." [2] Moreover, even sympathetic critics
rarely do more than take the book through its paces and show more
or less how Quarles's literary theory matches Huxley's literary practice; what they do not seem to be able to explain convincingly is
why Huxley used the method in the first place (except as a demonstration of technical virtuosity) and *how* that method is related to
the thematic content of the book.[3] But it is clear that no matter how

---

* Since this was written, a number of good analyses of the novel have appeared,
notably that of Peter Bowering's *Aldous Huxley* (New York, 1969), pp. 77–97.

2 Daiches, *The Novel,* p. 209.

3 For example, Frank Baldanza, "*Point Counter Point*: Aldous Huxley on 'The
Human Fugue,'" *South Atlantic Quarterly,* 58 (Spring 1959), pp. 248–257. To date
the most complete analyses of the musical structure of *Point Counter Point* are
Maren Selck, "Der Kontrapunkt als Strukturprinzip bei Aldous Huxley," Ph.D.
dissertation (University of Cologne, 1954); and chap. 3 of Alden Dale Kumler's
"Aldous Huxley's Novel of Ideas," Ph.D. dissertation (University of Michigan,
1957).

virtuosic, no work of fiction whose form and content are not directly and organically related can be considered a major work of art, which one instinctively feels this novel is.

Point Counter Point is not the first novel in which Huxley makes use of a contrapuntal technique. He had used it in the three preceding novels, primarily in order to expose the isolation of the characters, to indicate, in other words, the lack of any kind of communication among them. One recalls in this connection Denis Stone's conversation with deaf Jenny Mullion in *Crome Yellow.* In that conversation, as Denis himself remarks, their thoughts run along parallel lines with no possibility of ever meeting (except perhaps in infinity)—and the same thought in similar circumstances and identical phraseology occurs to Elinor in *Point Counter Point.* For all it matters, they might as well be talking to themselves. Or, in terms of the musical analogy, their conversation is counterpointed, with Denis's point of view in one register and Jenny's in another. Like the parallel lines, the two registers never meet; they are scored simultaneously, but the parts remain separate. The essential characteristic, consequently, of this type of counterpoint is that it is disharmonious. However, because the purpose of musical counterpoint is obviously to achieve harmony, Huxley's literary counterpoint is therefore a misnomer, though from the point of view of satire the name is most appropriate, since it is precisely out of the dissonance that the satire arises: where there ought to be harmony and significant contact, there is only discord and meaningless noise. To reveal this discord and noise is one of the basic functions of this technique in the early novels.*

Another, and closely related, purpose is to achieve an accurate portrayal of reality and of various conceptions of reality. Evidently, if one could counterpoint the homemade universes of a sufficiently large number of characters, one could thereby attain a kind of *Gesamtbild* of reality itself, with each character contributing his fragmentary vision to form a complete picture of the human condition. In the conversation between Denis and Jenny this was possible only to a very limited extent, since only two characters and two points of view were counterpointed. It was a very simple form of

* It is this satirical, disharmonious dimension of Huxley's use of literary counterpoint that is usually overlooked. So, for example, Theodore Ziolkowski in *The Novels of Hermann Hesse* (Princeton, 1965), p. 198, can praise Hesse's contrapuntal technique at the expense of Huxley and Gide. But is the revelation of nearly universal dissonance to be equated with the revelation of universal harmony?

counterpoint, with only two instruments making the "music." Even in *Antic Hay* only a few more instruments were added, as, for example, in the counterpointing of the conversations of Gumbril's friends with the account of the "black bundle's" and her husband's wretched existence. The same essentially holds true for *Those Barren Leaves,* though here there is already one section of the book which is structured according to this method (namely part III, "The Loves of the Parallels"). *Point Counter Point,* however, is a full orchestration, with an entire complement of instruments, which enables Huxley to present a more accurate and thorough transcription of his understanding of the human condition than was hitherto possible.

To arrive at an accurate portrayal of a manifold reality is also one of the fundamental reasons why Quarles wants to "musicalize" fiction. It is for this reason, certainly, that he plans to meditate on the example of Beethoven, who in his symphonies is able to alternate "majesty" and "joke," or, in other words, is able to present a complete picture of human existence and not merely a fragmentary one. Huxley explicitly raises the same problem—that of an artistic portrayal of the "whole truth"—in an essay published three years after *Point Counter Point* entitled "Tragedy and the Whole Truth" (1931). There he praises Homer and Fielding precisely because they were able to alternate majesty and joke, because they were willing to sacrifice what he calls "chemically pure art" for the (to him more worthwhile) purpose of achieving a total vision of reality. In an even earlier essay, originally an introduction to the younger Crébillon's *The Opportunities of a Night,* Huxley indicates that he may have held this preference for *Wahrheit* to *Dichtung* as early as 1925. In this essay, while speaking of the tragedies of Crébillon père, Huxley comments in passing that Racine and Corneille—"chemically pure" artists if ever there were such—are of rather doubtful artistic interest. At the same time he quotes with evident relish Crébillon fils' confession "qu'il n'avait encore achevé la lecture des tragédies de son père, mais que cela viendrait. Il regardait la tragédie française comme la farce la plus complete qu'ait pu inventer l'esprit humain." [4] From these comments it may be inferred with considerable certainty that Huxley viewed with approval Philip Quarles's attempts to put the "whole truth" into a novel.*

---

[4] Reprinted as "Crébillon the Younger," in *The Olive Tree* (1936).

* In a letter to Robert Nichols dated November 14, 1926, Huxley admits as much: "I work away on a long and complicated novel, which I want to make a

It is an inference all the easier to make because this is in fact what Huxley does in *Point Counter Point.* Quarles's simultaneous hypothetical juxtaposition of Jones murdering his wife with Smith wheeling his perambulator in the park is, for example, matched by Huxley's simultaneous juxtaposition of Spandrell's suicide with Burlap and Beatrice Gilray's frolicking in the bathtub, or by Lord Edward Tantamount's* grafting tails on asymmetrical tadpoles with Lady Edward's and John Bidlake's remarks on "asymmetrical" human beings.

This simultaneous juxtaposition is, of course, not restricted merely to the alternatives of majesty and joke, for instance, to Spandrell's perverse nobility and Burlap's ludicrous asininity. Rather, it embraces a large number of variations between these two poles; it modulates, as Quarles observes, "not merely from one key to another, but from mood to mood" (page 408). To be sure, the number of themes that are (and can be) modulated in this way is limited; it would be clearly impossible to handle all the possible human themes in a novel even of the length of *Point Counter Point.* For this reason Quarles and Huxley limit their themes to the most basic ones, to "love, or dying, or praying in different ways" (page 408). The controlling themes of *Point Counter Point* are precisely these three, and every individual in the novel experiences them in one way or another, though never in the same way. Each character is like an instrument in an orchestra—an equation Huxley specifically makes —which takes up at various points one or another of these themes and "plays" it according to the properties peculiar to its construction, or, in different terms, according to the limitations of the character's own individual conception of reality.

There is no need to show in any great detail how these three main themes run through the novel—it should be obvious enough that all of the major and most of the minor characters represent variations on them. For example, the theme of death is stated and varied and modulated in the horrible and seemingly senseless death of little Philip Quarles, the murder of Everard Webley, the farcical pseudo death of the elder Quarles, Spandrell's climactic suicide, and John Bidlake's cancer. And, naturally, the deaths or dyings of these characters affect almost all the other people in the novel. The same

picture of life in its different aspects, the synchronous portrait of the different things an individual simultaneously is—atoms, physiology, mystic, cog in the economic machine, lover, etc" (*Letters*, 276).

* Based, according to Ronald Clark, on John Scott Haldane. See his *JBS*, p. 57.

holds true for the theme of religion: one need only think of Marjorie's vapid mysticism, Burlap's Jesus perversion, Rampion's Hellenism, Quarles's skepticism, Spandrell's diabolism; and the theme of love: Lucy and Walter, Walter and Marjorie, John Bidlake and virtually everybody, Spandrell and his mother, Philip and Elinor, Elinor and Webley, Rampion and Mary, Burlap and Beatrice. There is no need to continue the list; it should be sufficiently apparent already that Huxley has practically infinite possibilities for the statement and repetition of themes, for their variation in tragic and comic and tragicomic modes.

By means of the technique of counterpoint Huxley skillfully manages to weave all these themes together, thereby developing a variety of characters and giving the novel a solid structural and thematic unity. He uses the technique, however, for another purpose as well: to satirize the narrow conceptions of reality which isolate most of the characters in the novel. Huxley almost directly admits as much in at least two passages usually neglected by the critics. The first incident occurs during the party at Tantamount House. Huxley describes Pongileoni's playing of the flute part in Bach B-minor suite, which is then repeated with variations by other instruments in the orchestra: "The parts live their separate lives; they touch, their paths cross, they combine for a moment to create a seemingly final and perfected harmony, only to break apart again. *Each is always alone and separate and individual.* 'I am I,' asserts the violin; 'the world revolves about me.' 'Round me,' calls the cello. 'Round me,' the flute insists. *And all are equally right and equally wrong; and none of them will listen to the others"* (page 32, my italics). In the next paragraph Huxley completes the identification. The individual is an instrument, humanity an orchestra: "In the human fugue there are eighteen hundred million parts" (page 32). Each character of the novel, consequently, like each instrument of the orchestra, has a different mode of seeing things, produces a different noise, and plays a different variation. Each character, like each instrument, is insulated in his own conception of reality, in his own kind of music. To be sure, as Huxley admits, it would be impossible to transcribe the score of the entire "human fugue." Eighteen hundred million parts are simply too many, and the artist must therefore necessarily select: "The resultant noise means something perhaps to the statistician, nothing to the artist. It is only by considering one or two parts at a time that the artist can understand anything" (page 32). This is precisely what Huxley does in the novel;

he considers one or two parts at a time, has one or two characters (sometimes a few more) embody and vary one of the principal themes. It is for this reason—and not by analogy to cinematic technique as is sometimes thought—that *Point Counter Point* is broken up into what Frank Baldanza calls relatively short "scenes." [5] In this way, and perhaps in this way only, Huxley can impose an artistic order upon the great many characters and events in this work.

Somewhat later in the book, Huxley offers another important statement on the isolation of his characters and its relation to the technique of counterpoint. This comment is made, unlike the previous one, through Philip Quarles. Quarles and his wife are on board ship returning from India to England, and he is telling her that he might like to use the situation of Walter Bidlake's amatory entanglements with Marjorie Carling and Lucy Tantamount as the basis for a new novel. It would serve, he thinks, as "a kind of excuse . . . for a new way of looking at things" (page 265). While they are speaking, their conversation is counterpointed with the conversations of several other passengers on the ship. In one of them a Frenchwoman is talking of the price of *camisoles en flanelle* at the Galeries Lafayette; in another an English girl is telling her admirers of the "wonderful time" she had at Gulmerg the previous summer; in still another two women missionaries are discussing the number of Chinese and Malays the bishop of Kuala Lumpur made deacons during the year. Quarles seizes on the example of these conversations to illustrate his new method of seeing reality in fiction: " 'All these *camisoles en flanelle* and pickled onions and bishops of cannibal islands are really quite to the point. Because the essence of the new way of looking is multiplicity. Multiplicity of eyes and multiplicity of aspects seen. For instance, one person interprets events in terms of bishops; another in terms of the price of flannel camisoles; another, like that young lady from Gulmerg . . . thinks of it in terms of good times. And then there's the biologist, the chemist, the physicist, the historian. Each sees, professionally, a different aspect of the event, a different lay of reality. What I want to do is to look with all those eyes at one. With religious eyes, scientific eyes, *homme moyen sensuel* eyes . . .' " (page 266). The result of such a new mode of novelistic point of view, Philip concludes, would be "a very queer picture indeed." Throughout the novel, Philip is preoccupied with trying to get at this "queer picture": he reads Burtt's

[5] Baldanza, "Point Counter Point," p. 254.

Metaphysical Foundations of Modern Science during the sea voyage and, much later, Bastian's *On the Brain,* while on the way to
London. His purpose is to gather material to document one of the
multiple modes of seeing things; in this case the scientific mode. It
is the same desire to see things from a multiplicity of viewpoints
that motivates him later to take an interest in the kitchen and cook
of the Bidlake country estate, or in the different ways in which
Everard Webley's political demonstration might be perceived. Even
more important in this respect is the entry in Philip's notebook
which immediately precedes his statement on the "musicalization"
of fiction. There Philip explicitly returns once again to the plan
to use the Walter Bidlake–Marjorie Carling–Lucy Tantamount situation as the basis for a novel. He plans to begin his story with Walter suddenly seeing Lucy's laughing mouth transformed into a gap-
ing maw of a crocodile, thereby "striking the note of strangeness
and fantasticality at once" (page 407); or, in other words, getting at
the queer picture of reality through yet another point of view (in
this sense, the title of the novel refers not only to the musical
method, but also to the countering of one *point* of view against
another). Somewhat later in this passage Quarles touches on the
same idea again, and this time states it directly: "The novelist can
assume the god-like creative privilege and simply elect to consider
the events of the story in their various aspects—emotional, scientific,
economic, religious, metaphysical, etc." Such a multiplicity of points
of view, either on the part of the isolated characters of the novel, or
on the part of the novelist within the novel, or on the part of the
novelist himself—*or all three*—would, Philip realizes, necessarily
involve the introduction of ideas. For, if the characters are to be
isolated within their private conceptions of reality, they must, as a
minimum, have the intelligence to formulate such conceptions,
must, in short, have ideas. But this requirement, as Philip is perfectly aware, would exclude all but one tenth of one percent of
humanity.*

---

* This exclusivity has always been considered one of the weak points of Huxley's fiction. In a different novel, and a different context, and wearing a different
mask (that of Anthony Beavis), Huxley retorts that all fiction is necessarily exclusive. "Life's so ordinary that literature has to deal with the exceptional. Exceptional talent, power, social position, wealth. Hence those geniuses of fiction, those
leaders and dukes and millionaires. People who are completely conditioned by
circumstances—one can be desperately sorry for them; but one can't find their
lives very dramatic. Drama begins where there's freedom of choice. And freedom

Of course, all the characters in *Point Counter Point* have "ideas" or—like Quarles senior and Marjorie Carling—at least think they do. These ideas are not, however, presented primarily for their own sake, but, rather, to enable Huxley to portray a large spectrum of as many points of view as possible, and to enable him artistically to represent by means of the technique of counterpoint the isolation of his characters within their closed systems of thought.

These ideas also are included to enable him to represent that isolation satirically. This is clear from an essay in *Music at Night,* "And Wanton Optics Roll the Melting Eye," written three years after *Point Counter Point.* In this piece Huxley specifically comments on the method employed in this novel: "The facts and even the peculiar jargon of science can be of great service to the writer whose intention is mainly ironical. Juxtapose two accounts of the same human event, one in terms of pure science, the other in terms of religion, aesthetics, passion, even common sense; their discord will set up the most disquieting reverberations in the mind. Juxtapose, for example, physiology and mysticism (Mme. Guyon's ecstasies were most frequent and most spiritually significant in the fourth month of her pregnancies); juxtapose acoustics and the music of Bach (perhaps I may be permitted to refer to the simultaneously scientific and aesthetic account of a concert in my novel, *Point Counter Point*) . . ." (*Music at Night,* page 40). What Huxley is analyzing here is essentially the same technique which Philip Quarles discusses under the heading of the "musicalization of fiction," namely the alternation of majesty and joke, coupled with the technique of multiple points of view. It is the juxtaposition of different points of view that is stressed here, not merely the juxtaposition of scientific imagery with musical or mystical imagery. It is a juxtaposition of the scientific "slice" of reality with the other "slices" that produces the satire, not the imagery itself. That this is Huxley's meaning is plainly apparent from the continuation of his analysis: "This list of prolonged incompatibles might be indefinitely prolonged. We live in a world of *non-sequiturs.* Or rather, we would live in such a world, if we were always conscious of all the aspects under which any event can be considered. But in practice we are almost never aware of more than one aspect at a time. Our life is spent first in one

---

of choice begins when social or psychological conditions are exceptional. That's why the inhabitants of imaginative literature have always been recruited from the pages of *Who's Who*" (*Eyeless in Gaza,* p. 313).

water-tight compartment of experience, then in another. The artist can, if he so desires, break down the bulkheads between the compartments and so give us a simultaneous view of two or more of them at a time. So seen, reality looks exceedingly queer. Which is how the ironist and the perplexed questioner desire it to look" (*Music at Night*, pages 40–41). What this analysis means is that the fragmentary conceptions or points of view of the individual characters add up to something approaching a total vision of reality, but that each fragmentary vision *is* fragmentary and must remain so, just as each instrument of the orchestra plays only a fragmentary portion of the total piece of music. The irony (and, to generalize, the satire) of this is, as Huxley here implies and as he directly states in *Point Counter Point,* that each instrument and each character thinks he is the total music and the total reality. The point of the satire is that each character is in fact isolated.*

In another essay, "Sermons in Cats," Huxley makes an even more direct and general statement on the isolation of man: "In spite of language, in spite of intelligence and intuition and sympathy, one can never really communicate anything to anybody. The essential substance of every thought and feeling remains incommunicable, locked up in the impenetrable strong-room of the individual soul and body. Our life is a sentence of perpetual solitary confinement" (*Music at Night*, pages 267–268). It is this isolation which *Point Counter Point* attempts to represent. Each character is confined to his solitary cell and has only one window through which he may look out upon the outside world. What he sees from his limited vantage point he generalizes into a picture of the whole of the external world, a picture which is almost always bound to be distorted and false.† It is a portrayal of the human condition similar to that

---

* In his preface to *Art and Artists,* ed. Morris Philipson (New York, 1960), pp. 7–8, Huxley returns again to the question of literary counterpoint. Though he clearly admits that "there is no equivalent in literature of sustained counterpoint or the spatial unity of diverse elements brought together so that they can be perceived at one glance as a significant whole," he still sees the need for some way of rendering the experience of "falling perpetually between half a dozen stools." Since the writer cannot say "several different things at once, he must, willy-nilly, say them successively." This means that he must choose between a more or less straightforward mathematically progressive method, or a "kind of directional free association" which is more realistic but less well ordered. This latter type of "melodic modulation" is the one Huxley prefers, even though it is much more difficult. "Hence," he concludes, "the essentially unsystematic nature of most of what I've written."

† The essay on El Greco in *Music at Night* is a detailed exposition of this insight.

described by Ortega y Gasset in *El tema de nuestro tiempo,* in which everything is relative and each man sees only a small slice of the totality of existence. Or, in Huxley's own words, everyone sees only the reality he likes best and passes over all the rest.

There are, however, in this novel at least two characters who do not pass over all the rest: Philip Quarles and Mark Rampion. Both of them realize that they are only individual instruments in the vast human fugue and that man's understanding of reality is usually limited and therefore untrue. Philip Quarles is aware that his window looks out on a reality that is too exclusively intellectual and that he in consequence neglects the emotional and sensual aspects of life.* Rampion, on the other hand, has consciously attempted to avoid seeing reality with only a part of his being. He wants to perceive as much of the totality of life as possible; he wants to become himself an instrument which would be a substitute for the whole orchestra, which could play the whole human fugue and not simply an isolated part. It is precisely for this reason that Philip Quarles admires him: "He lives more satisfactorily, because he lives more realistically than other people. Rampion, it seems to me, takes into account all the facts (whereas other people hide from them or try to pretend that the ones they find unpleasant don't or shouldn't exist), and then proceeds to make his way of living fit the facts, and doesn't try to compel the facts to fit in with a preconceived idea of the right way of living (like these imbecile Christians and intellectuals and moralists and efficient business men)" (page 440).

Rampion does not commit the fatal error which Denis in *Crome Yellow* had complained of in almost the same terms as Philip Quarles's; Rampion suits his way of living to reality, not to a preconceived notion of reality. In short, he tries to achieve what Huxley in "The Reef" had called the "triune peace," the perfect harmony of "soul, will and body." Like Gumbril senior in *Antic Hay* and Calamy in *Those Barren Leaves,* he is the positive point set counter against a great many negative points. He wishes to transform the noisy discord which is the common music of humanity into an ideal harmony.

Rampion's ideal of "intergral living," however, differs in at least one important respect from the ideals of the old Gumbril and Cal-

---

* Quarles's name is apparently an esoteric and ironic allusion to a work attributed to Peter Longueville, *The English Hermit; or, Unparalleled sufferings, and surprising adventures, of Mr. Philip Quarll. Who was lately discovered on an uninhabited island in the South-sea; where he had lived above fifty years, without any human assistance* (London, 1786).

amy. Both Gumbril's "crystal world" and Calamy's mysticism take only minimal cognizance of the importance of the life of the senses. Both, in fact, would seem to be proposed primarily as solutions to the dreariness and sterility of that life; and Calamy actually at one point in the novel states explicitly that sexual activity is not compatible with an attempt to see reality in all its facets. Rampion's solution, however, is solidly based on the inclusion of the life of the senses. To be sure, it is at the same time opposed to a life exclusively sensual, such as the sterile hedonism of Lucy Tantamount. It calls, rather, for a complete bodily harmony and postulates that only through such balance can a consequent spiritual harmony be achieved. Like Gumbril, Rampion demands proportion and balance, but unlike him, he does not demand a proportion and balance of the spirit alone. What Rampion strives for is, to use a phrase Huxley employed later in a direct exposition of this same philosophy, "a balance of excesses" (*Do What You Will*, page 279), a balance including both body and spirit. Only through this kind of harmony and balance, Rampion asserts, can one escape the "wearisome condition of humanity" of which the epigraph to the novel speaks. Man must no longer be self-divided between passion and reason but combine both into a harmonious unit. Only if he succeeds in this can he escape the isolation which is otherwise the wretched lot of humanity.

Rampion's criticism of the other characters in the novel is based on this perception. His pictures portray monsters with heads of men, or bodies of men with monstrous heads; he focuses his entire attack on what he sees as the perversion (only incidentally sexual) of the wholeness of man: hence he assails Burlap for being a "Jesus pervert," Spandrell for being a "morality-philosophy pervert," and Quarles for being an "intellectual-aesthetic pervert" (page 564). Still, though his criticism is—and is meant to be—brutally and personally frank, it is directed not so much at particular individuals as it is at the society which nurtured and shaped them. Rampion's diagnosis of the disease of imbalance or perversion is that it is universal, an epidemic which threatens to destroy all mankind.

But it is curable—or so Rampion thinks. Otherwise, why his constant condemnation, why his own "pedagogue perversion"? If Rampion did not believe that individuals and society could change or be made to change, there would surely be no point in criticizing them so heatedly. And indeed his continual harking back to Greece as an ideal society indicates that in Greece his concept of balance demonstrably took on a real and historical form. So that which was, may be again.

Rampion believes that man is master of his fate, believes it implicitly, unquestioningly—so much so in fact that he never bothers to defend or even articulate this position. His first line of defense is several logical miles further on: at when and how, not if. His success in argument, however, is—perhaps significantly—minimal, at least in this novel (that is, to the extent that he is the fictional character Rampion and not merely a mask for D. H. Lawrence). Though he speaks persuasively and "wins" most of the arguments he takes part in, he and his wife, and to some degree Quarles, are the only real believers. Rampion's optimism about amelioration and his struggle to effect it may be admirable, but the evidence of the novel does not suggest that he will be practically successful.

The negative, pessimistic point set counter to Rampion's positive, optimistic one is most clearly propounded by Spandrell, a character who seems consciously intended by Huxley to be a kind of foil to Rampion.* The fact that when we first encounter them they are together is perhaps an indication of this; certainly the final scene of the novel, with its confrontation of Spandrell and Rampion, shows that Huxley is consciously working out a contrast, leading up to some final resolution of opposites.

In Rampion's eyes, Spandrell is a "morality-philosophy pervert," though in spite of this he is still a person eminently worth saving. In his own terminology, Spandrell is an Augustinian; and, as every good Augustinian, ergo good determinist, must, he believes in the existence of a first cause, in God. Indeed, like Rampion and Rampion's balance, he is more concerned with proving the existence of God to others than with proving it to himself. More precisely, his primary preoccupation is not so much the fact of God's existence as the meaning of His creation.

The fullest account of Spandrell's philosophy is given at a lunch in Philip's club, where Rampion is pointedly absent. Here Spandrell maintains that "everything that has happened to [him] was somehow engineered in advance" (page 290), a perception that soon leads him to proclaim the correctness of "old Augustine's" understanding

---

* Just as Rampion's name suggests a bridging of the gap between man and man, and man and nature, so Spandrell's evokes the "spandrel," which *Webster's* defines as "the triangular space between the outer curve of an arch and the rectangular figure formed by the mouldings or framework surrounding it." In short, where Rampion supports, Spandrell is useless ornament.

of life. The upshot of this is that Spandrell disclaims ultimate responsibility for what he is and does, and disclaims further any ability to change, to become anything other than what he is. Indeed, all of Spandrell's life—or rather all that portion of it following his mother's marriage to the mustachioed Major Knoyle—consists of a continual attempt (or series of experiments) to find out who God is. Spandrell tries to force God to come out of hiding, and reveal to him the meaning of his life. Hence he turns to the devil as the easiest way of coming into contact with God, for, as he perceives, an absolute quantity at one end of the scale posits another and opposite absolute on the other end; and further, an understanding of the one must eventually confer an understanding of the other.

Seen from this perspective, Rampion and Spandrell are the two poles within which *Point Counter Point* operates: the poles of Hellenic humanism and Christian diabolism. Put somewhat differently, Spandrell stands for the acceptance of the human condition as wearisome, for the inevitable duality or plurality of life and the inexorable separation of man from man, a condition that can only be transcended by death. Rampion, on the other hand, is the champion (Rampion/champion) of life, the bridge or "ramp" to the spiritual and social integration of man.* Rampion, unlike Spandrell, does not see man's nature as inherently double, that is, half body and half spirit, with the body evil and spirit good; he sees man as a continuum of bodily and spiritual elements which, when properly balanced, become a single unit, become that marvelous and rare thing, a human being.

The problem which the novel poses, when understood in this way, is: who is right, Spandrell or Rampion?

There are a good many overt indications in the novel that Rampion is right—or that we are meant to think so. For example, he is the one character (with the possible exception of Webley) who seems fully satisfied with what he has made of life. And Webley's satisfaction, interestingly enough, may be seen to arise from sources broadly similar to Rampion's: Webley, after all, seeks integration, not separation, though he seeks it on a social, not individual level. What Webley wants is the balance of society, the harmony of the social orders. This fact surely serves, at least in part, to account for having Illidge participate in Webley's murder; for Illidge, the Marxist dia-

---

* Specifically, however, a rampion is a European bellflower (*Campanula rapunculus*) whose roots are edible. Another hint that Rampion is rooted deeply to the earth?

lectician, the proponent of class warfare and social imbalance, stands in almost the same relation to Webley that Spandrell does to Rampion.

Furthermore, Rampion is at least respected, if not liked, by almost all the major characters of the novel—an indication surely that we are meant to respect him as well, a suspicion confirmed by Rampion's uniqueness in not being subjected to any sort of obvious satire. The fact that the author likes him seems to suggest that we should too, and that we should accept his philosophical position as the most correct one. Moreover, Rampion has an uncanny gift for perceiving what is wrong with the other characters in the novel— and subsequent events confirm the rightness of his diagnoses. Finally, of course, Huxley was advocating a philosophy remarkably like Rampion's—"the balance of excesses"—in a number of essays published at roughly the same time as *Point Counter Point.*

There are nonetheless signs (largely implicit to be sure) that Rampion/Lawrence's philosophy is not so wholeheartedly accepted in the novel as it is in the essays. The beginning of the novel is concerned with the fetal development of man, the progress of worm to fish to mammal and so on, something Rampion's static Hellenism is incapable of dealing with. Is it possible for an ex-fish to become a "balanced" human being? Such a question does not occur to Rampion, but Huxley, Lawrence or no, must still ask it. Rampion's philosophy cannot explain the curious and ironic twists—not of man—but of fate. Why, for example, should a cart have run over Philip's foot and maimed him—and maimed him not merely physically but emotionally as well? Only the Topiarist God of the early Huxley or the Augustinian determinism of Spandrell can interpret such happenings, certainly not Rampion's idea of a man-made and man-run universe. Neither can Rampion account—and, significantly, is not made to account—for the horrible and unexplained death of little Philip Quarles. Is it possible to achieve balance, or worthwhile to try to achieve it, if nature or God or fate can strike one down, maim or kill one at any moment? Rampion remains curiously silent.

Spandrell's moral-philosophical perversion, it is clear, cannot be dismissed from the novel as easily as it is from Rampion's mind. And it is consequently not at all coincidental that the story concludes with a final confrontation of Spandrell and Rampion: this is the culminating point of the novel. Just as it is no coincidence that the final scene but one opens with a recording of Beethoven's *Heiliger Dankgesang* which is described in the same duality of spiritual and material terms as the playing of the Bach B-minor suite at Tantamount House during the second scene of the novel. The two musical performances provide the frame for the novel, and their description provides also a symbol for the two primary ways of viewing life: Rampion's and Spandrell's. Rampion's: that the music is basically man's, hence fundamentally material and of this world. Spandrell's: that it is essentially spiritual, a revelation of God's existence in man; and that man perceives, not himself, but God in the beauty and harmony of the music, just as he perceives the devil, and not merely himself, in the ugliness and dissonance of life.

The conclusion of *Point Counter Point* seems on the more obvious level to confirm Rampion's position. In the silence following the shots, we no longer hear the music of divinity but only the music of the machine, the pointless scratchings of the needle on the inner grooves of the record. *Deus* has degenerated into *deus ex machina,* as from Rampion's intermediary human position, God inevitably must. Superhumanity and subhumanity are both enemies of humanity. The Spandrell who failed earlier in his attempts to become a devil by seducing virgins and murdering Edward Webley, now seems to have failed again in trying to become an angel by having himself killed—becoming to that high requiem a sod. Rampion is apparently right because he stands in between, because he balances, rather precariously to be sure, between God and devil, because he hears the music of neither divinity nor machine, but only of humanity.

Still, lurking doubts seem to remain in Huxley's mind, if Rampion's humanity is in the final analysis a gift of the gods, or if its continued existence depends too heavily on such fortuitous matters as good health, a good wife, the absence of carts that run over one's feet or cancers that gnaw at one's stomach. Furthermore, the central, controlling image of the novel—that of the orchestra—seems at once to affirm and deny Rampion's position. For if, on the one hand, each individual man contains within himself all the instruments of the orchestra, then it is at least possible for him to achieve a harmony of the separate, individual parts. Therefore Rampion is right. But if, on the other hand—the hand Huxley implicitly shows us at the end of the novel—each man is not a sum of the musical instruments but merely a single, solitary instrument within the vast orchestra of humanity, then he will obviously only be able to play his own part and make his own noise; or rather not his own, but that which fate has noted down for him. And it will only be the conductor—God—who will be able to make sense out of the resulting noise.

If this is the case, then *Point Counter Point* ultimately returns full circle to the position Huxley enunciated in his early poems—despite all the affirmation of Rampion. For, though there may be a final harmony, perhaps like that which Claude Bernard saw as the guiding principle of the universe, or else the concordant interconnection of all aspects of life which Philip Quarles perceives, there still will be no harmony for man, at least for individual man. For the individual can be only a part, a very small part, of this greater harmony. In the final analysis, the achievement of harmony, as Rampion knows, depends on man's being God: only then can he be the whole musical score and not merely a fragment of it. But is man, is Rampion, a god? To himself and to his wife, perhaps; to his readers, whether in the guise of Rampion or of Lawrence, probably not.

This division of the novel—whether conscious or unconscious does not much matter—into one level of obvious affirmation and another of residual skepticism mirrors the other divisions that run, like great chasms, through the novel, beginning with the epigraph from Fulke Greville and its vision of man born to one law and bound to another. It is the "irony of being two" all over again, but this time scored in many registers, with multiple variations, played in many keys, and symphonically orchestrated.

Nearly all the characters are plagued by this divisiveness within their own personalities. All, with the exception of Rampion, are schizophrenic, split between the claims of the body and those of the spirit; or else monomaniacs who have succeeded, for the time being at any rate, in suppressing one half of themselves in order to devote themselves entirely to the other. Only Rampion seems not to be content with a duality or moiety of self; only he demands and achieves unity.

The division, too, runs in a rather different direction through the novel as a separation between the real and the unreal. For this novel, like Huxley's earlier ones, only perhaps more so, is autobiographical. Quarles, even without Huxley's later explicit confession that he was "in part a portrait of me," clearly—to those who knew anything at all about Huxley—is the author himself (with Spandrell possibly making up some of the other parts of the self-portrait).[6] That Huxley does what Quarles in his journal proposes to do should be a sufficient clue that Huxley is here working out fictionally many of the

6 *New York Times,* May 6, 1933, p. 14.

problems, aesthetic, philosophical, personal, that concerned him in actual life. And there is the further and by now notorious circumstance that both Rampion and Burlap are based on real people: the former on the man who in the years immediately preceding this novel had become Huxley's intimate and respected friend, the latter on his old chief editor (and perhaps chief enemy) at the *Athenaeum,* John Middleton Murry.*

Part of the sense of incompletion or division that one feels in reading this novel may arise from Huxley's attempt to transport these (and other) real beings into his fictional world. They—or at least Rampion—do not seem to have traveled well. Rampion does not fit in comfortably with the other inhabitants of Huxley's imagination, people whom we have met before, though bearing different names, in earlier works. Burlap is not nearly so much out of place, perhaps because he reminds us of similar characters like Barbecue-Smith in "The Farcical History of Richard Greenow," but also, I think, because he is somehow more acclimatized to the world of *Point Counter Point.* He is present there to the extent that he can *act* (in a double sense) in it, not merely talk in and about it like Rampion.

This distinction can be appreciated more fully if we compare Rampion with an earlier Huxley portrait of Lawrence, that of Kingham in the title story of *Two or Three Graces* (1926). There Kingham/Lawrence comes alive as Rampion/Lawrence never does in

---

* In *Figures in the Foreground, Literary Reminiscences, 1917–40* (London, 1963), p. 71, Frank Swinnerton feels compelled to "testify to Huxley's laughing, disgusted perception that Murry was auto-intoxicated, and in the habit of mystically identifying himself with whatever saint or genius was his latest enthusiasm." Murry himself comments less enthusiastically on Huxley's "distinctly pointed" portrait of himself in *Between Two Worlds: An Autobiography* (London, 1935), p. 438. According to F. A. Lea, *The Life of John Middleton Murry* (London, 1959), pp. 115–116, the story of Burlap's involvement with his secretary, Ethel Cobbett, is almost literally true, right down to her dismissal. Though Murry later pretended that Huxley's caricature had not wounded him, Lea reports that his first impulse was to challenge him to a duel—"a vision," as Lea says, "to which Max Beerbohm alone could do justice" (p. 159). That Huxley felt some real personal animosity against his former editor at the *Athenaeum* is clear from his reaction to Murry's biography of Lawrence, *Son of Woman*: "Murry's vindictive hagiography was pretty slimy—the slug's-eye view of poor L: and if you knew the intimate history of his relations with L and Mrs. L, you'd really shudder. One day it really ought to be published" (*Letters*, 352). Very likely a good deal of it had already been published in *Point Counter Point*. In a mellower mood, he later observed that "there is something of Murry in several of my characters, but I wouldn't say I'd put Murry in a book," *Writers at Work: The Paris Review Interviews*, 2nd ser. (New York, 1963), p. 210.

Point Counter Point, partly because Huxley is here poking fun at him ("King Ham"), partly because we are made more aware of his faults. The main point of difference, however, is that in Kingham/Lawrence (as in Burlap/Murry) Huxley is intent on transporting a personality from one realm of being to another; and he knows that to reassemble a personality in the realm of fiction one has to present it in action, not merely in contemplation or conversation. Kingham/Lawrence is alive because we see him act to become what he is at the end of the story; Rampion/Lawrence is dead (as a character) because he is fixed and finished when he enters the story. There is no more growth left in him—and the few flashbacks to his youth are not enough to resuscitate him.

What Huxley has done in Rampion, in other words, is to bring Lawrence's ideas across the gulf without bringing along Lawrence's vitality and personality. Out of a man whose life consisted of self-contradiction and growth and change, Huxley has created a man who is incapable of any sort of change. Lawrence, therefore, was certainly justified in criticizing Rampion as a "gas-bag," [7] though perhaps he should have remembered that at least one aspect (and that not a minor one) of his own personality was a profound windiness, as his autobiographical character Birkin in *Women in Love* amply testifies. But even in *Women in Love* we can discern that the difference between Birkin/Lawrence and Rampion/Lawrence is not a difference in gases, either in kind or volume (in both cases much the same and often equally inert) but in the ability, shared by Birkin and Kingham but not by Rampion, to drop the conversational bag and free their hands for physical and emotional action.

To be sure, the gaseousness of Rampion ought not to be exaggerated. Too often critics of *Point Counter Point* harp on him and on his relation to Lawrence to the exclusion of all else. They forget that Rampion actually appears only a few times in the novel, even though his penchant for lecturing tends to make him seem more prominent. Of course, *Point Counter Point* might have been a more amusing and perhaps "better" novel if, as G. U. Ellis suggests, Huxley had focused his satire on Burlap and left Rampion out altogether.[8] By the same token, *David Copperfield* would have been a much "better" book if Dickens had left out the protagonist and focused his attention on Micawber. But it would not have been the

7 *The Collected Letters of D. H. Lawrence,* ed. Harry T. Moore, vol. 2 (New York, 1962), p. 1096.
8 G. U. Ellis, *Twilight on Parnassus,* p. 278.

same book. It is futile to think about what might have been. The point is that Huxley, beginning with this novel, has started to move, openly and consciously, in the direction of constructive satire. He no longer lashes mankind simply for the painful pleasure of lashing it and hence himself; he now hopes to achieve a definite end through his satirical means (though how optimistic that hope is, the ambiguous figure of Spandrell is there to tell us). In practicing this new mode of explicitly constructive satire, Huxley runs certain risks—those, for example, that Fielding encountered in *Tom Jones*. There Allworthy is almost as much of a "gas-bag" as Rampion is here, but Allworthy cannot be removed without distorting the whole moral context of the novel. He must remain to provide at least the overt standard by which all the other characters are to be judged. And so must Rampion—though one might wish for a less obtrusive and more interesting standard.

Point Counter Point is doubtless marred by its "Rampionism," but it still remains the apex of Huxley's satirical achievement. It is his only novel (and one of the few novels *tout court*) which succeeds in portraying relatively succinctly and convincingly the main social and intellectual outlines of an era. In the manner of Stendhal's *The Red and the Black,* it could, without evoking undue surprise, have been subtitled "A Chronicle of 1928." Furthermore *Point Counter Point,* because of the possibilities of unity in diversity offered by its musical technique, focuses its satiric thrust in a way unprecedented by Huxley's earlier novels and perhaps equaled subsequently in the Huxley canon only by *Brave New World.* The whole force of the satire is now directed almost exclusively on an incisive exposition of the preconceptions of characters—to the point even of extending, as we have seen, to the author himself.

This kind of self-satire, to bring up one of the perennial clichés about Huxley, is something he supposedly borrowed from Gide's *Les Faux Monnayeurs.* Perhaps he did, but not very likely. Huxley was well versed in French literature (well enough to translate a novel by Remy de Gourmont and Mallarmé's "L'Après-midi d'un faune"); he knew Gide personally, admired *The Counterfeiters,* but held certain reservations about him as man and artist, as Gide seems to have realized.*

---

* Huxley opens his review of *La Symphonie pastorale* for *The Athenaeum* (September 24, 1920), p. 422, with the observation that "Gide is one of the problems of literature," and then proceeds to give a lengthy and biting answer to the question of how it is that "a man can possess so many of the qualities that go to

Even in the early and mid-twenties, Huxley was by no means unknown in France: T. S. Eliot had written about him in the *Nouvelle Revue Française*; and Proust had mentioned him favorably—the only contemporary English novelist to be so honored—in *Remembrance of Things Past*. Hence, to demonstrate or at least to suggest persuasively that Huxley's novel was a mere pastiche of Gide's would certainly have shed reflected glory on Gide's work in France and elsewhere, though Gide possibly did not intend his accusation to appear either so complete or so malicious. Still, he might have mentioned that Huxley had used the basic device of *The Counterfeiters*, the inclusion of a novelist within a novel, in a short story, "Nuns at Luncheon" (1922) and in *Those Barren Leaves* (1925), both published before Gide's novel. Furthermore, it is clear that Huxley uses this device in *Point Counter Point* primarily for satirical purposes, and in this respect imitates *The Counterfeiters* practically not at all. Ironically, Gide himself provides the best reply to those critics who would reduce literature to a game of who came first, when—appropriately in his *Journal des Faux-Monnayeurs*—he declaims against "cette manie moderne de voir influence (ou 'pastiche') à chaque ressemblance que l'on découvre, manie qui transforme la critique de certains universitaires en police et qui

---

make a great writer and yet be so definitely not an immortal, so certainly not great?" *The Counterfeiters* is the only novel of Gide that he liked. On January 18, 1927, he wrote to Robert Nichols: "Gide, as you say, is disappointing. He has a faculty for always touching on interesting subjects and never really getting hold of them. He attacks great moral problems and then, before the campaign has well started, beats an elegant, literary and genteel retreat. The only good book he has written is the last, *Les Faux Monnayeurs*, which is very interesting and in its way very good. It is good, I think, because it is the first book in which Gide has ventured to talk about the one thing in the world that really interests him —sentimental sodomy" (*Letters*, 281–282).

That Gide was by no means unaware of Huxley's opinion (or disposed to overlook it) emerges clearly from the account of a brief meeting with Gide in Clive Bell's *Old Friends* (London, 1956), p. 148. Sometime in the twenties, Bell was in a Paris restaurant dining alone when Gide came in with a large party, paused at Bell's table, and asked to join him later for coffee. His object was not small talk, but the answer to a very specific question. " 'Why does Aldous Huxley refer to me as a "faux grand ecrivain?" ' he demanded; adding traditionally 'I have never done him any harm.' I could not say; but we passed the five minutes he had to spare well enough, speaking ill of Aldous presumably. Later I asked Aldous whether he had said anything of the sort. Yes, he had—some twenty years earlier in a magazine, possibly an undergraduate magazine. But Gide had the eyes of a lynx and the memory of an elephant."

For an exhaustive (and at times exhausting) discussion of the influence, or lack of it, of *The Counterfeiters* on *Point Counter Point*, see Gerd Rohmann, *Aldous Huxley und die französische Literatur* (Marburg, 1968).

précipite tant d'artistes dans l'absurde par crainte d'être soupçonnés de pouvoir ressembler à quelqu'un." * [9]

Point Counter Point, as far as the development of Huxley's satire is concerned, "points" in a new direction. It closes off the period of predominantly destructive satire, and begins the period of predominantly constructive satire. Huxley has now momentarily found— and not much later will permanently find—ideals which he considers both desirable and practical and which he hereafter expounds not merely novelistically but also essayistically. He begins to abandon that detachment which was by and large characteristic of the earlier novels and becomes *engagé.* Though never (with the possible exception of *Island*) mere *romans à thèse,* Huxley's later novels sometimes become so preoccupied with preaching the doctrine of humanity (or nonattachment or mysticism) that they become less than human. But even though the later Huxley turns to propaganda, he never loses his gift for brilliantly corrosive and destructive satire. All of the later novels are full of marvelously satirical parts, even if they now remain only parts and must alternate with extensive passages of almost direct exposition. With one notable exception, however: *Brave New World.*

* He declaims against "this modern mania of seeing influence (or 'pastiche') in every resemblance that one finds, a mania which transforms the criticism of certain academics into detective work, and which leads so many artists into the absurd, because they are afraid of being suspected of resembling somebody" (my translation).

[9] André Gide, *Journal des Faux-Monnayeurs* (n.p., NRF, 1927), p. 112.

Eyeless in Gaza

by Peter Bowering

In "Uncle Spenser," one of his short stories of the early twenties, Huxley wrote "Some day, it may be, the successful novelist will write about man's relation to God." *Eyeless in Gaza,* Huxley's "conversion" novel, was in every sense a beginning. Huxley's return to contemplative mysticism, in the context of 1936, was totally unexpected. Alexander Henderson, whose critical work on the writer had been published in the previous year, had expressed the hope that "Much would be done to remove the imperfections of English Communism if our own Brahmins, men of the quality of Huxley and Aldington and E. M. Forster, would look more carefully into Communism and consider whether they cannot, after all, find it worthy of support. They would in all probability discover, as André Gide did, that they could support it." [1] In actual fact Huxley had already come under the influence of Gerald Heard, whom he had first met in 1930.[2] Dr. Miller, the first of Huxley's "men of good will," was undoubtedly a portrait of Heard; while the events recorded in Anthony Beavis's journal relate directly to Heard and Huxley's activities in the Rev. H. R. L. Sheppard's peace movement and must have occurred at approximately the time when they were written. Their common interests were further reflected in the two parallel tracts, Huxley's *Ends and Means,* and Heard's *The Third Morality,* both published in 1937.

In terms of form, *Eyeless in Gaza* represents Huxley's most complete departure from the original "novel of ideas." To dramatize the conversion theme it was necessary to show a character at different stages of his career; and, in contrast to the earlier novels, *Eyeless*

"*Eyeless in Gaza*" by Peter Bowering. From *Aldous Huxley: A Study of the Major Novels* (London: The Athalone Press, University of London, 1968), chapter 8. Copyright © 1968 by Peter Bowering. Reprinted by permission of the author and publisher.

1 *Aldous Huxley,* p. 196.
2 See Ronald W. Clark, *The Huxleys* (1968), pp. 231-2.

in Gaza spans a period of over thirty years from the hero's boyhood to middle life. Instead of a chronological sequence, there is a counterpoint of four narratives describing different epochs of Anthony Beavis's life; the earliest shows him as a schoolboy at the turn of the century shortly after his mother's death; next, as an adolescent at Oxford in the years immediately preceding the first world war, when his irresponsibility leads to the death of his best friend; then, in London during the late nineteen-twenties, when his career is well established; and finally between 1933 and 1935, when he comes to the crisis which makes him reject his previous life and seek a new one. The various episodes are woven together so that the novel shifts backwards and forwards in time; thus a scene from 1926 is followed immediately by one of 1902, an event from 1914 by one of 1933 and so on. In spite of this, there is a general forward movement in time throughout the novel as a whole; the first half concentrates on the events of the years 1902 to 1926, while the latter half is largely devoted to the events of the years 1927 to 1935, which include Anthony Beavis's Diary. The separate narratives are, of course, related in a chronological order.

The opening chapters give a clue to the method. The novel begins on the occasion of Anthony's forty-second birthday, the day which is to change the whole course of his existence. Anthony, who is having an affair with Helen Ledwidge, the wife of one of his former schoolfellows, has accidentally discovered a heap of snapshots. Depicting scenes from his early life, they evoke memories of his mother and father, Mary Amberley (his first mistress), and by implication his dead friend, Brian Foxe. Their significance becomes clear as the chapter unfolds. Anthony, like Philip Quarles, is the sceptic of a scientific age, the detached philosopher, "the preoccupied man of science who doesn't see the things that to everyone else are obvious" (ch. i). What is patently obvious, in this case, is Anthony's share in Helen's unhappiness. He has no time for emotions and responsibilities; he has denied his ability to love for what he believes to be freedom and in consequence Helen exists for him only in a context of pleasure. His love, as she puts it herself, is really a swindle, a trick for getting something for nothing. Anthony's attitude to Helen typifies his attitude to life; at the cost of denying his responsibility to others, his freedom is complete, complete that is except for the superfluous memories, "the corpses" that turn up inopportunely to remind him of the past. The faded snapshots, then, symbolize all the buried past Anthony would rather forget. Later, when he is making love to Helen on the sun-roof, the memories come swarming back: "The thirty-five years of his conscious life made themselves immediately known to him as a chaos —a pack of snapshots in the hands of a lunatic." There is no order, no purpose: somewhere in the back of his mind a lunatic shuffled the pack of cards and dealt them out at random. In spite of Freud, it was all a matter of chance:

> Unless, it now rather disquietingly occurred to him, unless of course the reason were not before the event, but after it . . . What if that picture gallery had been recorded and stored away in the cellars of his mind for the sole and express purpose of being brought up into consciousness at this present moment? Brought up, today, when he was forty-two and secure, forty-two and fixed, unchangeably himself, brought up along with those critical years of his adolescence, along with the woman who had been his teacher, his first mistress, and was now a hardly human creature festering to death, alone, in a dirty burrow? And what if that absurd childish game with the flints had had a point, a profound purpose, which was simply to be recollected here on this blazing roof, now as his lips made contact with Helen's sun-warmed flesh? In order that he might be forced, in the midst of this act of detached and irresponsible sensuality, to think of Brian and of the things that Brian had lived for; yes, and had died for— died for, another image suddenly reminded him, at the foot of just such a cliff as that beneath which they had played as children in the chalk pit. Yes, even Brian's suicide, he now realized, with horror even the poor huddled body on the rocks, was mysteriously implicit in this hot skin. (ch. iii)

To allay these disquieting thoughts he begins to count the movements of his hand as he caresses Helen's warm body and, by an easy transition, the reader is taken back to 1902, when Anthony as a child is counting the wayside advertisements from the train window on the way to his mother's funeral.

The method is now apparent: from this point the chapters unfold like the heap of snapshots and the images of Anthony's memory—without chronology. The story of the growth of the hero from boyhood to his discovery in middle life that his imagined freedom is no freedom at all is presented through the episodes, the spots in time which are significant to his moral development; his conversion is only complete when he has finally accepted responsibility for the past events which he has formerly denied. The return to the experience of the past, beginning with the snapshots and memories on his forty-second birthday, is thus the start of a process which eventually restores meaning to his life. In spite of this, most critics felt when the novel appeared that the method was unjustified. It must be admitted that the device of the time shift is too mechanical; that the events of the past are recorded from outside by an impersonal narrator, whereas the treatment of time in the first chapter suggests a psychological method more after the manner of Virginia Woolf's *Mrs. Dalloway,* in which the "remembrance of things past" takes place in the mind of the protagonist. However, an early critic observed that the method does serve "to increase the suspense, because the chief event in the story, the suicide, which chronologically comes early, is not completely related until the end." [3] Furthermore, the presence of the journal or diary necessitated some method of this kind; placed at the end of the novel it would have confronted the reader with a huge indigestible framework of ideas, like the second epilogue to *War and Peace.* For the purposes of analysis, on the other hand, it is convenient to unravel the main narrative and restore the chronology, beginning with the events of Anthony's boyhood.

The first of the snapshots is one of Anthony's mother taken shortly before her death, the young woman who stood in a garden at the turn of the century "like a ghost at cockcrow." As Anthony wrote later in his journal, "most infantile and adolescent histories are disastrous"; perhaps Anthony's was more disastrous than most. Certainly, his Hamlet's eye view of his father's second marriage is still with him in middle life. The snapshot inscribed "Grindelwald 1912," showing his father, stepmother and two half-sisters carrying alpenstocks against the dim background of the mountains, has deeper associations going back to the months immediately after his mother's funeral. "I would wish my days to be separated each from each by unnatural impiety," he exclaims as he puts the picture down (ch. i). The misquotation is an echo of his father, recalling a conversation, just five months to the day after his mother's death:

> "Today's the second," said his father in the same slow voice.
> Anthony felt apprehensive. If his father knew the date, why had he asked?
> "It's exactly five months today," Mr. Beavis went on.
> Five months? And then, with a sudden sickening drop of the heart, Anthony realized what his father was talking about. The Second of

November, the Second of April. It was five months since she had died.
"Each second of the month—one tried to keep the day sacred."
Anthony nodded and turned his eyes away with a sense of guilty
discomfort.
"Bound each to each by natural piety," said Mr. Beavis. (ch. ix)

The first trip to the Bernese Oberland with Anthony's future stepmother took place only three months later; and Anthony's attitude
to his father was irrevocably fixed. "The dramas of memory," as he
observed later, "are always Hamlet in modern dress." The marriage
for the sake of the motherless child is portrayed in vivid terms by
Anthony's uncle:

> The house positively reeked of matrimony. It was asphyxiating! And
> there sat John, fairly basking in those invisible radiations of dark
> female warmth, inhaling the stuffiness with a quivering nostril, deeply
> contented, revoltingly happy! Like a marmot . . . a marmot with its
> female, crowded fur to fur in their subterranean burrow. Yes, the
> house was just like a burrow—a burrow . . . and that unhappy little
> Anthony like a changeling from the world of fresh air, caught and
> dragged down and imprisoned in the marmot warren. (ch. xv)

His father's hypocrisy and repulsive sentimentalism foster a cynicism
towards marriage and all it implies. He is to rationalize the attitude
in terms of his work; later he admits that he could have accepted
Helen's love; he could have even loved in return, but he had deliberately chosen to be free, to remain free for the sake of his writing. Finally, he comes to realize that his own position is as false
as the one he has rejected; that having spent his whole life reacting
away from his father's standards, he had become precisely what his
father was—"a man in a burrow." In his case the burrow happened
to be intermittently adulterous instead of connubial. If Anthony's
revolt against the connubial burrow has its origin in his father's
second marriage, his scepticism towards religion and its ethical off-
shoots is also a family inheritance. For his father there could be no
immortality after Darwin; his uncle, James Beavis, held similar
views—he had grown up as a Bradlaugh atheist who ought to have
been blissfully happy parading his cosmic defiance. Needless to say
he was not. Much to his brother's horrified amazement, he died
with all the consolations of the Catholic faith.

The first challenge to the standards Anthony has acquired from
his father and uncle comes from the liberal Christianity of Mrs.
Foxe and her son, Brian. Brian, the child of an unsatisfactory mar-

riage, has no father and his close relationship with his mother has disastrous consequences. The main function of Brian and his mother, however, is to serve as a foil to Anthony's cynicism. Brian's emotional temperament and nervous disposition prove an easy target for his friend's detached and sceptical view of life. Their relationship is worked out symbolically in the movement of the tiny, three-masted schooner with paper sails that spans the guttering between the two boys' bedrooms. It has been carved by Brian and, like their friendship, is a little "lop-sided." Brian has been consoling Anthony over his mother's death:

> Balanced precariously in the tall embrasure of the windows, the two children stood there for a long time in silence. The cheeks of both of them were cold with tears; but on Anthony's wrist the grip of that consoling hand was obstinately violent, like a drowning man's.
>
> Suddenly, with a thin rattling of withered leaves, a gust of wind came swelling up out of the darkness. The little three-master started, as though it had been woken out of sleep, and noiselessly, with an air of purposeful haste, began to glide, stern-foremost, along the gutter. (ch. vi)

A few years later the roles are reversed. It is Brian who now stands in need of consolation but this time Anthony fails to span the gap between them. He frees himself from the "obstinately violent" hand, even though it means his friend's death. Brian's grip, then as always, is a stranglehold on his conscience.

Brian's immediate role, however, is to restore some significance to the natural order of things in the face of Anthony's negation. Tutored by Mrs. Foxe's radical Christianity, he tries to explain that it is God who counts, not the church; it is caring for people that really matters. Anthony resists; his uncle does not believe in God and for that matter he doesn't either. But in spite of Anthony's defiance, the figure of his friend remains before him, an unwelcome example of the behaviour he should imitate, continually awakening an unpleasant and repressed sense of guilt. When Brian protests about the ragging of young Ledwidge,

> . . . they all laughed—none more derisively than Anthony. For Anthony had had time to feel ashamed of his shame; time to refuse to think about that hole in Lollingdon churchyard; time, too, to find himself all of a sudden almost hating old Horse-Face. "For being so disgustingly pi," he would have said, if somebody had asked him to explain his hatred. But the real reason was deeper, obscurer. If he hated Horse-Face, it was because Horse-Face was so extraordinarily

decent; because Horse-Face had the courage of convictions which Anthony felt should also be *his* convictions—which, indeed, would be his convictions, if only he could bring himself to have the courage of them. (ch. vi)

Anthony's sense of moral guilt is bound up with his desire to forget "the hole in Lollingdon churchyard." Every act of moral cowardice is a betrayal of his dead mother—it is Hamlet in modern dress again; and on an ethical plane this is the central theme of the novel; the gap between belief and action, between knowledge and experience and the problem of transforming one into the other. Or as Anthony writes on the first page of his journal: "Five words sum up every biography. *Video meliora proboque: deteriora sequor.* Like all other human beings, I know what I ought to do, but continue to do what I know I oughtn't to do" (ch. ii). Rachel Foxe imposes herself on Anthony as a kind of spiritual substitute for his mother, one he bitterly resents; and after her son's death she continues to act as the keeper of a conscience he would rather ignore. But for the moment her reading from Renan's *Life of Jesus*, during the Easter holidays, has the effect of a momentary conversion: "The tears came into Anthony's eyes as he listened, and he felt an unspeakable longing to be good, to do something fine and noble". (ch. ix).

The second section of the novel covers the years 1912–14, when Anthony and Brian are at Oxford; his affair with Helen's mother, Mary Amberley, and his share in Brian's death. The forces exerting themselves on Anthony during his childhood, Mrs. Foxe's Christianity on the one hand and his uncle's agnosticism on the other, are now replaced by Brian's Fabianism, with its implicit commitment to something "fine and noble," and Gerry Watchett and his aristocratic friends. Anthony's view of life has hardened somewhat and any form of moral obligation is seen as a threat to his concept of personal freedom. He rejects Brian's Shavian equation of poverty with evil and the organization of society so that the individual couldn't commit sins because he refuses to bind himself. He professes a belief in the fundamental theory of mysticism, but he doesn't want to achieve anything—he is quite content only to know about the way of perfection. While recognizing that known truth is not the same as experienced truth, he does not consider the experience to be worth the price he would have to pay for it. When Brian points out that one has to be a prisoner to become free, Anthony is forced to admit that he is, in fact, a prisoner of knowl-

edge; but he will always be ready to stay in that prison. The irony
is not immediately apparent. To Brian the implication is of a moral
rather than a spiritual nature. It is too much of a luxury, an exploitation of one's privileges; for him Fabianism is only a beginning. He meant to go on with philosophy and literature and history until he was thirty. Then it would be time to do something
else, something more direct in getting at people, in realizing the
Kingdom of God. Anthony's reply is one of automatic ridicule, but
after Brian has gone he feels ashamed and humiliated. It was a
brainless response.

Nevertheless, the fundamental weakness in Anthony's character
triumphs; Brian and the Fabians are left to their own resources and
Anthony joins Gerry and his friends. Anthony's emancipation, or
what he likes to think of as emancipation, is largely intellectual;
the irresponsibility of the young aristocrats belongs to a social and
economic order of which he has no part. They do, however, represent an aspect of freedom to which he would readily aspire:

> They faced life, not diffidently and apologetically, as Anthony faced
> it, not wistfully from behind invisible bars, but with the serenely
> insolent assurance of those who know that God intended them to
> enjoy themselves and had decreed the unfailing acquiescence of their
> fellows in all their desires. (ch. ix)

But they, like Anthony, have their own prison. In a later conversation with Staithes, he suggests that people with money or power
are freer or at least less completely conditioned by their environment than the poor. This is somewhat naïve and, as Staithes is
quick to point out, if he really knew rich and powerful people, he
would soon feel differently. However, in spite of this, we find
Anthony writing in a notebook entry for 1933, that personal freedom can only exist in the political context of an aristocrat or pluto-
cratic society. But in fairness one must add that he was beginning
to have doubts.

To return to Anthony and Brian: for a time the slight Mephis-
tophelian influence that Anthony exerts over Brian—he had introduced him to Baudelaire, "the words that remained in the memory
like a crime"—is more than counterbalanced by Anthony's sense of
shame and betrayal. Mrs. Foxe, whose pseudo-scientific Christianity
is beyond "the pale of rationality," still strikes an unpleasant chord
in his conscience. This delicate balance is upset by the advent of
Mary Amberley, who Anthony has not seen since his mother's

funeral. Mary Amberley, "the very embodiment of desirability," was the subject of one of the snapshots taken in 1912. She belongs with the "femme fatale" sketches of the earlier novels, Mrs. Viveash and Lucy Tantamount, whose chief function is to deprive the hero of all normal concepts of morality. Mrs. Amberley is no exception; she has all the ruthlessness of her predecessors and under her guidance Anthony's cynicism is allowed full rein. As he tells Helen, when looking at the snapshots, she delivered him from the worst perils of "Darkest Switzerland"—she also delivers him from the perils of darkest Fabianism. He becomes the "enlightened and scientific vivisector" of Brian's adolescence:

> "Poor old Brian!" By his tone, by the use of the patronizing adjective, Anthony established his position of superiority, asserted his right . . . to anatomize and examine. Yes, poor old Brian! That maniacal preoccupation of his with chastity! Chastity—the most unnatural of all the sexual perversions . . . Mary's appreciative smile acted on him like a spur to fresh efforts. Fresh efforts, of course, at Brian's expense. But at the moment, that didn't occur to him. (ch. xxvii)

The same image is used to describe Helen's flirtation with Hugh Ledwidge: "It was an experiment, made in a spirit of hilarious scientific enquiry. She was a vivisector—licensed by perfection, justified by happiness," (ch. xx) In his eulogy to Crébillon le Fils, written in 1925, Huxley had elaborated on the spirit of detachment applied to sexual behaviour:

> . . . Crébillon's attitude towards the phenomena of sex seems to me precisely that of the true scientific investigator . . . He contrives to forget that love is a matter of the most intimate human concern . . . Making a clean sweep of all prejudices, he sets to work, coolly and with detachment, as though the subject of his investigations were something as remote, as utterly divorced from good and evil, as spiral nebulae, liver flukes, or the aurora borealis. (*The Olive Tree*)

It is clear from *Point Counter Point* that Huxley saw this as one of the dominant attitudes of the time and, like Lawrence, he felt it was to be deplored. In Anthony it is a vice; from a detached observation it becomes a detached participation. He recognizes that his seduction of Joan is the result of a momentary sensuality; while his reply to Joan's innocent question about Iago, "Men don't tell themselves that the wrong they're doing is wrong. Either they do it without thinking. Or else they invent reasons for believing it's right" (ch. xxxiii), simply reflects on the sheer irresponsibility of his behaviour. But, in spite of this, he vacillates right to the end; his final refusal to take any responsibility comes when Brian confesses his own sensual weakness for Joan and asks his friend's advice. Anthony concludes that the decision had made itself and he evades the issue once and for all by telling Brian that he ought to come to terms with reality, the same meaningless platitude he is to offer many years later to Mary Amberley, financially ruined and addicted to morphia.

Anthony's refusal to face reality is brought home to him in the light of Mrs. Foxe's admission of guilt, the acceptance of her own share of responsibility for Brian's suicide. For a brief moment Anthony had been determined to tell the truth, but now he was pinned irrevocably to his own lie. The bars of Anthony's cage are forged to his own design: knowledge, detached sensuality, and the role of the vivisecting comedian; so that when Miller tells him that "what we're all looking for is some way of getting beyond our own vomit," some way of getting beyond "this piddling, twopenny-half-penny personality . . . with all its wretched little virtues and vices, all its silly cravings and silly pretensions," Anthony translates it into terms of his own immediate experience:

> Some way, Anthony was thinking, of getting beyond the books, beyond the perfumed and resilient flesh of women, beyond fear and sloth, beyond the painful but secretly flattering vision of the world as menagerie and asylum. (ch. xlix)

Of the three spots of time recalled in the sun-roof scene, the last belongs to Helen, the incident at the midwife's in the rue de la Tombe-Issoire. This forms the climax of the third section of the novel which describes the events of the years 1926–28 and is largely devoted to the lives of Helen and Mary Amberley. Helen is perhaps the most attractive and successful piece of characterization in the novel. She inherits some of her mother's qualities, her flippant sense of humour, her ability to give herself completely to the sensation of the moment:

> Dancing, she lost her life in order to save it; lost her identity and became something greater than herself; lost her perplexities and self-hatreds in a bright harmonious certitude; lost her bad character and was made perfect; lost the regretted past, the apprehended future, and gained a timeless present of consummate happiness. (ch. xviii)

In her irresponsible flirtation with Hugh Ledwidge she resembles

Mary Amberley, but she is more sensitive and intelligent—her handling of Hugh's party to launch "The Invisible Lover" is one of the humorous high spots of the novel. Further she shows some development, from her disastrous marriage to Hugh to a fuller and more mature relationship with Ekki Giesebrecht. But her progress, like her mother's, is one of increasing bondage and disillusionment. Her momentary vision of "a timeless present of consummate happiness," like Mary's divine moment in the shadow of the Pascin nudes, is of the same order of experience as the St. Matthew Passion or the Hammerclavier Sonata: they give a taste of the next world, but they are not enough. What is enough, is one of the questions Huxley is trying to answer, but clearly any form of sensual experience is suspect. Anthony in his drunken dissertation on St. Thomas and mystical experience concludes that

> Even St. Thomas is forced to admit that no mind can see the divine substance unless it is divorced from bodily senses, either by death or by some rapture. Some rapture, mark you! But a rapture is always a rapture, whatever it's due to. Whether it's champagne, or saying OM, or squinting at your nose, or looking at a crucifix, or making love . . . (ch. x)

But a rapture is not always a rapture; the Baroque Saints may be portrayed writhing in ecstasies of physical passion, but this is a direct misrepresentation of fact. Mere sensuality is wrong, whether it is Anthony's detached amusement or Helen's joyous abandonment, because it invariably results in enslavement to the self; and this leads to irresponsibility and moral degradation. Physical passion can be made compatible with responsibility, Anthony decides, but "only when it ceases to be an end in itself and becomes a means towards the unification through love of two separate individuals" (ch. xv). This is suggestive of the Laurentian relationship of *Point Counter Point*, but again there is no active demonstration of it within the novel (Anthony himself settles for celibacy as the only safe course); and it is not until *Island* that Huxley is able to offer a satisfactory compromise between sensuality and the claims of moral rectitude.

The failure of Helen's sensual life, her progressive disillusionment and enslavement to the self are expressed symbolically in three closely related scenes: the theft of the kidney, the death of her kitten, and her subsequent seduction by her mother's lover; there is finally the climax in the rue de la Tombe-Issoire where desire, shame and physical revulsion become fused together in a nightmare of delirium. On the couch in Mme. Bonifay's sitting-room, she sees Gerry making love to her again:

> And Gerry was there, sitting on the edge of her bed, kissing her, stroking her shoulders, her breasts. "But Gerry, you mustn't! . . . Gerry, don't!" But when she tried to push him away, he was like a block of granite, immovable; and all the time his hands, his lips were releasing soft moths of quick and fluttering pleasure under her skin . . . (ch. xxxix)

Later she imagines herself with her sister, Joyce, and her baby:

> She took the baby from Joyce, she pressed him close against her body, she bent her head so as to be able to kiss those adorable little fingers. But the thing she held in her arms was the dying kitten, was those kidneys at the butcher's, was the horrible thing which she had opened her eyes to see Mme. Bonifay nonchalantly picking up and carrying away in a tin to the kitchen.

On returning to consciousness, she likens herself to the dying kitten, reduced "to a dirty little rag of limp flesh, transformed from a bright living creature into something repellent, into the likeness of kidneys, of that unspeakable thing that Mme. Bonifay . . ." For a brief while with Ekki she escapes from this enslavement to the self but after his death everything is the same as before; her continuing allegiance to Communism is little more than an emotional projection of her feelings for her lover, and a hatred for his torturers. A year after Ekki's disappearance, she is wishing that they had taken her too, instead of leaving her there, "rotting away, like a piece of dirt on a rubbish heap. Like a dead kitten" (ch. liv). Her words were spoken with a vehement disgust. Such is the measure of Helen's progress. In his essay on Swift, Huxley notes that, considered as comments on reality, Gulliver and Prometheus, for all their astonishing difference, have a common origin—"the refusal on the part of their authors to accept the physical reality of the world" (*Do What You Will*). Intense disgust with physiological phenomena is always associated, in Huxley, with a refusal to face reality. Almost all the characters in the novel are guilty in their respective ways. For Helen and Anthony life is a constant evasion of facts, while Brian's refusal to come to terms with his physical passion has disastrous consequences. John Beavis and Hugh Ledwidge make their protest by deliberately mimicking the attitudes of childhood. John Beavis takes refuge in an abject and repulsive kind of sentimentalism; while the "invisible lover," like the author of the *Jour-*

nal to Stella, desires Helen to be a bodiless abstraction, and is furi-
ous with her for being otherwise.

Further, the thematic symbols associated with Anthony and Helen
are always presented in a moral context and intense feelings of disgust are invariably linked with a sense of guilt and shame. Implicit
in their physical revulsion is a feeling of betrayal, whether it be
the hole in Lollingdon churchyard, Helen's unborn child, or "the
millions going cold and hungry." The refusal to face up to physical
reality is just another way of evading responsibility, of refusing to
accept the full consequences of one's thoughts, feelings and actions,
and in the final analysis, the fact of death itself. For, on another
level, the associated symbolism depicts decay and mortality,[4] as
Helen was carrying her kitten across the lawn, she thought how

> . . . it was not only the declining sun that made everything seem so
> solemnly and richly beautiful; it was also the thought of the passing
> days, of human limitations, of the final unescapable dissolution . . .
> The tears came into her eyes; she pressed the sleeping kitten more
> closely to her breast. (ch. xxiv)

Helen, like the other main characters in *Eyeless in Gaza,* approxi-
mates to one of W. Sheldon's physiological types referred to in *Ends
and Means.* She is the viscerotonic, whose experience of life is
largely emotional; Anthony, the cerebrotonic, the intellectual who
can only express himself in terms of ideas; while Staithes is the
somatotonic, the man of action. Each is a prisoner of his predomi-
nating tendency; Helen of her emotions, Anthony of his knowledge,
and Staithes of his futile schemes to reform himself and the world.
Staithes, in fact, is hardly a character at all. There is little to con-
nect the rugby playing type at Bulstrode with the Fabian at Oxford
or the misanthropist who reads *Timon.* But his function as a mouthpiece is important; as the man of action he voices the theme of
political as opposed to personal freedom. It is perhaps an indication
of Huxley's desire to answer his left-wing critics that Anthony, while
preoccupied with his own concept of personal freedom, is always
opposed by someone expounding its political counterpart. The ban-
ner of political reform is handed on through the novel from Mrs.
Foxe's Liberalism to Brian's Fabianism; from Staithes's revolutionary Marxism to Ekki's Communism, to fade away finally with Ekki's
death and Helen's disenchantment. The political theme is never

4 It will be recalled that to Mrs. Viveash kidneys were a *memento mori.*

realized dramatically; the abortive Mexican revolution merely pro-
motes discussion and provides Miller with an excuse to propound
his ideas. Nevertheless it is essential to the working out of the
theme; in the end, under Miller's guidance, the concepts of personal
and political freedom are resolved into one. Meanwhile Staithes
carries the main burden of political disillusionment: as a Marxist
revolutionary, he is opposed to Gerry Watchett's aristocratic
"ideal"; but by the third phase of the novel his fervour has
turned to cynicism. Revolution is all right in the preliminary stages
when it is just a matter of getting rid of the people at the top. But
afterwards, he argues, echoing Chelifer's more pessimistic strictures
on the utopian society, if society is changed, what then? "More wire-
less sets, more chocolates, more beauty parlours, more girls with
better contraceptives . . ." (ch. xxii). In brief, simply more opportunities to be piggish. Staithes's puritanical dislike of pleasure, like
Chelifer's, invites criticism; but this, of course, was only one side
of the utopian picture—*Brave New World* had already provided
the other. Staithes's Mexican expedition with his destructive slogan
of "Revolution for my sake" is the final measure of his disenchantment.

The fourth narrative phase returns to the events of the opening
chapters of the novel, and the occasion of Anthony's forty-second
birthday. This section describes the events which change the pattern
of Anthony's life and lead to his conversion at the hands of Miller.
Anthony, who is making love to Helen on the sunroof, has returned
to his detached sensualities to avoid the unpleasant implications
of the past. Into this context, "the dog from the skies" appears like
the thunderbolt of a wrathful Jehovah. The carcass of the fox
terrier is a unifying symbol: it partakes of the same qualities as the
thematic symbols associated with Helen—like the kitten it is "another dirty little rag of limp flesh, transformed from a bright living
creature into something repellent," and it is another object evoking
a deep sense of physical disgust allied with feelings of guilt and
shame. In his meditation on unity, Anthony integrates it into his
total experience of physical reality: fear, shame, guilt and disgust
are unified in "the drunken Mexican's pistol . . . the dark dried
blood on that mangled face among the rocks, the fresh blood spat-
tered scarlet over Helen's naked body, the drops oozing from the
raw contusion of Mark's knee" (ch. liv). Further, like the other
associated symbols, it depicts mortality; Anthony compares the fly-
covered carcase with Brian's battered body at the cliff's foot, and

Helen links it with death. At Hugh's party Staithes asks Croyland whether he found that even *Macbeth,* even the Mass in D, or the El Greco *Assumption* were adequate against death, to which Helen adds with irony that "Father Hopkins won't keep dogs off." Finally, it is almost literally the *deus ex machina*—dog "interpreted kabbalistically backwards, signifies God." The other thematic symbols are woven into the narrative: the almost "shapeless carcase" appears from nowhere with the moral force of a heavenly visitation:

> Anthony opened his eyes for just long enough to see that the aeroplane was almost immediately above them, then shut them again, dazzled by the intense blue of the sky.
> "These damned machines!" he said. Then, with a little laugh, "They'll have a nice God's-eye view of us here," he added.
> Helen did not answer; but behind her closed eyelids she smiled. Pop-eyed and with an obscene and gloating disapproval! The vision of that heavenly visitant was irresistibly comic. (ch. xii)

Then comes the thunderbolt of the angry Jehovah: like the snapshots, it is another corpse that turned up very opportunely to shatter Anthony's complacency, and force him to re-examine once more the burden of the past.

This scene has been described as the moral pivot of the novel.[5] Certainly Anthony is never the same again. His first genuine feeling is one of pity followed by "an almost violent movement of love" as he sees the hurt and suffering Helen as a human being for the very first time. It is too late. Helen after her baptism of blood has resolved to leave. As she is going both pause to examine a butterfly settled on a cluster of buddleia:

> The spread wings were tremulous as though from an uncontrollable excess of life, of passionate energy. Rapidly, ravenously, but with an extraordinary precision of purposeful movement, the creature plunged its uncoiled proboscis into the tiny trumpet-shaped flowers that composed the cluster . . . Again, again, to the very quick of the expectant flowers, deep to the sheathed and hidden sources of that hot intoxicating sweetness! Again, again, with what a tireless concupiscence, what an intense passion of aimed and accurate greed. (ch. xii)

It is too much for Helen to watch; she flicks it away and departs almost at once. The moral is obvious to both of them. That night Anthony has a nightmare, a familiar dream that had haunted him

5 Elizabeth Bowen, *Collected Impressions* (1950), p. 147.

since boyhood; now, it has a "vague but horrible connection with the dog." As he lies awake afterwards he is faced with "a huge accumulation of neglected memories . . . Those snapshots. His mother and Mary Amberley. Brian in the chalk pit, evoked by that salty smell of sun-warmed flesh, and again dead at the cliff's foot, among the flies—like that dog . . ." (ch. xii).

A few days later, in the course of another sleepless night, Anthony reads Lawrence's *The Man Who Died*. At long intervals the distant crowing of a cock and the cicadas, endlessly repeating the proclamation of their existence, remind him, like the butterfly, of the irresponsible stream of energy of natural life. For Lawrence the animal purpose had seemed enough, had seemed better than "the squalid relationships of human beings advanced half-way to consciousness, still only partially civilized" (ch. xxvi), but then Lawrence had never looked through a microscope.[6] He recalls a film of the fertilization of a rabbit's ovum: "the horror of that display of sub-mental passion, of violent and impersonal egotism! Intolerable, unless one could think of it only as raw material and available energy," raw material that could be worked-up for other ulterior purposes. Anthony suddenly realizes that his own pursuit of knowledge, which he had once thought of as an end in itself, was only the means, was only a part of the evolutionary process like the spermatozoa struggling towards their goal, as definitely raw material as life itself, to be worked-up, but to what end? He knows what the finished product would have to be and with one part of his being he revolts against the knowledge; but with another he is miserably reflecting that he would never be able to succeed. He has no idea where or how to begin and, in the end, he is afraid of making a fool of himself. A few hours later he is telling Staithes that since the death of Brian his life has been without purpose. He had rejected the concept of an integrated personality, for

> "how can there be freedom—so long as the 'you' persists? A 'you' has got to be consistent and responsible, has got to make choices and commit itself. But if one gets rid of the 'you,' one gets rid of responsibility and the need for consistency. One's free as a succession of un-

6 Huxley comments on *The Plumed Serpent*, ". . . in the end, we are asked to renounce daylight and fresh air and immerse ourselves in 'the grand sea of the living blood' . . . We cannot accept the invitation. Lawrence's own incomparable descriptions of the horror of unadulterated blood have made it impossible. It was impossible even for himself; he could not accept his own invitation" (*Beyond the Mexique Bay*). This was written in 1934 following Huxley's visit to Central America. Lawrence's influence was already beginning to wane.

conditioned, uncommitted states without past or future, except in so far as one can't voluntarily get rid of one's memories and anticipations." (ch. xxvi)

This was an essential part of the doctrine of *Do What You Will*, a kind of philosophical extension of Lawrence's "non-stable ego," which Anthony had described some seven years earlier:

> It was left to Blake to rationalize psychological atomism into a philosophical system. Man, according to Blake (and, after him, according to Proust, according to Lawrence), is simply a succession of states. Good and evil can be predicated only of states, not of individuals, who in fact don't exist, except as the places where the states occur. It is the end of personality in the old sense of the word. (ch. xi)

Or as one critic put it, the chief contention of *Do What You Will* was that there was no persisting self, and "there being no persisting self there is of course, no Universe—none, that is, of which any consistent truth can be predicated." [7] For Anthony this had become a doctrine of irresponsibility but, as he admits to Staithes, the memory is the rub. The lunatic who shuffles the cards at the back of his mind has the last word. It is Miller who provides the answer: there is a moral order "where every event has its cause and produces its effect—where the card's forced upon you by the conjuror, but only because your previous actions have forced the conjuror to force it upon you" (ch. xlix), or as the author of the *Dhammapada* wrote, "All that we are is the result of what we have thought." This is the last of *Do What You Will* and the beginning of the neo-Buddhism of *Ends and Means*.

On Anthony's return to London, he accidentally meets Helen and Ekki Giesebrecht; her happiness with her new lover is an immediate reminder of his own sense of failure. To return to his old way of life is now out of the question and he decides to throw in his lot with Staithes and go to Mexico. The Mexican expedition provides Anthony with a series of experiences, paralleling those of Helen, which reveal the true nature of his imagined freedom; like Helen, he has no answer to the problem of physical suffering. The first incident which reveals his inadequacy occurs at Puerto san Felipe where the daughter of the agent lies sick with meningitis. The screaming child with her head rolling from side to side reminds him of Helen on the sun-roof; there he observed "the symptoms of that death-bed in which he had his part as assassin and fellow-

7 E. P. Hart, *New Adelphi*, XIII (November 1936), p. 101.

victim," Helen's face twisted in grief like one of Van der Weyden's Holy women at the foot of the Cross (ch. iii). It was all one and the same: "Tortured by pleasure, tortured by pain. At the mercy of one's skin and mucus, at the mercy of those thin threads of nerve," and there was nothing whatever one could do about it (ch. xli). There are further examples of Anthony's inadequacy: the incident in the bar at the Hotel at Tapatlan and the amputation of Staithes's leg have a common background for which Huxley once coined the phrase, "the human vomedy." The first suggestion of something more positive comes when Anthony observes Staithes's face, serene and almost smiling, under the chloroform; it was the face of one who had made himself free.

> But in fact, Anthony reflected, in fact he had had his freedom forced upon him by this evil-smelling vapour. Was it possible to be one's own liberator? There were snares; but also there was a way of walking out of them. Prisons; but they could be opened. And if the torture-chambers could never be abolished, perhaps the torturers could be made to seem irrelevant. (ch. xlix)

"Was it possible to be one's own liberator?" Helen on the sun-roof, the screaming child, Staithes under the anaesthetic—all stretched out supine on their beds of torment, suggest no answer. Only the picture of the martyrdom of St Erasmus in the museum at Basel indicates the way:

> An executioner in a fifteenth-century costume, with a pale shell-pink codpiece, was methodically turning the handle of a winch . . . winding the saint's intestines, yard after yard, out of a gash in the emaciated belly, while the victim lay back, as if on a sofa, making himself thoroughly comfortable and looking up into the sky with an expression of unruffled equanimity. (ch. liii)

For Anthony the final moment of truth occurs when Staithes quotes Rochester. Suddenly, he is faced with the realization:

> After a search so painful and so long
> That all his life he had been in the wrong.

He resolves to go and make himself look ridiculous with Miller.

The final section of the novel covers the events of the twelve months following Anthony's return to London with Miller. It is written in the form of a diary and serves as a record of Anthony's spiritual growth. Self-knowledge, he declares, is an essential preliminary to self-change. The journal was the first step. It begins and concludes with a confession and repudiation of his past way of life:[8] the way of "detached sensualities" and "sterilised ideas." His life's work had been:

> A picture of futility, apparently objective, scientific, but composed, I realize, in order to justify my own way of life. If men had always behaved either like half-wits or baboons, if they couldn't behave otherwise, then I was justified in sitting comfortably in the stalls with my opera glasses. (ch. ii)

He himself had chosen to regard the whole process as either pointless or a practical joke; as he admits in the closing chapter of the novel, it had been a deliberate act of the will. This avowal is to some extent autobiographical and is paralleled by a similar confession in *Ends and Means* where, posing the question of "significance," Huxley says that, like so many of his contemporaries, he took it for granted that there was no meaning; but as he also concedes, most ignorance is vincible ignorance. We don't know because we don't want to know. The knowledge, as Anthony so frequently insists, had always been there, but knowledge is not enough. The problem, as always, is how to transform it into a practical way of life. This is the function of Dr. Miller, the first of Huxley's exemplary characters who were to point the way.

James Miller, as it has previously been suggested, is essentially a mouthpiece for the ideas of Gerald Heard. In *The Third Morality* (1937), Heard outlines the training he considers necessary to fit the facts of the "new cosmology." The three physical means consist of diet, psycho-physical re-education and co-ordination on the lines propounded by F. M. Alexander, and lastly control of the respiration. These functions, although generally subconscious, can be brought into full consciousness and re-ordered to produce a better pattern of basic psycho-physical behaviour. Bodily training is to be practised in conjunction with meditation, the fundamental technique of Hindu and Buddhist mysticism whereby the individual achieves a state of self-awareness and non-attachment. Here are the main features of Dr. Miller's system: "a non-theological praxis of meditation which he would like . . . to couple with training, along F. M. Alexander's lines, in use of the self, beginning with physical control and achieving through it (since mind and body are one) control of impulses and feelings" (ch. ii). To which Huxley has

---

8 This is a structural feature of the novel: the two confessions belong to the second and final chapters respectively.

added the form of pacifism known as passive or nonviolent resistance; this is the political correlative of the ethic of non-attachment.

The idea that there is a persisting self which can be re-educated represents an important advance in Huxley's thought. Anthony, we recall, had finally reached the point of rejecting the concept of the self as a "succession of unconditioned, uncommitted states." This marked Huxley's final break with Rampion's or Lawrence's doctrine of "life-worship." Just how far Huxley had committed himself to this theory it is hard to say; less one might suppose than most critics have imagined. In *Point Counter Point,* the characters far from being free as a "succession of states" were at the mercy of their bodily functions—the very existence of the body was a cynical comment on the soul; and there was little to suggest that any kind of radical change were possible. In fact, it is precisely this lack of freedom, so painfully manifest in Helen and Anthony, that lies behind so much of Huxley's pessimism. Bernard's cry of "what would it be like . . . if I were free—not enslaved by my conditioning" is not restricted to the confines of *Brave New World.* It would have seemed indeed at times that Huxley had succumbed to the Behaviourist view that "mind is merely an epiphenomenon of matter." Anthony certainly sees the mind as determined by the body, "at the mercy of one's skin and mucus," at least he does so before he meets Miller. Then in the journal a new note of optimism appears:

> Conditioned reflex. What a lot of satisfaction I got out of old Pavlov when first I read him. The ultimate debunking of all human pretensions. We were all dogs and bitches together . . . No nonsense about free will, goodness, truth and all the rest. Each age has its psychological revolutionaries . . . The nineteenth century had to begin again. Marx and the Darwinians. Who are still with us—Marx obsessively so. Meanwhile the twentieth century has produced yet another lot of debunkers—Freud and, when he began to flag, Pavlov and the Behaviourists. Conditioned reflex: it seemed, I remember, to put the lid on everything. Whereas actually, of course, it merely restated the doctrine of free-will. For if reflexes can be conditioned, then, obviously, they can be re-conditioned. Learning to use the self properly, when one has been using it badly—what is it but re-conditioning one's reflexes? (ch. vii)

This is the secret of F. M. Alexander's method. In his introduction to Alexander's *The Use of the Self,* John Dewey writes: "The school of Pavloff has made current the idea of conditioned reflexes. Mr.

Alexander's work extends and corrects the idea. It proves that there are certain basic, central organic habits and attitudes which condition *every* act we perform, every use we make of ourselves . . . This discovery corrects the ordinary conception of the conditioned reflex. The latter as usually understood renders an individual a passive puppet to be played upon by external manipulations. The discovery of a central control which conditions all other reactions brings the conditioning factor under conscious direction and enables the individual through his own co-ordinated activities to take possession of his own potentialities. It converts the fact of conditioned reflexes from a principle of external enslavement into a means of vital freedom." [9] In *Ends and Means* Huxley goes further and states that the physical attributes achieved by Alexander's method lead ultimately to greater mental and moral self-awareness and self-control. This was a completely new concept of the conditioned reflex, the importance of which need hardly be emphasized here.

Meditation can also be conceived as another method of self-education, a further means of gaining greater self-awareness and self-control; but it is, of course, more than this: it has always been the primary means of achieving what Huxley has called man's final end and purpose, the unitive knowledge of the Godhead, or as he puts it somewhat more tentatively in *Ends and Means,* "the direct intuition of, and union with, an ultimate spiritual reality that is perceived as simultaneously beyond the self and in some way within it" (ch. xiv). Miller, like Heard, wanted meditation practice to be strictly "non-theological" to attract the widest possible following and, as Anthony insists, meditation in no way necessitates the belief in a personal Deity: "God may or may not exist. But there is the empirical fact that contemplation of the divinity—of goodness in its most unqualified form—is a method of realizing that goodness to some slight degree in one's life . . ." (ch. xliv). Whether one believes in a personal God or not is a matter of taste. The psychological results will be the same.

In the final chapter, Anthony's meditation on unity draws together the threads of the novel; it is a movement away from individual separateness to a merging with the spiritual reality of the universe. It begins with the physical facts of Anthony's life, the importunate memories that pinpoint his weaknesses and failures; it dwells on the "almost nightmarish vision of a more-than-Berg-

9 *The Use of the Self* (1946), p. xxi.

sonian life force" of the sub-microscopic world; then it spirals upwards to higher forms of life and existence, moving away from evil
—all that emphasizes the separate self, towards goodness, love and
compassion. "Step by step towards the experience of being no longer
wholly separate, but united at the depths with other lives, with the
rest of being," to merge finally in an ultimate vision of peace, unity
and liberation:

> Peace from pride and hatred and anger, peace from cravings and
> aversions, peace from all the separating frenzies. Peace through
> liberation, for peace is achieved freedom. Freedom and at the same
> time truth. The truth of unity actually experienced . . . Peace in
> this profound sub-aqueous night, peace in this silence, this still emp-
> tiness where there is no more time, where there are no more images,
> no more words . . . For now there is only the darkness expanding
> and deepening, deepening into light: there is only this final peace,
> this consciousness of being no more separate, this illumination . . .[10]

The personal and political themes merge together at the point
where the individual takes responsibility. Personal and political
freedom are compatible in the form of non-violent resistance or
"positive pacifism." Here again, the material is largely autobiographical. Huxley's pamphlet, *What Are You Going to do About
It?*, the case for constructive peace, was published in the summer
of 1936. Asking for recruits for the Rev. H. R. L. Sheppard's peace
movement,[11] Huxley warned that the formation of another sub-
scription-collecting, literature-distributing and pledge-signing society would not be enough. The constructive peace movement had to
be all these things; but it also had to be a kind of religious order
in which the members were dedicated to a definite way of life. The
organization would take the form of an affiliation of small groups
of five to ten individuals, such as those adopted by the early Christians, the Quakers, the Wesleyans and the Communists. Intensive
training would be necessary because peace and social justice can
only be realized by means that are just and pacific. And human
beings will only behave justly and pacifically if they have been
trained to do so. Miller, who had learned his technique of non-

---

10 Gerald Heard, *The Third Morality*, p. 258, states: "The first contemplation
must be of the unifying life to which the individual belongs and into which he
may be delivered by pushing through and beyond his individualistic arbitrary
frontiers."

11 The Peace Pledge Movement which included such well-known figures as
Bertrand Russell, Middleton Murry, Siegfried Sassoon, George Lansbury and
Donald Soper.

violence as a field anthropologist, provides Anthony with a practical demonstration while addressing the meeting at Tower Hill, when he allows himself to be assaulted by an angry heckler; but it is clear that Huxley envisaged far more of the peace movement than mere resistance to hostile crowds. In *Ends and Means* he foresees trained groups that would "go out into the world" where they would organize non-violent resistance to domestic oppression, and intercede between hostile armies.

All other means of social reform will ultimately fail because they do not make sufficient allowances for the freedom of the individual. Brian's Fabian concept of a society organized "so well the individual couldn't commit sins" is limited because preventative ethics are not enough. Prevention is good but it cannot eliminate the necessity for a cure. One is external to the individual, the other, the individual teaching of right use, gets rid of the cause of maladjustment and therefore of the occasions giving rise to bad behaviour. What is needed is a method of achieving progress from within as well as from without. Progress, not only as a citizen, a machine-minder and machine-user, but also as a human being. Staithes rejected Communism because he thought the ultimate end unworthy: "Millions and millions of soft, piggish Babbitts, ruled by a small minority of ambitious Staitheses" (ch. xxii), but Anthony rejects it because he believes that the means would finally defeat the ends: "One of the first discoveries . . . one makes," he tells Helen, "is that organized hatred and violence aren't the best means for securing justice and peace" (ch. liv). If reform is to be regarded simply as a matter of politics, then it seems one must approve and practise liquidation; governments with comprehensive plans for the betterment of society have invariably been governments that have used torture, but a solution is possible if one thinks in terms of individual men and women. All the evils of society are performed not in the name of individuals but in the name of the nation. In the end, Anthony concluded, there is "no remedy except to become aware of one's interests as a human being" (ch. xxxv).

The Later Novels of Huxley

by Joseph Bentley

Brave New World marks the end of Aldous Huxley's career as a major satiric novelist. After 1932 he abandoned the mask of the fashionably disenchanted ironist and began his drift toward mysticism and responsible involvement in public issues. The game most popular with the pyrrhonic esthetes of the 'twenties, the sport called *Épater le bourgeois,* had finally gone stale, after it had dominated five of Huxley's novels and scores of short stories, poems, and essays, not to mention countless reviews and a play. Under the influence of a congeries of insights too complex to deserve the simplistic label "mysticism," Huxley's later novels changed radically in structure, tone, and style; they attempted unsuccessfully to merge and unify widely divergent areas of experience and thus created a formal discontinuity that can only be called an esthetic disaster. Huxley's reputation plunged catastrophically during the last quarter-century of his life, but the stylistic and structural causes of the decline have never, it seems to me, been satisfactorily defined.

We must begin the exploration in Huxley's early attitudes and stances. He argued in "Vulgarity in Literature," his artistic credo and apologia for his early period, that to "shock the stupid and morally reprehensible truth-haters" into an acceptance of reality is not only a solemn duty of the satirist; it is also a great and rare pleasure, for, as Baudelaire put it, *"le mauvais goût"* is the aristocrat's prerogative—it provides in abundance *"le plaisir aristocratique de deplaire."* The exquisite bad taste of some of Huxley's early passages is indeed a rare pleasure for the connoisseur of negativity. One is not likely to forget Gumbril's idea at the beginning of *Antic Hay* for trousers with an inflatable seat to make religious commitment easier for people who are obliged to worship on those flesh-mortifying pews in college chapels; nor the disquisition upon reli-

"The Later Novels of Huxley" by Joseph Bentley. From *The Yale Review,* 59 (1970), pp. 507–519. Reprinted by permission of the author and the editor of *The Yale Review.*

gion, architecture, and plumbing in *Crome Yellow,* in which we discover that a great Renaissance house was designed with the privies in the towers so that men, while performing their basest functions, could have the spiritual advantage of being as close as possible to God. The gratuitous outrageousness of Philip Quarles's novelistic technique in *Point Counter Point* is another memorable Huxleyan maneuver: Quarles studies the sexual processes of rare fish as preparation for a novel about the amorous intrigues of Bloomsbury sophisticates, and notes in passing that the figure of a dominating and peevish wife should be contrapuntally merged with descriptions of certain species of fish in which the male exists only as a microorganism attached to his "fair one's" lower digestive tract. Quarles is pleased to accept the title, "The Zoologist of Fiction," and so, at that stage in his career, was Huxley. On virtually every page of those early novels the scientific or scatological image intrudes into contexts of romance, spirituality, or esthetic high seriousness. No one since Swift had so consistently manipulated a continuous parallel between exalted spirit and vile flesh. But Swift had usually made his moral ground clear; we can sense that those "Aeolists" in *A Tale of a Tub,* who attain heights of spiritual intensity by dancing in a circle, each applying a bellows to his neighbor's breech and pumping him full of inspiration, represent not only Swift's pleasure in aristocratic bad taste but also, quite clearly, his genuine conviction that the dissenters were perverting true Christianity. In the early Huxley no clear moral grounds are discoverable; his mood alternates between dismal negativity and amusing negativity, between the image of life as doomed foppery and the image of life as a knockabout farce among the dustbins. To paraphrase Baudelaire's line, Huxley's grotesque anatomical vision was, in the decade of *The Waste Land,* an oasis of outrage in a desert of boredom.

When *Eyeless in Gaza* appeared in 1936 it was suddenly clear that a dramatic change had occurred in Huxley's attitudes and style. The Zoologist of Fiction still functioned and the anatomical image still intruded into incongruous contexts, but overwhelming the familiar Huxleyan moments were long introspective meditations on the meaning of life, tedious speculations on the nature of Christian love and goodness of heart, and incomprehensible assertions about ultimate reality and the Divine Ground of All Being. Even the flourishes of physiological satire had a transformed quality. Instead of pneumatic trousers we have the image of pullulating maggots; in place of breaking wind in a cathedral we have a ruptured child surprised while awkwardly masturbating in his truss; scenes merging modern love with the image of Fabre among the Coleoptera are replaced by the scene in which a dog falls from a passing airplane, explodes on a roof, and covers a pair of nude lovers with blood and gobbets of flesh. Vile flesh in *Eyeless in Gaza* has become doubly vile.

Another difference in his use of the physiological image is that from *Eyeless in Gaza* onward Huxley focuses far more often on pain, torture, and death. In his fiction before 1936 we are not made vividly aware of physical pain in his characters. True, there are various suicides, murders, diseases, and mortifications of the flesh in his earlier books; but those earlier physical horrors are not dwelt upon at great length. In *Those Barren Leaves,* for example, a girl dies miserably from food poisoning, but we are spared, for the most part, a close description of her agony. Murder and death and disease figure prominently in *Point Counter Point,* but here again the descriptions are distant and abstract. The death of Webley, for example, is seen as a species of chemical rearrangement; the emphasis is not on the pain he might have felt—actually, he did not know what hit him—but on the mechanics of cellular decomposition and rigor mortis. The death, in the same book, of Philip Quarles's child is indeed a vivid and painful passage; specific references to certain symptoms—blindness, headaches, screaming—emphasize the brutal reality of pain and physiological destruction. This, however, is the only scene in Huxley's earlier books which makes a careful attempt to depict vividly the reality of physical pain. The Savage's self-flagellations in *Brave New World,* like his suicide, are abstract events—painless because lacking in specific detail.

But in the later books pain becomes truly painful. In *Eyeless in Gaza* the disease and degradation of Mary Amberley, a middle-aged siren of the Lucy Tantamount variety, are described in minute detail, and Mark Staithes's gangrened leg forms the basis for several very specific chapters. We are invited to view such things as raw flesh, yellow and purple bruises, blood-soaked sheets, pus, the grating of the saw during the un-anesthetized amputation. In *Time Must Have a Stop* (1944) we follow every physiological disruption as Eustace Barnack falls dead with a heart attack, every outrage as Jim Poulshot is bayoneted in the face, the stomach, and the genitals. In *Ape and Essence* (1948) we also have a close view of tortures and an overpowering orgy of physical degradations. *The Genius and the Goddess* (1955) is the least violent of Huxley's late novels, but it ends with an accident which not only kills but demolishes the central character. Katy Maartens is killed in a highway crash, "destroyed . . . with every refinement of physical outrage—an eye put out by a splinter of glass, the nose and lips and chin almost obliterated, rubbed out on the bloody macadam of the road. And there was a crushed right hand and a broken shinbone showing through the stocking." The flesh in Huxley's late work is not only vile; it is also no longer funny. The aristocratic pleasure of displeasing has for the most part evaporated.

Another change in method can be seen in the ways in which Huxley manipulates the contexts of his satiric passages. The technique of injecting a low physiological value into a high cluster of values continues, at times, to recall his old method, but since it operates in a different context it has different effects. A passage from *Eyeless in Gaza* will clarify this difference. Mark Staithes, when asked at a social gathering why he, an extreme despiser of women, earns his living as a perfume manufacturer, answers that making scent is the best way he knows to express his lack of gallantry.

> Leaning forward, he took Mary's hand, raised it as though he were about to kiss it, but, instead, only sniffed at the skin—then let it fall again. "For example," he said, "there's civet in the stuff you've scented yourself with."
>
> "Well, why not?"
>
> "Oh, no reason at all," said Staithes, "no reason at all, if you happen to have a taste for the excrement of polecats. . . . In Abyssinia . . . they have civet farms. Twice a week, you take a stick and go and poke the cats until they're thoroughly angry and frightened. That's when they secrete their stuff. Like children wetting their knickers when they're afraid. Then you catch them with a pair of tongs, so that they can't bite, and scrape out the contents of the little pouch attached to their genital organs. You do it with an egg spoon and the stuff's a kind of yellow grease, rather like ear-wax. Stinks like hell when it's undiluted. We get it in London packed in buffalo horns. Huge cornucopias full of dark brown stinking ear-wax. At a hundred and seventeen shillings the ounce, what's more. That's one of the reasons why your scent costs you so much. The poor can't afford to smear themselves with cat's mess. They have to be content with plain isoeugenol and phenyl acetic aldehyde."

This passage uses Huxley's familiar technique; a configuration of images is distorted and devalued by the insertion of images with lower values. But here, as in the earlier passages, we are faced with a satiric ambiguity; no specific victim of the satiric thrust is clearly

implied. The target seems to be the image, the entire *Gestalt,* of re-
fined female eroticism; but, on second thought, the character of the
speaker, Staithes, seems to be the target. Both, in such satiric passages, receive the force of the devaluation. It is difficult or impossible
to decide which is *the* victim, and as a result we often have an un-
resolvable tension. But in *Eyeless in Gaza* we find certain clues, certain implied judgments about Staithes's character which prompt us
to take his comments as self-satire. Physiological and scatological
imagery follows Staithes throughout the book; it is his identifying
leitmotiv. His actions and the expressions on his face are consistently
described in scientifically physical terms. He does not smile, he
"demonstrates the anatomy of a smile," and he vigorously contracts
the "sphincters" at the corners of his eyes and mouth. Many of his
speeches are grossly scatological—his description of his family, for
example: they are "turds to the core. . . . So they can't think anything but turdish thoughts. And above all, they can't conceive of
anyone else thinking differently. Turd calls to turd; and, when it's
answered by nonturd, it's utterly at a loss." Staithes, then, is the
anatomical and scatological satirist in the novel; for the most part
Huxley's anatomical vision operates only through this one character.
Few of the others speak this way, and Huxley, as narrator, seldom
employs the technique on his own. He employs it through the mask
of Staithes. The satire, though still ambiguous and unresolved, is to
an extent more clearly directed backward against the speaker. Huxley has taken steps to make the reader understand that the physiological satirist satirizes himself.

Similar passages occur in *After Many a Summer* and *Time Must
Have a Stop.* In the former, Jeremy Pordage is the sophisticated
cynic who employs the physiological technique; and, like Staithes,
he is clearly an object of satire himself. In the later book it is Eustace
Barnack who becomes the victim of his own satiric monologues. In
these books we are still faced with satiric ambiguity, with dual-
directed satire; but the passages are managed so as to emphasize the
point that the satirist has satirized, not only his victim, but also himself. This is *Tendenz Witz,* in Freud's convenient term, with a vi-
cious boomerang quality, with a tendency in two directions at the
same time. To an extent, then, Huxley in his later books continues
to use his old technique, but in using it he takes steps to dissociate
himself from it. By emphasizing the reverse tendency of the technique he has found a way to retain an old method while renouncing
the mental structures upon which it is based.

We should see this as a crucial maneuver in Huxley's late fiction. He feels the need to avoid the implications of his former characteristic methods and yet he cannot entirely avoid the methods themselves. Apparently, the implication of the anatomical vision which he is most anxious to renounce is the idea that physiological phenomena are necessarily ignoble, obscene and hilarious. His kind of mysticism required a different evaluation of flesh from the old quasi-Manichaean concepts which seemed to underlie his early work. True spiritual enlightenment, he suggests, can be obtained not by ignoring or hating the body, but by learning to use it more sensibly. In most of Huxley's later novels and essays we are given to understand that the Divine Ground can be reached only through certain physical exercises and disciplines. Before one can alter the state of one's soul one must alter the state of one's body. In *Eyeless in Gaza* Anthony Beavis embarks on a course of spiritual exercises in how to sit, stand, breathe, and walk. He is taught by his friend Miller that intestinal poisoning induced by too much meat is the cause of negativism, despair, and the impulse toward violence. So he becomes a vegetarian and subjects himself to daily colonic irrigations, and eventually emerges as a soul in direct contact with the Divine Ground. In several of Huxley's later books we discover that the lower intestines are of paramount importance to the state of one's spirit—more so, in fact, than any other parts of the body. In *After Many a Summer*, Dr. Obispo and the Fifth Earl of Hauberk conclude that immortality can be obtained by altering the sterol chemistry of the lower digestive system. The dismal fact that this chemical alteration also causes the immortal one to lose his humanity and to become an ape emphasizes the point that physiology determines spiritual and intellectual levels. "Matter over mind" is also the implication of certain passages in *The Devils of Loudun*. In this historical study we discover that seventeenth-century nuns possessed by devils were "cured" by means of public enemas forcibly administered, with holy water and syringes shaped like crucifixes. In most cases this treatment discouraged a sufficient number of devils to be called a stunning success.

Huxley's two books on psychedelic drugs, *The Doors of Perception* and *Heaven and Hell,* suggest a similar concept of the interrelatedness of soul and body. When he discovered that certain easily obtainable drugs, like mescaline and lysergic acid, created a state analogous to the mystic's trance, he became interested, experimented with them, and recorded his experiences. The drugs appear to reduce the oxygen content of the blood, thus eventually reducing the conscious efficiency of the brain. Since the brain is among other things a filtering organism which rejects sensations, perceptions, and thoughts irrelevant to survival or practical interest, the decrease in efficiency frees the mind from its quotidian affairs and allows it to receive intuitions of "ultimate reality." (So, at least, goes the theory as Huxley states it in the middle 1950's; its scientific validity is less important here than the fact that it was what Huxley considered the most reasonable approach to the drugs.) These drugs, however, are significant not only because they provide us with the means to spiritual experiences, but also because they suggest explanations for the widespread mystical experiences of the past. It has been found, Huxley notes, that a chemical almost identical to mescaline can occur spontaneously, under the proper physiological conditions, in the endocrine systems of both children and adults. The spontaneous synthesis of the vision-inducing drug within the body can result from fatigue, strenuous exercise, malnutrition, or skin infections. After fasting has produced malnutrition and anemia, after flagellation has covered large areas of the body with infected sores, after the infection has released large quantities of histamine and adrenalin into the blood stream, and, finally, after periods of chanting, singing, and rhythmic incantations have reduced the supply of oxygen to the brain, the drug might occur in the endocrine system and cause the saint to see visions of eternity, the Godhead, and the Divine Ground. The implications arising from Huxley's commentary on mescaline suggest scientific sanctions for the traditional mortification of the flesh, and at the same time they suggest that mortification of the flesh is no longer necessary.

The most significant aspect of Huxley's treatment of physiological data in his later books is that, unlike the "amused pyrrhonic aesthete" of the 'twenties, he can no longer accept physiological data as satiric agents, as a means of devaluing an image. If chemistry is evoked as the operational key to religious insight, the mystic Huxley cannot consistently respond with his old derisive smirk, for he has spent most of his later years training himself to see the chemistry, the electricity, the glandular functions of the body as extraordinarily beautiful and marvelous phenomena—objective correlatives of spiritual reality. All of his spokesmen for mysticism—Miller in *Eyeless in Gaza,* Propter in *After Many a Summer,* Rontini in *Time Must Have a Stop,* and Rivers in *The Genius and the Goddess*— insist that the satiric irony which arises from the incongruity of physical and spiritual images is symptomatic of the diseased state of Western culture. They insist, further, that the enlightened individual cannot participate in that dance of negativism and despair which arises from the dislocation of man's flesh from his spirit. If we feel, with Darwinists, that man the image of God has been replaced with man the image of baboons, then we must feel not that man has been degraded but that baboons have been upgraded. Similarly, if Freudianism is correct in replacing man the rational animal with man the anal-erotic animal, then we must accept the anal-erotic animal with gratitude and delight. The constant implication of Huxley's early books is that vile flesh makes nonsense of ideals, but his mysticism purges flesh of its pejorative overtones and thus hinders its operation as a satiric agent. It can function as a *memento mori,* as an image suggesting "the body of this death" which might eventually be transcended; but it will not function in the old Baudelairean way as an allotrope of the absurdity and meaninglessness of existence.

Huxley's upgrading of the flesh might well have released him from a large measure of personal tension; it might have made him in his later years a saner and happier man; but it was a major disaster for his art. His satiric technique had depended on the connotative lowness of flesh. When, in *Point Counter Point,* he had described the development of a child from worm to fish to foetus and then had shifted to a scene fifteen years later where the ex-fish could be seen passionately engaged in a high-church confirmation ritual, the result was wickedly incisive nihilistic satire. But the later Huxley, when consistent with his new evaluation of flesh, is obliged to see the physiological fact as merely that—a fact. The mystic is forced to relinquish the aristocrat's prerogative of bad taste. Huxley's later sense of the facticity of flesh blurs and distorts his style; it creates a radical discontinuity in his work between meanings and rhetorical effects. When Huxley sets out to explore the physiological correlates of spiritual experience or other kinds of emotion, he creates against his will satiric or derisive overtones. In *Eyeless in Gaza,* for example, Miller argues that "a man thinks as he eats" and thus should avoid poisoning himself into skepticism by eating meat. Further, he says,

> Prayer makes you more yourself, more separate. Just as rump steak does. Look at the correlation between religion and diet. Christians eat meat, drink alcohol, smoke tobacco; and Christianity exalts personality, insists on the value of petitionary prayer, teaches that God feels anger and approves the persecution of heretics. It's the same with the Jews and Moslems. Kosher and an indignant Jehovah. Mut-

ton and beef—and personal survival among the houris, avenging
Allah and holy wars. . . . In the past only members of the upper
classes were thoroughly sceptical, despairing, negative. Why? Among
other reasons, because they were the only people who could afford
to eat too much meat. Now there is cheap Canterbury lamb and
Argentine chilled beef. Even the poor can afford to poison themselves into complete scepticism and despair.

Christianity and rump steak, God and guts—the result, whatever
the intention, is satire, even though we have excellent evidence that
Huxley took seriously the religious ideas that seem to receive the
force of the satire. Huxley was seriously a mystic and sincerely a
religious man, and Miller, the prophet who delivers this lecture
upon metabolic salvation, is a portrait of Gerald Heard, Huxley's
close friend and mentor in vegetarian mysticism. Miller appears in
other sections of *Eyeless in Gaza* as a modern saint; he is wise,
heroic, deeply aware of spiritual reality. He is so boringly admirable
that, like Huxley's other spokesmen for mysticism, he has been universally denounced by critics because his monologues destroy the
novel's continuity.

Huxley, then, is condemned in his later books to suffer the consequences of being misunderstood; he is condemned to be cynical
in his books even though he is not cynical in his attitudes. In his
last few years he was acutely aware of the phenomenon. In *The
Genius and the Goddess* he writes of Ruth Maarten's development
into adolescence, a period characterized by extremes of physiological
and emotional change. Her pubescence is a time of painful self-
doubt, menstruation, Swinburne, spirituality, Oscar Wilde, consti-
pation, and violent, hopeless love. "How impossibly crude our language is!" Huxley writes, in a digression from his description of
Ruth's problems:

> If you don't mention the physiological correlates of emotion, you're
> being false to the given facts. But if you do mention them, it sounds
> as though you were trying to be gross and cynical. Whether it's ten-
> derness or adoration or romantic yearning—love is always accom-
> panied by events in the nerve endings, the skin, the mucous mem-
> branes, the glandular and erectile tissues. Those who don't say so
> are liars. Those who do are labeled as pornographers. It's the fault,
> of course, of our philosophy of life; and our philosophy of life is the
> inevitable by-product of a language that separates in idea what in
> actual fact is always inseparable. It separates and at the same time it

evaluates. One of the abstractions is "good," and the other is "bad."
. . . What we need is another set of words. Words that can express
the natural togetherness of things. *Muco-spiritual,* for example, or
dermato-charity. . . . Why not viscerosophy? But translated, of
course, out of the indecent obscurity of a learned language into something you could use in everyday speech or even in lyrical poetry.
How hard it is, without those still nonexistent words, to discuss so
simple and obvious a case as Ruth's.

In the context of Huxley's plea for objectivity, it is particularly illuminating to note the responses of reviewers to *The Genius and the
Goddess.* Most of them found in it a disturbingly cynical and coarse
attack on the ideals of Western culture, filled with gratuitous strokes
of destructive satire; and one was moved to indignation by what he
understood as Huxley's fondness for "slapping the reader once again
with the stinking fish of puritanism." A critic for the Manchester
Guardian put it more mildly: "Nor does the narrator, who speaks
with all the paradoxes and physiological imagery of Mr. Huxley's
early works, seem to have persuaded himself out of the heresy of the
Manichees for all his talk of the need to transcend the duality of
body and soul." These comments, among many others, emphasize
the impossible stylistic situation that the late Huxley found himself
in. Against his best efforts—and even against his direct statements
to the contrary—his books persisted in saying things that he did not
wish to say.

In *The Perennial Philosophy,* Huxley diagnoses the problem: a
writer is "to some extent the victim of his own literary talents. *Le
style c'est l'homme.* No doubt. But the converse is also partly true.
L'homme c'est le style. Because we have a gift for writing in a certain way we find ourselves, in some sort, becoming our way of writing. We mould ourselves in the likeness of our particular brand of
eloquence." Huxley's talent is for a kind of art which depends for its
intrinsic value and extrinsic effect on a mode of consciousness that
he no longer finds acceptable. In his later books he is thus forced
often into a style for which he has no particular talent, the style of
the calm, professorial, deeply committed spokesman for an idea. His
efforts to be seriously and sincerely informative about the mystic's
way to salvation produce long sermons that are pedantic, dry, and
almost unreadable. Some commentators on Huxley's late works
maintain that they fail because they move too far in the direction
of the essay; but this point is not, it seems to me, a particularly

important one, for Huxley had in his early period also loaded his novels with generalizations about life. The primary difference is one of style; the ideas in his early books are largely negative and thus harmonize with the negativistic implications of his anatomical vision, but the later, affirmative ideas demand a style with affirmative implications, and that kind of writing is foreign to Huxley's literary personality. The stylistic failure of *Island,* Huxley's last novel, is an excellent case in point. More than any of his later works *Island* is purged of the dualistic irony characteristic of his best novels; his efforts to be entirely positive in this utopian antithesis to *Brave New World* render the book almost entirely devoid of esthetic value. The facts of the book are these: he could not write a "positive" utopian fantasy in the style of his best works; he could not write an esthetically coherent and balanced work in any other style; and, ergo, he could not make *Island* both "positive" and effective. One suspects that the novel took so long to write—more than six years, despite the fact that it contains little if anything his readers had not seen in others forms before—primarily because it was clearly a hopeless task. Hopeless and—to Huxley perhaps as much as to most readers —uninteresting and pedestrian.

Huxley, then, suffered the misfortune of outgrowing his own technique. He changed his view of the world, the flesh, and himself, but he was unable to find a style suitable to the new attitudes. The pleasures of *mauvais goût* clash violently with the mystic's insight, but the style charged with the spirit of *mauvais goût* was the only one available to him. During his last quarter-century of writing Huxley tried a number of strategies for solving this dilemma: he shifted his anatomical emphasis from the absurd and comic to the painful and horrible, he limited the satiric use of physiological imagery to specific personae in an attempt to dissociate himself from it, he made direct appeals to his readers to take the flesh-spirit mergers seriously, and, in ever increasing instances, he abandoned the ineluctably ironic anatomical vision in favor of bluntly direct sincerity. The result was in most cases disunity and esthetic incoherence. The discontinuity between his attitudes and the implications of his techniques prevented him from achieving a synthesis of that vast wit and brilliance of his early books with the spiritual affirmations implicit in his later ones. Satire in most of its traditional literary manifestations has made a synthesis of one kind or another between the militantly destructive and the morally constructive—in a word, between outrage and moral outrage. Huxley has been in his career both outrageous and morally affirmative; the only difficulty is that he was never able, like the great satirists of the past, to be both at the same time.

Huxley as Biographer: *Grey Eminence* and *The Devils of Loudun*

by Harold H. Watts

Separated by eleven years—*Grey Eminence* appeared in 1941 and *The Devils of Loudun* in 1952—are two works of Huxley's that are in a class by themselves, or appear to be at first inspection. Unlike the novels, they are accounts of events that actually happened rather than calculated manipulations of Huxley's own experience of his era. Unlike the utopias, *Brave New World* and *Ape and Essence,* they represent an attempt to read aright sections of the real past rather than to arouse shudders in the presence of an imagined future. And unlike many of the essays, the two biographies represent a prolonged and careful discipline of study rather than brilliant insight stimulated by a leafing through of Goya's *Desastres de la Guerra,* a contemplation of the Breughels in Vienna, or a visit to Sabbioneta,[1] a planned town in Italy.

This contrast offered by *Grey Eminence* and *The Devils of Loudun* is real. They are studies of seventeenth-century French religion and politics. By length at least they are even set apart from other instructive studies of sections of the past, like the essays on the religious charlatan, the Reverend Henry James Prince; on the French philosopher, Maine de Biran; on the Italian composer Gesualdo; and on the twentieth-century American Socialist, Job Harriman.[2]

"Huxley as Biographer: *Grey Eminence* and *The Devils of Loudun*" [editor's title] by Harold H. Watts. From *Aldous Huxley* (New York: Twayne Publishers, Inc., 1969) chapter 6 [originally "Two Biographies"]. Copyright © 1969 by Twayne Publishers, Inc. Reprinted by permission of the author and publisher.

1 "Variations on Goya" appears in *Themes and Variations* (1950). "Breughel" and "Sabbioneta" are included in *Along the Road* (1925).

2 The essay dealing with Prince is entitled "Justifications" and appears in *The Olive Tree* (1936). Maine de Biran is the subject of "Variations on a Philosopher" in *Themes and Variations* (1950). Harriman's story is told in "Ozymandias, the Utopia that Failed." This essay and "Gesualdo: Variations on a Musical Theme" appear in *Tomorrow and Tomorrow and Tomorrow* (1956) (English title: *Adonis and the Alphabet*).

But like these shorter studies, the two biographies manifest an attitude toward the past that one should expect of Huxley. The past, for him, does not so much exist as an object worthy of study in its own right but is an opportunity to recognize some moral or esthetic disease or disorder that works unrecognized in some section of the present. He continues, in these long books, the sort of inspection that one encounters in an early essay like "Comfort," [3] in which the study of the Renaissance taste for space and grandeur allows a more just estimate of the modern taste for coziness. The art of such an essay lies in taking up a subject, establishing a contrast that creates a startling but justifiable *aperçu*, and then quickly concluding. In *Grey Eminence* and *The Devils of Loudun,* Huxley does not conclude.

Instead, Huxley pushes in these two books his investigation of a selected section of the past to some length. He sustains his dogged analysis of the meaning of two segments of seventeenth-century experience as, of course, he has no need to do in an essay like the one on the seventeenth-century Italian composer Gesualdo. But in the two heroes of the biographies he finds just the sort of oddity that challenged him more briefly in the experience of Gesualdo, a man whose passional and religious experience contained the sort of quaint abnormality to which Huxley's attention veers as readily as a weathercock in a sudden breeze. Gesualdo killed his faithless wife and her lover; and, in a picture that his late-blooming piety caused to be painted, he had himself represented as rising to the heavenly embrace of Christ while his dead wife and her paramour endured the torments of hell in a lower corner of the picture.[4] This piquant detail is not alien in its preposterousness to the deformations of the religious experience which drew Huxley to Père Urbain Grandier, the hero of *The Devils of Loudun,* and to Père Joseph du Tremblay, the subject of *Grey Eminence.*

Yet, contrasts admitted, striking relations between these two books and Huxley's other work exist. As a biographer, he remembers and uses skills he acquired as a novelist and an essayist. He is an historian who, more often than most professional historians, suspends the onward march of event to compose paragraphs and even chapters of discursive analysis of the meaning, the sheer human sense or nonsense, of the events that he has just been relating.[5] He exercises,

---

3 "Comfort" appears in the collection of essays entitled *Proper Studies* (1927).
4 *Tomorrow and Tomorrow and Tomorrow* (New York, 1956), pp. 273f.
5 See the long chapter, "The Religious Background" (iii), which interrupts

in such passages, the essayist's prerogative to intersperse a narrative with circling elaborations that alter the shape of an event from what it apparently was to what it is or may be. And it is a novelist's prerogative to go beyond explicit evidence and to fill it out as the source materials do not—all with the intent of giving the richness of folly, misery, and acutest suffering not supplied by crumbling documents.

An analysis of the two books quickly indicates that Huxley goes beyond the work of sober historical reconstruction which, at many points, they do indeed contain. On his work of reconstruction Huxley erects a thesis. Perceptions are not followed up simply because they have come to an author rich in ingenuity; they are explored as part of the unfolding of the chosen thesis. The grotesque ceases to be esteemed for its own amusing sake. (Such soberness is not habitual with Huxley. One recalls that no tears are shed for the idiotic Miss Elver in *Those Barren Leaves* and that only an amused stare is offered the victims of a nineteenth-century religious impostor in the essay entitled "Justifications." [6]) In the two biographies, Huxley's pleasure in dazzling himself and others with the lightning of his own perceptions is in abeyance. Rather do both biographies participate in the elaboration of theses that dominate Huxley's mind from the mid-1930's onward—theses that receive a more general treatment in *Ends and Means, The Perennial Philosophy,* and other books.

It is with *The Perennial Philosophy* that the two biographies are most closely linked. *The Perennial Philosophy*—useful also for understanding *Time Must Have a Stop* and other later novels—is an exposition of the synthesis Huxley has made from his mental travels in many directions: in the regions of science, esthetics, and literature, and in the widespread terrain of mystical experience. The two biographies mine the past to demonstrate the soundness of the convictions arrived at in *The Perennial Philosophy.*

The convictions, briefly, are these. The redemption of man rests not on ritual observance or orthodoxy, not on conscious pursuit of suffering in an imitation of a savior named Jesus. Instead, redemption comes from a radical reorientation of human awareness that renders a future kingdom of heaven unnecessary and dogmas about a transcendent deity an irrelevance. The reorientation also trans-

---

the biographical presentation in *Grey Eminence.* Chap. iii in *The Devils of Loudun* is devoted to a similar inspection of the seventeenth-century forms of religious knowledge and activity.

6 *The Olive Tree,* p. 174.

forms one's estimate of whatever has seemed important in "the world"; much that has seemed important—politics, physical pleasure, or knowledge *per se*—moves to the periphery of attention or beyond it. For at the center of attention lies an incommunicable awareness of a new relationship to a principle of unity that binds together all experience. This awareness, rather than the death of a divine-human savior on a cross, redeems distressed and distracted men.

Huxley, in illustration of this crucial point, remarks of the inacceptable mysticism of Bérulle, a seventeenth-century teacher of the arts of religious meditation:

> Bérulle no doubt sincerely believed that the soul could adhere to the Incarnate Word or to the Virgin in exactly the same way as it could adhere to God, and with the same consequences. But, psychologically, this is impossible. There cannot be adherence to persons or personal qualities without analysis and imagination; and where analysis and imagination are active, the mind is unable to receive into itself the being of God.[7]

Bérulle and all religious teachers who try to center the deepest mystical experience on a suffering savior or a weeping Mother are setting up a discipline of an inferior order. The most Huxley will concede of such a path is that "It was a path that would lead them [the pupils] to virtue. . . . It was also a path that would lead them to intense, affective devotion to divine persons, and to untiring activity on their behalf. But it was not a path that would lead to union with ultimate reality."[8] Ultimate reality, as Huxley has learned to think of it—learned chiefly from Eastern instructors—lies beyond the personality of any nameable being, no matter how august.

Both *Grey Eminence* and *The Devils of Loudun* are negative demonstrations of this truth. Both books—implicitly in the tales which Huxley resurrects from the past and explicitly in the full commentary he provides—show the cost in misery and the sadness of neglected possibilities that come from faulty estimates of man's position. *Grey Eminence* is the more thoroughgoing demonstration; it concerns a protagonist who has the truth in his grasp (or nearly) and thinks that he can go on reaching for other things—power in particular. In contrast, *The Devils of Loudun* is chiefly concerned with persons who have little inkling that they have missed their

---

7 *Grey Eminence*, p. 97.
8 *Ibid.*

chance to live fully, to achieve a relation with unity that underlies diverse, discontinuous human experience. For Huxley, of course, this unity is a deity without face or form and cannot flatter man's interest in his individual existence. Like the Divine of the four-teenth-century German mystics, or the Principle venerated by the Gnostics, or the nullity at the heart of much Hindu and Buddhist spirituality, Huxley's One is without face or form, or qualities of any kind.

I *The Devils of Loudun*

The dramatis personae of the two books overlap. The hero of the second book, the rash and worldly Père Urbain Grandier of *The Devils of Loudun,* has the misfortune to add to his local troubles the antipathy of Richelieu and Richelieu's "grey eminence," Père Joseph.[9] A more important overlapping than this one is the fact that the two books share a background: France in the first half of the seventeenth century, recovering from the civil warfare of the previous century.

This warfare was in part occasioned by the confusions created in France and elsewhere by the Protestant Reformation and the Cath-olic Counter Reformation. Added to this change was the difficulty caused in France by disputes about the royal succession. Under Richelieu, power was being centered in the throne, at the expense of the nobles; the king of France and his ministers needed this power to challenge the Austrian and Spanish forces that surrounded them. In particular, the international problems that created and protracted the Thirty Years' War in Germany bulk large in *Grey Eminence*; these demanded the attention of Richelieu and his aide, the Capuchin monk Joseph du Tremblay. Less concerned with these inclusive matters is *The Devils of Loudun*; at the fore in this book are the perverted religious sensibilities of the time.

But both books, whatever their contrasts in range, drive toward the main point which is Huxley's concern: the mystery of man's re-jection of his great opportunity—the chance to be aware of the divine unity, and to unite himself with that unity by prayer and meditation. Both books are tragedies if, indeed, it be a tragedy to fail to be a saint. Huxley's estimate of what it is to be a saint differs from the traditional Catholic one, as he points out especially in

[9] *The Devils of Loudun,* pp. 167f.

Grey Eminence. The conventional Catholic saint of recent centuries turns toward the specific figures of the Christian pantheon—particularly toward Jesus and Mary. These figures, revere them as one may, are barriers to the "Clear Light" that shines for the mystic who is free—as some Catholic mystics are not—of devotion to adored, specific figures and of dogmas with which orthodox mystical experience has to be aligned.

Huxley remarks that an older group of Christian mystics—those who followed Dionysian traditions—"had adapted dogma to their own experience, with the result that, in so far as they were advanced mystics, they had ceased to be specifically Catholic." The possession of such liberty is crucial for the mystic; to see the importance of this freedom is to grasp what Huxley has in mind whenever he speaks of spiritual fulfillment and ultimate reality. Only such freedom "provides the basis for a religion free from unacceptable dogmas, which themselves are contingent upon ill established and arbitrarily interpreted historical facts." [10]

This important passage—important for understanding the concern that animates much of Huxley's later work—casts light on Huxley's recurring impatience with Christianity long after he has ceased to be cavalier toward religion in general. The truly wise person is—must be—that person who moves beyond his devotion to Jesus and Mary. Instead, he seeks a relation with the immanent unity that informs every nook and cranny of the universe; this latter principle is simply waiting to be known, to be united with, by the man or woman who achieves a transformation of his own awareness.

Serving this insight, Huxley fashions two cautionary tales. The essential point of these tales is not different from that advanced in *Time Must Have a Stop* (1944), where the man who dies, Eustace Barnack, experiences the tragedy of being earthbound, of realizing that his sensuality has inhibited insights that go beyond the raptures provided by a pretty Florentine woman. Grandier's failure in *The Devils of Loudun* is that of a man who, despite his priestly calling, was hardly aware of the opportunities he was bypassing. Père Joseph's failure is, as Huxley reads it, more moving and horrifying. For Père Joseph was, as a young man, a person who had felt a call to the spiritual life; whereas Grandier, handsome and talented and yet relatively obscure, had regarded the church as a stage where his talents could be displayed and as an avenue which often led to the bedchambers of lovely penitents.

[10] *Grey Eminence*, p. 92.

The Devils of Loudun, then, is primarily a brilliant study in what might be called religious morbid psychology—morbid because the book is concerned with a great many persons who misunderstand the opportunities that various religious vocations offer them. There is the morbidity of Grandier, who easily dismissed from his mind the implications of the religion he served—dismissed them until it was almost too late, until he was broken on the rack and tied to the metal seat where he would be burned to death. The perversion of Grandier is horrifying enough, but not really a strain on the reader's powers of understanding. The history of religion is full of persons who answer the call of Christ as if it summoned one to a profession little more demanding than the iron-mongery and the contract-writing of the men of Loudun who were Grandier's enemies.

The real depths of perversity, of religion gone awry, are reached by the Ursuline nuns who, following the example of their unworthy prioress, Jeanne des Anges, court demonic possession. This occult invasion of foreign wills—so the hysterical nuns believe—has its immediate origin in Grandier's evil power. The nuns are convinced that this disturbance comes ultimately from Satan himself and not, as one might say today, from levels of the unconscious. With a relish that the reader must recognize, Huxley describes the contortions that the poor ladies undergo. With a relentless attention (not new to the readers of his fiction) Huxley traces the effects of the frustrated sexuality and religious ignorance that keep the convent in an uproar and transform it into an equivalent of the sword-swallower's booth at a fair.

But Huxley's contempt for the nuns and for Grandier is more qualified than it is in early novels where, for example, the self-deception of the "Franciscan" Burlap, in *Point Counter Point,* wins nothing but laughter because it is so obviously beyond the pale of common sense. The hysteria of the nuns and the complacent pursuit of sensuality and power on the priest's part are *not* beyond the pale. Instead, the failure of Mère Jeanne des Anges and the self-deception of the handsome priest are representative of the failures that men in all centuries encounter. The nuns and the priest are immersed in folly—true. And it is folly that leads to the grotesque inconsequence of the events at Loudun—to the hysteria-induced signs of special divine favor on the hand of the Prioress (the names of Jesus, Mary, St. Joseph, and St. François de Sales appeared there and were widely exhibited by the Prioress in her travels) and to the graver waste of priestly talent. But it is not folly that can be regarded as incomprehensible, as in much of the invented folly in the Huxley novels of the 1920's. In those novels, analogous folly is just *there*, to amuse the author and his intelligent readers. The folly of *The Devils of Loudun* is, in contrast, one that illuminates the pattern of folly in modern man's own experience, though he is possessed not by devils but by more reputable causes of alienation from his proper destiny. If the reader finds Grandier's misreading of his own purposes comically stupid, what of his own?

The Devils of Loudun is Huxley's most moving book. Despite the long, essay-like sections on satanic possession and the general uncertainty man has about his purposes,[11] Huxley's account of the priest and the insane nuns moves with authority. It escapes the defects of the novels, the chief of which are random improvisation of event, and comment on event that is forced and often (for the perceptive reader) gratuitous. There is, in *The Devils of Loudun,* nothing gratuitous or forced in the chapters which tell of the appalling mental disorders that overtake the poor sisters, the exorcists who come to drive out demons and establish their own clerical reputations, and the mass of townsmen and visitors who find the writhing sisters an enchanting but horrifying spectacle. The history of the poor, contemptible Urbain Grandier moves toward the rack and the stake with an inevitability that is lacking from Huxley's accounts of human action that he, rather than life and past history, invented.

The powerful effect of this book and of the scarcely less powerful *Grey Eminence* depends not only on life and past history but on Huxley's acute perception as he looks carefully into the documents and secondary sources he works from and adds to them believable explanations (for example, his analysis of the probable motives of the exorcists, who are charmed by the opportunity to please God by exercising absolute power over the nuns).[12] It is an artistic achievement of the first order to be able to reconstitute such a person as Grandier—and Père Joseph of the other book, for that matter. One does not ask—as one reads the harrowing narrative of Grandier's last days when the belated elevation of the priest's character is played off against the sadistic righteousness of his persecutors— whether it is Huxley the novelist or Huxley the essayist who is at work. His talents, however various and quite distinguishable they may appear in other work, achieve fusion or interplay as the shat-

11 *The Devils of Loudun*, pp. 167f.
12 *Ibid.*, pp. 108–80. For a discussion of the phenomena of possession, see Louis Monden, S. J., *Signs and Wonders* (New York, 1966), pp. 164ff.

tered and repentant Urbain endures his last hours.[13] One has no great temptation to ask whether the writer is following or going beyond his documentation. Esthetically, at least, he has achieved the accents of truth.

One might say that Huxley's advantage in the two biographies is this: the inventor of the situations that challenge his skill is not himself but God or the vital force—or, as Huxley himself might say, the friction set up when primal unity falls into diversity. Huxley's main task in these two books is not that of fabricating a world; instead, his labor is the reconstitution of relationships as they had once existed. The analysis of varieties of Christian religious experience puts into play erudition and cleverness that do not (as elsewhere in Huxley) call attention to themselves. The reader is likely to agree with Huxley that Grandier's tragedy *vis à vis* that of the frantic nuns is a historical event rich in instruction—provided—a very important proviso—he is convinced of the applicability of the insight which guides Huxley as he scans these sections of human experience. This insight suggests that the tragedy of Grandier and the nuns stems from their failure to rise above the false accounts of the religious life that they had accepted.

II *Grey Eminence*

The tragedy also appears in the earlier of the two biographies, *Grey Eminence,* where it unfolds with a kind of quiet intensity. Less sensational in its substance, the life of Père Joseph is still quite interesting to one who has some degree of sympathy with Huxley's conviction that the ultimate disaster of all men lies in their failure to exploit what they are. Père Joseph, as is revealed during Huxley's unrelenting pursuit of the mysterious and enigmatic Capuchin, was not just another cleric who, like Grandier, was indifferent to the high ranges of experience that Christian mysticism offered. Grandier's choice of power and lechery was made by a man who had never given a second thought to interior prayer and to other techniques for purifying the spirit. Père Joseph, in contrast, was a man who knew full well what paths led to mystical experience and sainthood.

Moreover, he was a man who aspired to follow these paths. Yet he was—and here is the quieter but just as intense tragedy of *Grey Eminence*—able to convince himself that political intrigue on be-

---

[13] *Ibid.,* pp. 224–62.

half of France was not a path opposed to the one which Father Benet of Canfield and others had revealed to his mind in his youth.[14] A career full of double-dealing, of actions that delayed by many years the conclusion of the bloody Thirty Years' War, was not at odds with the service of God and an approach to a full union with God. Or so Père Joseph persuaded himself. But pursuits like Père Joseph's are—readers of Huxley are already aware—full of danger. As Huxley points out in *Ends and Means*[15] and elsewhere, the habit of compromise and connivance with evil may dull other faculties.

From Père Joseph's obtuseness at a crucial point comes his failure. As traced out in *Grey Eminence*, the failure is tangled with the many "necessary" comings and goings of Richelieu's "left hand" in a troubled Europe; the very arrival of the "grey eminence" could arouse fear. Père Joseph's travels, which reached from Paris to Ratisbon, Madrid, and Rome, finally produced a man who was as much a monster to himself as he was to those who feared him. He was a monster to others because of the moral evil—lies, the use of force, an indifference to suffering—to which he contributed. He was doubtless a monster to himself because he—unlike Grandier and most thoughtless workers of evil—knew rather clearly what he had turned away from: the practice of the presence of God.

One says advisedly: "he knew rather clearly." For Huxley contends that the particular mystical disciplines of prayer and meditation that Père Joseph had access to were flawed disciplines—flawed in such ways that, even if followed conscientiously, they would not allow a person to enjoy the full benefits of the "perennial philosophy." They were marred, as already noted, by the inferior instruction and guidance which he had from his early master, and by the pattern his mature life took—by the conviction that he could serve both God and Cardinal Richelieu. The "grey eminence" thought that he could "annihilate" the activities he undertook on behalf of Richelieu and France and preserve untarnished the relation to deity to which he aspired: "Given over to unannihilable activities, he came to be possessed, in spite of his daily practice of mental prayer, by a sense of bitterness and frustration. Visions, it is true, and prophetic revelations were still vouchsafed to him; but the unitive life of his early manhood was at an end; he had the dreadful certainty that God had moved away from him." [16]

14 *Grey Eminence*, pp. 60ff., 77–89.
15 *Ends and Means*, pp. 1ff.
16 *Grey Eminence*, p. 270.

Père Joseph was cut off from the "philosophy" that opens the way to a union with deity that is the same everywhere, whatever the differences among the religious structures where it takes place. Most mysticisms speak of the "emptying out" of the personality and of the culturally conditioned knowledge of the seeker, of the dark night he must journey through if he is to cancel all traces of himself, all traces of his individual awareness and passionate will. Père Joseph's misfortune was to be uncritically immersed in the world which that savior and many other teachers wished to transform.

Such were the fatal errors of Père Joseph. It is useful, for a general understanding of Huxley's position, to underline the defects of a specifically *Christian* mysticism; for its errors define, in a negative way, the positive vision of what human powers can accomplish: the gospel—not new but just forgotten and overlooked in the twentieth century—which awaits the attention of each thoughtful man. For those who are not thoughtful, who will not listen, Huxley has no hope and, often, little sympathy. Christian mysticism had come to a focus on a deity who was an individual or had once been—an individual limited by a special history and a special time to one set of events. Branches of Christian mysticism—the mysticism, for example, expressed in the medieval treatise, *Cloud of Unknowing*—had expressed wiser insights. There is in all men a divine element of which they are unaware "because all their attention is fixed on the objects of craving and aversion. But, if they choose to 'die to self,' they can become aware of the divine element within them and, in it, experience God. For those who so desire and are prepared to fulfill the necessary conditions, the transcendent can in some way become immanent within the spark, at the apex of the higher will." [17] No counsel is given here that the human soul need, in its pilgrimage, linger at the foot of a particular cross in Palestine. Instead, the soul must court apprehensions of deity that are not visualized in images or expressed in words. Imageless, wordless illumination was mysticism pure and simple; away from it would drop such an adjective as "Christian."

Thus, the fatal error of Père Joseph's directors had been to inculcate in his mind the expectation that there was a unique way that mystics who happened to live in a *Christian* world had to follow. Instead, all human beings, simply because they were indeed human or "amphibious," had warrant to commence an ascent of a spiritual

---

[17] *Ibid.*, p. 62.

Mt. Carmel—a mountain open to all men, in the same way and without qualification. In meditating on the tragic destiny of Christ, a Christian could make a useful start, just as a Buddhist might in esteeming the heroic renunciation of the Buddha when he left the forest and returned to suffering mankind. But it was when a Christian persisted in his esteem for Jesus and regarded the figure of Christ as the terminus of the mystical journey that the Christian would find himself following a path that turned upon itself and indeed never went beyond a deadening concern with a particular human personality. Concern with personality—even though it might be that of a redeemer—could only, in Shelley's phrase, "stain the white radiance of eternity." If a seeker worked in the limiting way familiar to Père Joseph, he would never win a view of the indescribable light where the spirit of man is united with the unity of which man is an apparently diverse part.

Père Joseph never learned the real meaning of Jesus' utterance: "My Father is greater than I." [18] For Père Joseph, Jesus was a continuing model. Devoted to this model, Père Joseph never learned that there was a source of being and inspiration that was unstained by the marks of human personality—a source better than a god who became man, better even than a god who was a father to all mankind, for that god was concerned with the infinite value not only of the localized personality of his son, but also of the localized personalities and special histories of each created being who was only human. Gods who were saviors and gods who were fathers were but modes of apprehending deity and could serve as early milestones on the mystic's way. They were milestones that existed to be passed by and quite forgotten as one journeyed toward a deity to whom it would be an impiety to attribute human personality or, even, fatherly concern. The goal of the successful mystic was union with the superb indifference and the superb undiscussibility of a divine principle. Having reached the goal, the successful mystic could look back with sorrowing condescension at a mystic manqué like Père Joseph and at the order of Calvarian nuns which he founded to pray eternally at the foot of a cross. One could only smile sadly at the "grey eminence" and his nuns, wrestling with their all too human impressions as they kept their eyes resolutely fixed on the pierced hands and feet of a suffering god.

[18] John 14:28.

III   Estimates

In conclusion, one can say of *Grey Eminence* and *The Devils of Loudun* that they are works in which Huxley chanced upon tasks that brought his wide-ranging concerns into a steady focus that allows one to see a relation among attitudes that elsewhere in Huxley's work are not clearly connected with each other. Elsewhere, the popularization of knowledge, satire, moralism—the drive to be an enlightener of man and more than just a novelist or an essayist—point beyond themselves and what they actually achieve. In *Grey Eminence* and *The Devils of Loudun* one sees what they point to.

In other works Huxley is often too much involved in "politics" as was Père Joseph. By "politics," of course, is meant more than the usual sense of the word; it includes the distractions of ambition and "image" that a novelist must be concerned with. But for once, in the two biographies, Huxley moves singularly free of the cleverness, facetiousness, and misplaced erudition that are the signs of his particular immersion in imperfect existence.

In the remaining work of Huxley there is much to admire. There is much more that is typical, with the familiar blend of merit and defect. But in that work there is nothing which reaches the eloquence, sincerity, and justice of many passages that, in *Grey Eminence* and *The Devils of Loudun,* recreate destinies which, until Huxley touched them, were objects of only antiquarian interest.

Vision and Symbol in
Aldous Huxley's *Island*

by Donald J. Watt

In their own soil those acres found
The sunlight of a flowering weed;
For still there sleeps in every ground
Some grain of mustard seed.

Aldous Huxley's last printed poem, "The Yellow Mustard" (1945), is an epitome of what he envisions as the process of salvation. As the poem opens, Huxley describes an expressionist landscape where fields are "Cabined beneath low vaults of cloud. . . . Like one wrapt living in his shroud,/Who stifles silently." The scene is like a "silent tomb" walled in by "Grey mountain-heaps of slag and stone." Through this dreary setting, "this emblem of a mind/Dark with repinings," wanders the discouraged poet. But, surprisingly, a "sudden glory" catches his eye, "As though a single, conquering ray/ Had rent the cloudy sky." The "miracle of light" transfigures "that dull plain" into "one luminous field." Oddly, though, the poet observes that the clouds above are unbroken: "No loophole in the living air/Had let the glory through." The field of the mind, as it were, has found sunlight in its own soil: "For still there sleeps in every ground/Some grain of mustard seed." The crux of the poem is the realization that illumination comes from within. The grain of mustard seed represents that seed of goodness and insight which, Huxley insists, lies buried within the dark ground of individual consciousness. The way to enlightenment consists, not of some remote visitation from the sky, from outside the self, but rather of tilling the soil of one's individual soul. Salvation, Huxley's poem suggests, is a process of inward vision.

"Vision and Symbol in Aldous Huxley's *Island*" by Donald J. Watt. From *Twentieth Century Literature* 14 (1968): pp. 149–60. Reprinted by permission of the author and the editor of *Twentieth Century Literature*.

Island (1962), Huxley's last novel, presents as many facets of his comprehensive vision for man and community as he was able to commit to print before his death in 1963. Julian Huxley recently revealed that his brother regarded *Island* "as one of his major contributions to serious thought, and he was saddened and upset by the incomprehension of so many of its reviewers."[1] The book is Huxley's solemn and, in many ways, unique remedy for psychic atrophy and the specter of the bomb in the world of the 1960's. Huxley remarks on *Island*:

> It's a kind of fantasy, a kind of reverse *Brave New World*, about a society in which real efforts are made to realize human potentialities. I want to show how humanity can make the best of both Eastern and Western worlds. So the setting is an imaginary island between Ceylon and Sumatra, at a meeting place of Indian and Chinese influence.[2]

Huxley conducts his probe toward an ideal society through a mixture of description and symbolism which culminates, as in *Eyeless in Gaza*, with an account of a visionary experience by the newly converted hero. I should like in the present article to describe some of the leading principles of Huxley's ideal community and to explore the implications of the book's major symbols in an attempt to sketch his final approach to the problem of existence in the modern world.

Plainly, *Island* is less a novel as such than any of Huxley's other novels. It is rather in the tradition of books like *Gulliver's Travels, Rasselas, Erewhon* and *The Pool of Vishnu*. Huxley's perfunctory attitude toward art in the later novels stems from his notion that art is not an end in itself: "By itself, art can never be completely redemptive. It can only point in the direction from which redemption comes."[3] In fine, art for Huxley became secondary to vision. Like Orwell in *1984* and Bradbury in *Fahrenheit 451*, Huxley had already recorded, in *Brave New World* and *Ape and Essence*, his alarming visions of potential counter-Utopias. Now, in *Island*, Hux-

---

[1] *Aldous Huxley 1894–1963: A Memorial Volume*, ed. Julian Huxley (New York, 1965), p. 24. Mrs. Laura Archera Huxley's recently published book about her late husband, *This Timeless Moment: A Personal View of Aldous Huxley* (New York, 1968), confirms Julian Huxley's remark: "Aldous was appalled . . . at the fact that what he wrote in *Island* was not taken seriously" (p. 308). Mrs. Huxley's memoir includes much information helpful in understanding *Island*, especially her comments on dianetics and the "Art of Dying," two aspects of Huxley's vision which I do not discuss in detail in this essay.

[2] *Writers at Work: The "Paris Review" Interviews* (second series; New York, 1963), p. 198.

[3] *Themes and Variations* (New York, 1950), p. 120.

ley outlines his Utopian ideals. The plot of *Island*, consequently, is
bare, clearly a simple vehicle for expressing Huxley's thought. Will
Farnaby comes to Pala posing as an innocent traveler but secretly
hoping to obtain a contract for rights to the island's rich oil re-
serves. Farnaby, whom Huxley calls "the serpent in the garden," [4]
forms an underhanded alliance with forces within and without
Pala, even at the price of aiding and abetting the destruction of its
Utopian community. While waiting for the seeds of his plot to
ripen, however, Farnaby becomes more and more interested in the
Palanesian way of life. Farnaby is "the man who won't take yes
for an answer" [5] but, exposed to the radiant happiness, goodness
and affirmation of Pala's inhabitants, he succumbs to their benevo-
lence. Unfortunately, just as Farnaby is converted to Pala's mode of
existence, military forces from neighboring Rendang seize the island
and snuff out the ideal community. As Huxley noted while composing the novel, "I'm afraid it must end with paradise lost—if one is to
be realistic." [6] The main point of the plot, then, is to introduce
through Farnaby's guided tour of Pala a means of describing an
ideal society.

To begin with, Huxley's fairly complex vision stems from his conviction that any operative ideal would have to be based on a syncretic approach to the problem of existence. The need for an active
synthesis of many diverse elements is one of the fundamental tenets
of later Huxleyan thought: "Our disease has a mutliplicity of co-
operating causes and is not to be cured except by a multiplicity of
co-operating remedies." [7] Nurse Appu Radha stresses the need for a
multiplicity of remedies in *Island* in her recital of the rhyme in
Chapter VI:

> "I" am a crowd, obeying as many laws
> As it has members. Chemically impure
> Are all "my" beings. There's no single cure
> For what can never have a single cause (p. 76).

---

4 *Interviews,* p. 199.
5 *Island* (New York, 1962), p. 18. This and subsequent references in the text are
to the Harper and Brothers first edition.
6 *Interviews,* p. 199.
7 *Brave New World Revisited* (New York, 1958), p. 106. Huxley had insisted
on a syncretic approach in *Ends and Means:* "The remedy for social disorder
must be sought simultaneously in many different fields. . . . We shall never succeed in changing our age of iron into an age of gold until we give up our ambi-
tions to find a single cause for all our ills" (New York, 1937), pp. 10, 16.

In the 1950's Huxley expands that "minimum working hypothesis" of Sebastian in *Time Must Have a Stop* into a more inclusive vision of simultaneous reforms. Huxley provides a clue to his expanding idealism in *Tomorrow and Tomorrow and Tomorrow* (1956):

> If you were able to combine Jung with F. W. H. Myers, and if you were then to enrich the product with the theories of Tantrik Buddhism and the practices of Zen, you would have a working hypothesis capable of explaining most, perhaps indeed all, the unutterably odd facts of human experience and, along with the hypothesis, a set of operational procedures by means of which its unlikelier elements might be verified.[8]

Among the varieties of Eastern mysticism, Mahayanist thought especially offered to Huxley an attractive religious base on which to erect a correlated synthesis.

Huxley was evidently among the first of his critics to recognize that the mystical way of life could easily devolve into pure escapism. In the 1950's he appears to have discovered a type of mysticism which insisted on involvement rather than detachment. In *Tomorrow and Tomorrow and Tomorrow* Huxley declares that "enlightenment is not for the Quietists or Puritans who, in their different ways, deny the world, but for those who have learned to accept and transfigure it" (p. 170). Huxley distinguishes carefully the two main traditions of Hindu philosophy: the ancient Hinayana tradition, which taught total renunciation of the world and the quest for perpetual Nirvana; and the more recent Mahayanist tradition, which sought awakening through a responsible if delicate recognition of the world. In *The Devils of Loudun* Huxley protests: "For the Bodhisattva, according to the Mahayanist tradition, the world obliterating ecstasies of the Hinayanist Sravaka are not realization, but barriers to realization." [9] In Chapter VI of *Island*, Huxley emphasizes the notion that his religion accepts the phenomenal world in Ranga's explanation of the essential principle of Tantrik Buddhism:

> "If you're a Tantrik, you don't renounce the world or deny its values; you don't try to escape into a Nirvana apart from life. . . .

---

[8] New York, p. 134. In *Proper Studies* Huxley announced that Jung seemed to him the most gifted of contemporary psychologists, whose "books on psychological types and on the unconscious are works of cardinal importance. . . . By comparison with Jung, most other psychologists seem either uninspired, unilluminating, and soundly dull, or else, like Freud and Adler, monomaniacal" (New York, 1928), p. xviii.

[9] New York, 1952, p. 70.

No, you accept the world, and you make use of it; you make use of everything that happens to you, of all the things you see and hear and taste and touch, as so many means to your liberation from the prison of yourself" (p. 85).

One of the basic notions of recent Mahayanist teachings, bitterly contested by the older school, is the theory that anyone seeking true enlightenment must remain involved with the world: "The Mahayana stresses the necessity to help the world rather than merely abandon it, thus adding a touch of humanity and emotional warmth to the cold and stern doctrine of the Elders." [10] In its tolerance and flexibility, Mahayana offers enlightenment not only to the monk in isolation but to the layman in society as well. That branch of Eastern thought which Huxley pursued left him intellectual elbow-room to satisfy both his mystical and reformative urges. By its insistence on the power of contemplation, Mahayana exalts the individual capable of uniting with the Divine Ground. By its refusal to retreat from the world, it invites the concerned critic to attempt to improve the conditions of humanity. Such a philosophy offered Huxley a foundation upon which to correlate his ideals in a number of areas into a theoretically operative synthesis aimed at creating the good rather than the great society.

One of Huxley's strongest ideals promoted in *Island* is the desire that Western and Oriental worlds accept and learn from each other. Farnaby asks if the teachers of the West could learn what Pala has learned. " 'Why not,' " replies Mrs. Narayan in Chapter XIII, " 'no change except that God would have to be thought of as immanent and man would have to be thought of as potentially self-transcendent' " (p. 258). The founders of modern Pala, the Scottish doctor and the Old Raja, joined forces to make the best of both worlds. As a result, Pala adopts English culture and the English language, but practices the Buddhist religion and the Oriental art of living. Like Rabindrath Tagore, Huxley believed as early as in *Proper Studies* (1928) that, "Compared with Western science, Western politics and morals are rudimentary" (p. 116). In *Island* the Palanese wholeheartedly exploit the achievements of Western technology, but they derive their ethical standards from the East. The question of politics and government is treated rather vaguely. The island has a figurehead Rani, but internal affairs seem to be conducted by a core of policy-making wise men and administrators. The merger between

10 Erik Zürcker, *Buddhism* (New York, 1962), p. 40.

East and West in *Island* is not defined exhaustively. Like most sweeping ideals, it eludes complete description. But the direction of the union is toward a Tagorist synthesis of Western progress with Eastern spirituality.

An area in which such a merger appeared to Huxley eminently possible and desirable is that of psycho-sexual relationships between man and woman. In the "Epilogue" to *The Devils of Loudun* Huxley writes of a type of love idealized in India:

> In India there is a Tantrik yoga, based upon an elaborate psycho-physiological technique, whose purpose is to transform the downward self-transcendence of elementary sexuality into an upward self-trans-cendence. In the West the nearest equivalent to these Tantrik prac-tices was the sexual discipline devised by John Humphrey Noyes and practiced by members of the Oneida Community (p. 324).

Pala's answer to slums and over-population is contraception and "maithuna," the yoga of love. Maithuna is Pala's name for what the Oneidans called Male Continence, a form of *coitus reservatus*. The Huxley version, though, exalts the method by adding "dhyana" or contemplation to the process. The point appears to be that the aware-ness in the sexual act is what turns the relation into yoga. For those who may not care for maithuna, Pala's government distributes Wes-tern mass-produced contraceptives which are, says Radha in Chapter VI, " 'like education—free, tax-supported and, though not compul-sory, as nearly as possible universal' " (p. 95). In *Brave New World Revisited* (1958) Huxley warns that the new age will not be the Space Age, but the Age of Over-Population. The result of the Pala-nese program, Ranga ascertains, is " 'that our population is increas-ing at less than a third of one per cent per annum. Whereas Ren-dang's increase is as big as Ceylon's—almost three per cent. And China's is two per cent, and India's about one point seven' " (p. 90). Farnaby, representing the skeptic's reaction to the doctrine, manages to see "the whole thing as reassuringly ludicrous. What shall we do to be saved? The answer is in four letters" (p. 89).

Chapter XIII of *Island* outlines Huxley's ideals in the field of edu-cation. Farnaby concurs with Menon's contention that in America boys and girls exist for mass consumption, in Russia for strengthen-ing the national state, and in China for cannon fodder. But, Menon continues, in Pala they exist for " 'actualization, for being turned into full-blown human beings' " (p. 236). Adolescents are taught not only, " 'in their psychology and physiology classes, that each one of

us has his own constitutional uniqueness,' " but also " 'to experience
their transcendental unity with all other sentient beings' " (p. 237).
The ensuing recognition of human diversity leads to a recognition
of the need for mutual forbearance and mutual forgiveness. Children are taught morality by animal analogies, compassion by erosion
analogies:

> "We shall be permitted to live on this planet only for as long as we
> treat all nature with compassion and intelligence. Elementary ecology
> leads straight to elementary Buddhism" (p. 249).

Pala teaches Elementary Practical Psychology as a method of " 'liberating you from the hauntings of your own painful memories, your
remorses, your causeless anxieties about the future' " (p. 263). The
goal of the technique, as Huxley suggests through *Eyeless in Gaza*,
is to enable the subject to live only in the present, in the "now" of
immediate awareness. Palanesian education attempts to " 'reconcile
analysis with vision' " (p. 238), the innumerable differentiating fac-
tors of existence with the one common cause. Menon proclaims:

> "What we give the children is simultaneously a training in perceiv-
> ing and imagining, a training in applied physiology and psychology,
> a training in practical ethics and practical religion, a training in the
> proper use of language, and a training in self-knowledge. In a word, a
> training of the whole mind-body in all its aspects" (p. 243).

What Huxley prescribes through the Palanese theory of education
is a unified approach to reality and experience. Menon advises:
" 'Never give children a chance of imagining that anything exists in
isolation' " (p. 247). Huxley's comprehensive mysticism is not just a
Western retreading of Taoist ideology, but also a positive counterpoint to the problems of separation, alienation and incommunica-
tion which he delineates in his other novels. Huxley always sought
an ideal which would permit him to experience and express existence as an entity rather than a fragment, and the educative ideals of
Island aim toward a similar objective for Everyman.

Huxley also proffers a revised and ideal family system in *Island*.
In Chapter VII Susila MacPhail describes Pala's answer to Western
family problems between children and parents:

> "We all belong," Susila explained, "to a MAC—a Mutual Adoption
> Club. Every MAC consists of anything from fifteen to twenty-five
> assorted couples. Newly elected brides and bridegrooms, old-timers
> with growing children, grandparents and great grandparents—every-

body in the club adopts everyone else. Besides our own blood relations, we all have our quota of deputy mothers, deputy fathers, deputy aunts and uncles, deputy brothers and sisters, deputy babies and
toddlers and teenagers" (p. 102).

Pala's sociologists call the process "hybridization of microcultures"
(p. 103). For the children, free to roam at will among the parents
within their club, the system provides an outlet for discontent or
irritation, an exposure to a wider variety of people and views, and
an opportunity for greater self-expression. " 'Mutual Adoption guar-
antees children against injustice and the worse consequences of
parental ineptitude,' " Susila informs Will. " 'It doesn't guarantee
them against discipline or against having to accept responsibilities' "
(p. 104). For the parents and older deputies, the system provides
" 'healthier relationships in more responsible groups, wider sym-
pathies and deeper understandings' " (p. 103). Susila contrasts what
she calls Will's kind of family with Pala's kind:

> As though reading instructions from a cookery book, "Take one
> sexually inept wage slave," she went on, "one dissatisfied female, two
> or (if preferred) three small television addicts; marinate in a mixture
> of Freudism and dilute Christianity; then bottle up tightly in a
> four-room flat and stew for fifteen years in their own juice. *Our*
> recipe is rather different: Take twenty sexually satisfied couples and
> their offspring; add science, intuition and humor in equal quantities;
> steep in Tantrik Buddhism and simmer indefinitely in an open pan
> in the open air over a brisk flame of affection" (pp. 102–103).

The result, according to Susila, is " 'an entirely different kind of
family' " (p. 103). Instead of the exclusive, compulsory family of
Will's society, Pala creates an inclusive, liberated family. Evidently,
Huxley feels that much of the physical bullying and psychological
blackmail recurrent in a closed family life could be eliminated by
such a procedure as a MAC. Figures like Beavis in *Eyeless in Gaza,*
Pordage in *After Many a Summer,* Poole in *Ape and Essence* and
Rivers in *The Genius and the Goddess* would have benefited immensely from a Mutual Adoption Club.

One of the most striking practices of Pala is its widespread use of
artificial insemination to protect its inhabitants from hereditary disease and to improve the race. Vijaya tells Will in Chapter XII that
" 'we developed the techniques of AI about twenty years before you
did. But of course we couldn't do much with it until we had electric
power and reliable refrigerators. We got those in the late twenties.
Since then we've been using AI in a big way' " (p. 219). Shanta's

parents had her and her brother by AI because her father's family displayed a history of recurrent diabetes. Vijaya and Shanta, since they already have a set of natural twins, plan to have their third child by AI " 'to enrich the family with an entirely new physique and temperament' " (p. 218). Pala has " 'a central bank of superior stocks' " from which to choose. " 'In the early days,' " Vijaya tells Will,

> "there were a good many conscientious objectors. But now the advantages of AI, have been so clearly demonstrated, most married couples feel that it's more moral to take a shot at having a child of superior quality than to run the risk of slavishly reproducing whatever quirks and defects may happen to run in the husband's family. Meanwhile the theologians have got busy. AI has been justified in terms of reincarnation and the theory of karma. Pious fathers now feel happy at the thought that they're giving their wife's children a chance of creating a better destiny for themselves and their posterity" (p. 220).

The notion of an artificial stock of babies perhaps at first recalls, disturbingly, the bottled babies of *Brave New World.* But the crucial difference, for Huxley, is that in the earlier novel the State completely and ruthlessly controlled production, whereas in *Island* the decision to try AI and the choice of the stock rests entirely with the parents. Pala's community is founded on the principle of the freedom and liberation of the individual and, in Huxley's vision, all the facets of the ideal society follow that principle.

Huxley conveys to his readers some of his more difficult ideology in *Island* through an interesting use of symbol. In truth, the nature of Huxley's subject frequently requires a symbolic description because many of his mystical precepts elude literal explanation. In *Heaven and Hell* (1955) Huxley apologizes for writing of his mystical concepts analogously: "It is difficult, it is all but impossible, to speak of mental events except in similes drawn from the more familiar world of material things." [11] In *Time Must Have a Stop* and *The Perennial Philosophy,* Huxley maintains that the mystical process itself is neither expressible nor demonstrable except by direct personal experience. As the teacher in Pala's Elementary Applied Philosophy class says, " 'What Buddha was implying and what Mahakasyapa understood was that one can't speak these teachings, one can only *be* them' " (pp. 253–54). Accordingly, Huxley turns to

11 New York, p. 2.

a select but informing group of symbols in the novel in an attempt to suggest some of his more evasive mystical notions.

The very title of the book, *Island*, suggests a pattern of symbolism latent in Huxley's thought for many years. As far back as 1924 Huxley ponders the problem of the isolation of the individual as he describes Uncle Spencer: "He was imprisoned within himself. He was an island surrounded on every side by wide and bottomless solitudes . . . he thought of all the millions and millions of men and women in the world—all alone, all solitary and confined." [12] For Huxley in the 1920's existence seemed bewilderingly pluralistic; the world appeared to be inhabited by a group of irreconcilably heterogeneous individuals. Huxley seems never to have altered his belief in the multiplicity and confusion of unmystical experiential reality. In *Themes and Variations* (1950) he observes that everyone is "an island universe of private experiences." [13] Through his conversion to mysticism, Huxley arrived at the conviction that while relativity and isolation were part of the human condition, they were not necessarily the sum total of human fate. As he asserts in *The Devils of Loudun*, people "long to get out of themselves, to pass beyond the limits of that tiny island universe, within which every individual finds himself confined" (p. 67). In Huxley's last novel, the mystical ideals of Pala and the implications of the title combine to suggest larger meanings for the symbol of people as islands.

Farnaby relates the history of his aunt and uncle, Mary and Frank, in terms of island symbolism. " 'Two young people on their private Pala,' " he reflects aloud. " 'Even outside of Pala one can find occasional islands of decency. Tiny little atolls, or even, every now and then, a full-blown Tahiti—but always surrounded by the Essential Horror' " (p. 274). The Essential Horror for Huxley is suffering and death. Frank died of gangrene after being struck by shrapnel in World War I, and many years later Mary died horribly from cancer. The Essential Horror overwhelmed Will by reducing first his dog, then Aunt Mary, and finally his mistress, Molly, into alien and repulsive packets of garbage. Each successive experience of the death of someone close to him drove Will ever more deeply into the island

---

[12] *Young Archimedes and Other Stories* (New York, 1924), p. 126. Island references to illustrate a lack of personal contact occur in Huxley's 1948 play, *The Giaconda Smile,* and in his essay on G. B. Piranesi's *Prisons* (1949). In the 1950's Huxley evoked imagery of people as islands with increasing frequency, especially in *The Devils of Loudun* (1952), *The Doors of Perception* (1954) and *The Genius and the Goddess* (1955).

[13] New York, p. 175.

of his self, his phenomenal ego, confining him within "an isolated consciousness, a child's, a boy's, a man's, forever isolated, irremediably alone" (p. 276). As a result, he feels safer without human contacts. He endorses a separative existence and scoffs at a unity which will end inevitably in the Essential Horror. He rejects what the Palanese celebrate as "awareness" because he wants to be " 'less aware of my own excellent health in an ocean of malaria and hookworm, of my own safely sterilized sex fun in an ocean of starving babies' " (p. 277). The unreformed Will is his own island. Like Huxley's other irreligious heroes, his only answer to pluralism is an attempt to erect a private haven of cynicism, sensuality and detachment.

A more profound meaning underlies Huxley's island symbolism in the novel, though, a meaning which, in its implications and its contacts with Palanese idealism, suggests a counter to Will's self-enforced isolation and escapism. Almost thirty years earlier Huxley comments on "The Individual" in *Texts and Pretexts* (1933):

> Our successive states are islands—but, for the most part, "sister islands linking their coral arms under the sea." . . . But here and there, in midocean, rises some isolated peak; uninhabited, or peopled by races of strange men and unknown animals. . . . Between these and the oceanic islands, there exists, no doubt, some obscure, submarine connection. If in no other way, they are at least united in this: that they rise from the crust of the same globe.[14]

Huxley at this time was groping for an answer to the atomistic appearance of experience. In his later acceptance of a mystical philosophy, he perceived that experience, like humanity, was indeed anchored in a connective, submarine ground. The lesson that *Island* propagates through Pala's subculture and the connotations of Huxley's symbol is that, although people are admittedly alone on the surface of routine life, like islands, they are nevertheless united, like islands, beneath the uneasy, oceanic flux. Through their contact with a common base, their submarine connection with a more permanent, subsurface reality, they are joined in a unitive psychic land which, for Huxley, is the mystical "Divine Ground." The cynic, whose vision is limited to "outsight," to the surface, sees only separation and isolation in a pluralistic universe. The mystic, who is capable of genuine insight, perceives a unity beneath the heaving, relativistic chaos, a unity which is far more real than the separation

14 New York, pp. 56–57.

of surface reality. The symbolism behind Huxley's title is, in this way, functional to the Palanesians' emphasis on awareness and to Huxley's own mystical reading of life.

Huxley also constructs a symbolic pattern in *Island* based on the ancient tradition of mountains as emblems of aspiration and achievement. Susila anticipates the pattern in Chapter IV when she uses word therapy to bring peace to the distraught Will. She brings his restless mind " 'out of the hot plain . . . effortlessly, into the freshness of the mountains' " (p. 35). Through Susila's therapy, the figurative mountains become Farnaby's refuge from disturbing, intrusive memories of Molly, from the guilt which haunts him from his past. But the physical mountains of Pala, in their service as an educational proving ground for the young climbers, assume a meaning more relevant to Huxley's brand of mysticism. Dr. Robert reports in Chapter X that scaling the precipices is, for the young, " 'an ordeal that helps them to understand the world they'll have to live in, helps them to realize the omnipresence of death, the essential precariousness of all existence' " (p. 185). Like Hemingway in *A Farewell to Arms*, Huxley suggests that simple retreat to the mountains does not automatically solve the problems of suffering and death. Calamy, in *Those Barren Leaves*, goes to a mountain for a place to purge himself of selfishness and worldly preoccupations. But in *Island* the climax of the youngsters' climb, their liberation through the worship in the temple, strengthens them for a return to the jungle below. After the hard physical and mystical struggle to the summit of openness, sunlight and perspective, explains Vijaya, comes the inevitable descent back to

> "jungle life in all its exuberance and its rotting, crawling squalor . . . beauty and horror. . . . And then suddenly, as you come down from one of your expeditions in the mountains, suddenly you know that there's a reconciliation . . . beauty made one with horror in the yoga of the jungle" (pp. 192–3).

The jungle signifies life lived at the routine, everyday level of existence. It is ugly and chaotic, terrifying and self-destructive. The mountains signify the peak of the curative, illuminating mystical experience. It, in turn, is beautiful and unitive, uplifting and constructive. In *Eyeless in Gaza* Huxley uses images of cones in an ocean to etch the mystical process. In *Island* he uses references to mountains in a jungle to suggest the same process. In both novels, the guiding idea is the same: the individual should seek union with the

"Godhead" through a close mental and physical discipline, but the resulting exaltation should provide a means of confronting, not an excuse for denying, external reality. Through his symbolism of the mountains and the jungle in *Island,* Huxley insists that the Maha-yanist employment of contemplation and ecstasy does not constitute a Nirvana escapism.

A less traditional symbol of some consequence appears in Chapter XIII. Here, Huxley describes the application of scarecrows in a field to Pala's stance on the notion of an anthropomorphic divinity. The scarecrows resemble homemade gods because, Vijaya declares, the Old Raja wanted the children to understand that

> "it's we who pull their strings and so give them the power to pull ours . . . and when anyone looks up, even at a god, he can hardly fail to see the sky beyond. And what's the sky? Air and scattered light; but also a symbol of that boundless and (excuse the metaphor) *pregnant* emptiness out of which everything, the living and the inanimate, the puppet makers and the divine marionette, emerges into the universe we know" (p. 234).

Empty space, explains Dr. Robert in Chapter X, is " 'at once the most powerful symbol of death and the most powerful symbol of the fullest, intensest life . . . the Buddha Nature in all our perpetual perishing' " (p. 188). The scarecrows and the sky come to symbolize the diverse, traditional, personal images of God behind which, in the "perennial philosophy," exists the universal consciousness common to them all. The scarecrows and the sky serve to illustrate Huxley's belief, reiterated time and again after 1940, that there is a "Highest Common Factor" to all religions. In this sense, Huxley's angle of vision comprehensively embraces all religions as manifestations of "the One."

Island, like *Eyeless in Gaza,* ends with a vision by the repentant hero. Unlike that of Beavis, though, Farnaby's vision is stimulated by the *moksha*-medicine. Dr. Robert in Chapter IX describes the medicine as " 'the reality revealer, the truth-and-beauty pill' " (p. 157) which enables even beginners in contemplation " 'to catch a glimpse of the world as it looks to someone who has been liber-ated from his bondage to the ego' " (p. 158). The *moksha*-medicine in Pala is available to anyone, although the uninitiated take it only under careful supervision. Huxley's serious quest for a "reality re-vealer" pill and his personal experiments toward a perfect vision-producer are among the more controversial items in his efforts to formulate a suitable mystical system of life for the masses.[15] The goal of the perfect stimulant is total awareness of events and objects in the present, leading to the "awakeness" of the contemplative mind in meditation. Huxley contends in *Tomorrow and Tomorrow and Tomorrow*: "Total awareness opens the way to understanding, and when any given situation is understood, the nature of all reality is made manifest" (pp. 56–57).

Farnaby evidently experiences total awareness when, in the last chapter, he tries the *moksha*-medicine. At first, he feels undiluted identity with pure spirit: "Ultimately and essentially there was only a knowledgeless understanding, only union with unity in a limitless, undifferentiated awareness" (p. 309). But, consistent with Huxley's thinking, Susila warns against indefinite immersion in delicious Nirvana, asserting, " 'Bodhisattvas dilute their Nirvana with equal parts of love and work' " (p. 311). She puts on the Fourth Brandenburg Concerto, and Will feels that "tonight, for the first time, his awareness of a piece of music was completely unobstructed" (p. 312). He sees common objects in new ways charged with beauty and significance: "This breathing apocalypse called 'table' might be thought of as a picture by some mystical Cubist, some inspired Juan Gris with the soul of Traherne and a gift for painting miracles with conscious gems and the changing moods of water-lily pads" (p. 317). Susila, however, constantly the moderator, wants also to call Will's attention to " 'the still sad music of humanity' " (p. 318). She bids him to look down to the floor, at one of Tom Krishna's pet lizards: "A glow of sheer evil radiated from every gray-green scale of the creature's back, from its obsidian eyes and the pulsing of its crimson throat, from the armored edges of its nostrils and its slit-like mouth" (p. 319). In *Heaven and Hell* Huxley cautions that the visionary experience may be terrifying as well as illuminating, pointing to Kafka, Van Gogh, Goya and Browning's "Childe Roland" as examples of visionary terror in art. Will witnesses with sheer horror the incident of the copulating praying mantises, as the female sedately chews off the male's head during the sexual act. Then the symbol of the Essential Horror, the hulking lizard, devours them both in a pantomime of pain, malice and insane violence. A succession of frenzied mental scenes of cruelty and imbecility remind Will that there is no escape from the real world, as squalid a jungle as it may

---

[15] In *The Doors of Perception* Huxley proposes: "What is needed is a new drug which will relieve and console our suffering species without doing more harm in the long run than it does good in the short" (New York, 1952), pp. 64–65. See R. C. Zaehner's argument against Huxley's remarks on mescalin, "Mescalin and Mr. Aldous Huxley," *The Listener*, LV (April 26, 1956), pp. 506–7.

be. As if to confirm the truth of his realization, Will then stands by helplessly while the forces of Rendang, led by Murugan, invade the island and murder Dr. Robert.

The concluding pages of *Island* contain that ambivalent mixture of hope and despair which governs Huxley's final position. A passage of dogged hopefulness that enlightened man will not only endure but prevail keynotes Farnaby's last reflections:

> And always, everywhere, there would be the yelling or quietly authoritative hypnotists; and in the train of the ruling suggestion givers, always and everywhere, the tribes of buffoons or hucksters, the professional liars, the purveyors of entertaining irrelevances. Conditioned from the cradle, unceasingly distracted, mesmerized systematically, their uniformed victims would go on marching and countermarching, go on, always and everywhere, killing and dying with the perfect docility of trained poodles. And yet in spite of the entirely justified refusal to take yes for an answer, the fact remained and would remain, remain everywhere—the fact that there was this capacity even in a paranoiac for intelligence, even in a devil worshiper for love; the fact that the ground of all being could be totally manifest in a flowering shrub, a human face; the fact that there was a light and that this light was also compassion (p. 334).

In *Island*, Huxley's faith in the potentiality of man receives its clearest and most noble expression. Since *Eyeless in Gaza* Huxley was convinced that any improvement of existence in the modern world would have to begin with the individual. He believed that every individual has within him a latent fund of insight and compassion. He felt that a small but alert number of men, perhaps his own version of Milton's "few but fit," were capable of enlightenment without external aid. In a favorable environment, Huxley seems to have thought, this core of leaders would be able to assist large numbers of people in realizing their latent goodness and mystical potential. In *Island*, Huxley illustrates what could be done in a community if it were built on the premise of "goodness politics" rather than power politics.

But the modern environment, by conditioning man to the worship of Mars and Mammon, prostitutes the dormant goodness of his nature to false values. A world obsessed with militaristic and materialistic values is blind to pacific and mystical values. "In the popular philosophy of our own time," Huxley notes during World War II, "it goes without saying that . . . a minority of contemplatives is perfectly useless and perhaps even harmful to the community which tolerates it." [16] Huxley's final position remains grudgingly

realistic as he concedes regretfully that even the possibility of an
independent contemplative community is quite remote in the world
of the 1960's. As Farnaby listens to Murugan's ebbing procession,
Huxley's resignation to modern rejection of his thought, to the refusal of mankind "to take yes for an answer," becomes apparent.
Huxley's conclusion to *Island* is consistent with the advice from
Aristotle with which he prefaces the novel: "In framing an ideal we
may assume what we wish, but should avoid impossibilities." Huxley sought to frame an ideal knowing that its acceptance, perhaps
even its tolerance, in a materialistic world was impossible, yet believing that its relevance to men as individuals was supremely real.
And it is difficult not to wonder if *Island* is Huxley's final legacy to
posterity, if somehow he hoped that someday the quest toward such
an ideal on a more universal scale would not be so far removed from
reality.

Huxley concludes his preface to a 1959 edition of his *Collected
Essays* with a statement which is perhaps a summary of his life:
"For the writer at least, and perhaps also for the reader, it is better
to have tried and failed to achieve perfection than never to have
tried at all." [17] Whatever posterity's final judgment of Huxley's
achievement may be, it will surely recognize his positive concern for
that humanity which he so persistently scolds. It will clearly recognize the power and foresight of his vision, its continuing relevance
in the middle 1960's and, we may safely assume, later. It will certainly recognize his tireless quest for a new set of first principles in
what he regarded as an unprincipled world. In *Beyond the Mexique
Bay* (1934) Huxley quips, in a mutation of Voltaire, "Il faut culti-
ver notre oasis." [18] It is perhaps one of Huxley's most creditable
achievements that he cultivates his oasis tellingly, and yet patrols
unflinchingly into the wasteland problems of scientific, economic
and psychological reality in an intense effort to save mankind from
itself. If he has failed in his attempt to achieve perfection in his
vision, the attempt itself was decidedly salutary. Huxley's sad foun-
tain in one of his earliest poems, "The Garden" in *The Burning
Wheel* (1916), would seem to be a fit symbol of himself as he frames
his Utopian island almost fifty years later:

> There shall be seen the infinite endeavor
> Of a sad fountain, white against the sky
> And poised as it strains up, but doomed to break
> In weeping music . . .

17 New York, p. ix.
18 New York, p. 232.

Chronology of Important Dates

1894   July 26. Born in village of Godalming, Surrey, third son of Leonard and Julia Arnold Huxley.

1908   September. Enters Eton College.
November. Death of Julia Huxley.

1910   Autumn. An attack of *keratitis punctata* causes blindness and withdrawal from Eton.

1911   Partial recovery of sight after surgery.

1913   October. Enters Balliol College, Oxford.

1916   June. Receives a First in English Literature. Summer holidays at Garsington Manor.

1917   September. Teaching post at Eton (until February, 1919).

1918   August. *Defeat of Youth* (poems).

1919   July 10. Married to Maria Nys.
Joins editorial staff of *The Athenaeum*.

1920   April. Birth of Matthew Huxley.

1921   November. *Crome Yellow*.

1923   November. *Antic Hay*.

1925   January. *Those Barren Leaves*.
September. Round-the-world journey: India, Hong-Kong, U.S.A.

1926   Friendship with D. H. Lawrence.

1928   October. *Point Counter Point*.

1929   Friendship with Gerald Heard.

1932   January. *Brave New World*.
November. *Texts and Pretexts*.

1935   Active in pacifist movement.

1936   July. *Eyeless in Gaza.*

1937   April. Voyage to U.S.A.
            Friendship with W. H. Sheldon.

1938   Lives and works in Los Angeles.

1939   October. *After Many a Summer.*

1941   October. *Grey Eminence.*

1944   August. *Time Must Have a Stop.*

1945   September. *The Perennial Philosophy.*

1948   August. *Ape and Essence.*

1952   October. *The Devils of Loudun.*

1953   May. Takes mescalin under the supervision of Dr. Humphrey
            Osmand.

1954   February. *The Doors of Perception.*

1955   February. Death of Maria Huxley.
            June. *The Genius and the Goddess.*

1956   March 19. Married to Laura Archera.

1957   June. *Collected Short Stories.*

1959   August. *Collected Essays.*

1961   May. Huxley house in Los Angeles destroyed by fire.

1962   February–May. Visiting professor, University of California,
            Berkeley.
            March. *Island.*

1963   November 22. Death of cancer, Los Angeles. Cremation.
            Memorial service in London on December 17.

Notes on the Editor and Contributors

ROBERT E. KUEHN, editor of this volume, is Lecturer in English and Assistant Director of the Yale University Center for British Art and British Studies. He has also edited *Twentieth Century Interpretations of Lord Jim* and (with John G. Halkett) *This Powerful Rime: An Anthology of Ten Poets.*

JOSEPH BENTLEY is Professor of English at the University of South Florida, Tampa.

MILTON BIRNBAUM is Dean of the School of Arts and Sciences and Professor of English at American International College, Springfield, Massachusetts.

PETER BOWERING has worked for the British Council in Milan. Since 1970 he has been Lecturer for the Extra-Mural Department of the University of London.

PETER FIRCHOW is Professor of English and Comparative Literature at the University of Minnesota. He has published essays on numerous literary figures and he has translated Schlegel's novel *Lucinde.*

FREDERICK J. HOFFMAN was interested in many aspects of modern literature. His books include *Freudianism and the Literary Mind, The Little Magazine, The Twenties,* and *The Mortal No: Death and the Modern Imagination.*

CHARLES M. HOLMES is Professor of English at Transylvania University in Lexington, Kentucky.

JEROME MECKIER teaches the modern novel at the University of Kentucky, where he is Associate Professor of English. He is currently working on a bibliographical essay on Huxley.

SANFORD E. MAROVITZ is Associate Professor of English at Kent State University. At present he is writing a book on Herman Melville.

PETER QUENNELL's books include studies of Shakespeare, Pope, Byron, Ruskin, and other literary figures.

JOHN WAIN is Professor of Poetry at Oxford. He most recent book is *A House for the Truth.*

DONALD J. WATT edited *The Collected Poetry of Aldous Huxley* in 1971. He is currently at the School of English Studies, University of Nottingham.

HAROLD H. WATTS is on the faculty of Purdue University. He is the author of *Ezra Pound and the Cantos* and *Hound and Quarry.*

EVELYN WAUGH was the foremost satirist in English in the twentieth-century. He is the subject of a recent book of reminiscences by his friends, *Evelyn Waugh and His World,* edited by David Pryce-Jones.

ANGUS WILSON is the author of many works of fiction and literary criticism, including *Anglo-Saxon Attitudes, The Middle Age of Mrs. Eliot, and Late Call.*

FRANCIS WYNDHAM has contributed literary criticism to numerous British periodicals, including the *Observer,* the *New Statesman,* and *Encounter.* He is the author of the British Council pamphlet on Graham Greene.

Selected Bibliography

Bibliographical

Eschelbach, Claire John and Shober, Joyce Lee (foreword by Aldous Huxley). *Aldous Huxley, A Bibliography: 1916–1959.* Berkeley and Los Angeles: University of California Press, 1961.

Clareson, Thomas D. and Andrews, Carolyn S. *Aldous Huxley: A Bibliography, 1960–1964.* In *Extrapolation* 6, no. 1 (1964/65).

For items since 1964, see annual volumes of the *MLA Bibliography.*

Biographical

Bedford, Sybille. *Aldous Huxley: A Biography,* Volume One: 1894–1939, London: Chatto & Windus and Collins, 1973.

Clark, Ronald W. *The Huxleys.* New York: 1968.

Huxley, Julian, ed. *Aldous Huxley, 1894–1963: A Memorial Volume.* London: Chatto & Windus, 1965.

Huxley, Laura Archera. *This Timeless Moment: A Personal View of Aldous Huxley.* New York: Farrar, Straus & Giroux, 1968.

Smith, Grover, ed. *Letters of Aldous Huxley.* London: Chatto & Windus, 1969.

Critical

Atkins, John A. *Aldous Huxley: A Literary Study.* New York: Roy Publishers, 1956.

Birnbaum, Milton. *Aldous Huxley's Quest for Values.* Knoxville: University of Tennessee Press, 1971.

Bowering, Peter. *Aldous Huxley: A Study of the Major Novels.* London: Athelone Press, 1968.

Daiches, David. *The Novel and the Modern World.* Chicago: University of Chicago Press, 1939.

Firchow, Peter. *Aldous Huxley: Satirist and Novelist.* Minneapolis: University of Minnesota Press, 1972.

Greenblatt, Stephen J. *Three Modern Satirists: Waugh, Orwell, and Huxley.* New Haven: Yale University Press, 1965.

Henderson, Alexander. *Aldous Huxley.* London: Chatto & Windus, 1935.

Holmes, Charles M. *Aldous Huxley and the Way to Reality.* Bloomington, Indiana: Indiana University Press, 1970.

Meckier, Jerome. *Aldous Huxley: Satire and Structure.* London: Chatto & Windus, 1969.

O'Faolain, Sean. *The Vanishing Hero.* New York: Grosset & Dunlap, 1956.

Savage, Derek. *The Withered Branch: Six Studies in the Modern Novel.* London: Eyre & Spottiswoode, 1950.

Watts, Harold H. *Aldous Huxley.* New York: Twayne Publishers, Inc., 1969.

Webster, Harvey Curtis. *After the Trauma: Representative British Novelists Since 1920.* Lexington: University Press of Kentucky, 1970.

Woodcock, George. *Dawn and the Darkest Hour: A Study of Aldous Huxley.* New York: Viking Press, 1972.